Hic oculos similesq vultus, hic ora tueri
Poteris, nec vltra hæc artifex quivit manus

ANNALES ipsum celebrisq BRITANNIA monstrant
Perenniora saxo et ære avnuata.

Quisquis et Historiæ Cathedram hanc conscenderit esto
Benignitatis usque monumentum loquax.

HISTORIAE ECCE IVBAR LVX ET PRAECLARA VETVSTAE CLARENTIVS VITA SENEX NONO NOVEMBRIS XIIIT

CAMDEN'S BRITANNIA

KENT

From the edition of 1789 by Richard Gough

ANNOTATED AND EDITED BY

GORDON J. COPLEY

HUTCHINSON OF LONDON

Hutchinson & Co (Publishers) Ltd
3 Fitzroy Square, London W1

London Melbourne Sydney Auckland Wellington Johannesburg
and agencies throughout the world

First published 1977
This annotated edition © G. J. Copley 1977

Designed by Hans Schmoller R.D.I.
Set in Monotype Bembo

Printed in Great Britain by The Anchor Press Ltd,
Tiptree, Essex, on Smooth Wove 110 gsm paper supplied by
William Sommerville & Son Ltd, Croydon, Surrey
Bound by William Brendon & Son Ltd, Tiptree, Essex

ISBN 0 09 125240 7

To

'BILL' TIMMONS

best of friends

The Conquest of Wessex in the Sixth Century
1954

An Archaeology of South-East England
1958

Names and Places
1964, revised edition 1972

English Place-Names and Their Origins
1968, revised edition 1971

Camden's Britannia: Surrey and Sussex
1977

CONTENTS

The map on pages 24–25 is reproduced from Gough's edition of
Camden's Britannia

ILLUSTRATION SOURCES

William Camden (frontispiece), *Camden's Britannia*, edited by Richard Gough, 1789

Greenwich (pp. 8-9), Deal Castle (p. 61): British Museum

Eltham Palace (p. 12): *Archaeologia*, The Society of Antiquaries of London, vol. 6, 1782, pl. 51

Gravesend (p. 14): William Thornton, *New complete, and Universal history*, description and survey of the cities of London and Westminster, the borough of Southwark, and the parts adjacent, 1784

Maidstone (p. 19): Victoria and Albert Museum

Leeds Castle (p. 21), Allington Castle (p. 22), Kit's Coty House (p. 26), Halling House (p. 27), Rochester Castle (p. 31), Minster (p. 32), Faversham Abbey (p. 35), Chilham Castle (p. 39), Canterbury, St Augustine's Monastery (p. 45), Canterbury Castle (p. 51), Dover Castle (p. 66), Old Church in Dover Castle (p. 70), Saltwood Castle (p. 77), Ostenhanger House (p. 78), Lyme Castle (p. 79): Francis Grose, *The Antiquities of England and Wales*, vol. 2, 1774

Reculver (p. 36): *The Gentleman's Magazine*, part 2, 1809

View of Canterbury (pp. 40-41), Canterbury Cathedral (p. 47): William Somner, *The Antiquities of Canterbury*, 2nd ed. 1703, frontispiece and facing page 8, respectively

Richborough Castle (p. 57): William Stukeley, *Itinerarum Curiosum*, vol. 2, 1776

Roman warfare: a *testudo* (p. 68): Aylett Sammes, *Britannia Antiqua Illustrata: or the Antiquities of Ancient Britain*, 1676

PREFACE

Even though Camden's *Britannia* is one of the more important starting-points in the study of local history, there has been only one edition of it since Gough's of 1789 and that is a splendid, though necessarily very expensive, facsimile of Bishop Gibson's edition of 1695, a work to be consulted in a well-stocked institutional library, but far beyond the means of most researchers. In recent decades, however, the number of students of local history has increased greatly and there is an ever-growing body of general readers who find pleasure and interest in the study of their own localities.

The present edition has been prepared with these students and readers in mind; yet even the scholar has been hampered in his work by the lack of an accessible and up-to-date edition of the *Britannia* that takes into account the vast increments in knowledge of the last two hundred years. He, too, has been kept in mind, though he is obviously free to reject everything in the following pages apart from Camden's text itself. Relevant to this is Gough's remark in his Preface: 'The want of an improved edition of the Britannia has been long complained of, and it is not perhaps easy to assign a reason why one has not been undertaken.' Of course, there are those who, from a position of superior scholarship, will regard the present work as a belated essay in effete antiquarianism. High in their ivory towers, they are unaware of the busy, unpretentious students who find deep satisfaction in exploring the local past and who have it well within their power to save at least a few scraps of worthwhile knowledge from oblivion. It is with them that the present editor unashamedly ranges himself, for without the work of these amateurs and more serious students, scholarship would be much the poorer.

The use of the translation of 1789 needs little defence. Richard Gough was a classical scholar and an antiquary in the great English tradition that goes back at least to William Worcester (1415–82). Moreover, Gough had the advantage of two earlier translations, Holland's of 1610 and Gibson's of 1695, the latter correcting the former at many points; and, inevitably in a work of such magnitude, Gough found a few errors of translation in Gibson and his collaborators, as well as of fact in the Camden original. Indeed, he corrects each of them about a dozen times in the chapters describing the five south-eastern counties. But even Gough, as he himself foresaw, is occasionally in error and without doubt this new edition will not be free of faults in spite of careful revisions.

It is, then, the translation made by Gough that is used in the following pages, for it is unlikely that Camden's Latin text could be better rendered. Gibson's and Gough's 'Additions' to their translations have not usually been reproduced for several reasons. Firstly, they contain much that Camden omitted, often deliberately; secondly, the growth of specialist studies has gone so far since 1789 that corrections would in total be more lengthy than the 'Additions' themselves; and, finally, they would have so enlarged the volume as to make it unwieldy in both content and format. Nevertheless, wherever Gough's comments illuminate Camden's text, they have been cited; and Gough's practice has been imitated in the reproduction of passages from the *Itinerary in England and Wales* . . . of John Leland wherever they are relevant to that text. In fact many passages from Leland are included which Gough did not reproduce, for almost always they either add interesting details or reveal the *Itinerary* as Camden's source.

The present editor's notes are intended to illuminate the text, bringing to bear on it the fruits of modern scholarship. As a scholar of the Renaissance, Camden believed in the unity of learning and he ranged widely over much of the field of contemporary knowledge. The modern reader would have the inconvenience of recourse to many works outside the category of historical topography if it were not for this edition. The sources cited in the notes will serve as pointers to the fuller clarification of Camden's text. Inevitably, the notes reflect this wide range of topics, sometimes giving them the appearance of an *omnium gatherum* of snippets; yet it must be said that there is much in the notes that has not been culled from books. Over several decades, and more intensively in recent years, the editor has visited the places described in the *Britannia*, some of them many times; and the visits have required much walking and the subsequent discarding of much mud.

Emphasis in the notes has constantly been put on those things that are still to be seen, some still as Camden saw them; and it is astonishing how much of what he described yet survives. Scratch the surface of twentieth-century suburbia and there is a good chance that a fragment of Tudor England will show through. Go out into the countryside or into the country towns and the survivals are numerous. The continuity from palaeolithic to medieval England that the editor sought to demonstrate in his *Archaeology of South-East England* needs no demonstration when comparisons are made between Camden's England and that 'pleasant land' of the later twentieth century, widely despoiled though it is by the 'developers'. For the barbarians and the wealthy philistines of Matthew Arnold's day are still with us and they have inordinate power. Camden's England is being bulldozed into oblivion faster than at any time in the past and almost all that is being newly provided is like a leprous disease on the fair face of the landscape. Hardly a town or village in southern England has been spared from some egregious defacement or other, whether it be electricity pylons, oil depots, refuse dumps, former establishments of Her Majesty's forces, new roads and factories, incongruous multistorey office blocks or ordinary dwellings. Even the worst of what has been destroyed was better than almost all that has replaced it and vast profits have been indecently made at the expense of amenity. Yet it is something to be grateful for that generations of local worthies (some of them no doubt also despoilers in their time) and that national topographers such as Leland and Camden recorded what they did when they did.

Camden omits not a little that existed in his day and still exists, but generally speaking his omissions are not made good in the notes. On the other hand he includes much national history that the modern reader may be glad to ignore. Equally superfluous to any reader but a specialist are the lengthy passages of genealogy that break the thread of his narrative from time to time. But Camden knew well what he was doing. He was fully aware of the topics that would interest his literate contemporaries; and genealogy was certainly one of them.

The popularity of the *Britannia* is best attested by the number of times it was re-issued during his lifetime and soon after it. The first edition of 1586 was followed by a sixth as early as 1607; and Holland's translation of 1610 gave the work to a vastly greater number of readers. Five further editions in the original Latin had been published in Germany and Holland by 1662 as befitted the work of a scholar who was the correspondent of many of the most eminent European savants. Bishop Gibson's edition of 1695, with considerable additions to Camden's description of each county, was followed in 1722 by a further enlargement, reprinted in 1753 and 1772, the latter with minor corrections. Then came Gough, the greatest of the translators and editors.

The arrangement of the edition of 1789 is of some interest and requires description. The format was folio (17 × 10 inches) in three volumes, only the first of which is of present concern. John Nichols, the printer, was a friend of Gough and his companion on many of his travels. Nichols also wrote and published several works on historical topography.

The title-page is faced by a portrait of Camden engraved by James Basire from the original by Marcus Gheeraerts, painted in 1609 when the sitter was 58 years of age. The original is in the National Portrait Gallery. It had been presented by Camden to the History School at Oxford.

Following the title-page of the 1789 edition is a page of dedication by Gough to George III, 'Patron of Arts and Sciences, the Father of his People . . . , who has condescended to encourage researches into antiquity'. Gough's Preface comes next, with pagination v–viii. It includes two passages that are important for an understanding of his footnotes to Camden's text. In the present edition these notes appear at the foot of the text, lettered alphabetically. The new notes are numbered 01 to 99, 01 etc., and arranged in narrower columns. Gibson's and Gough's additions are not usually included.

The passages of Gough's Preface to be borne in mind are:

'All the bishop's [i.e. Gibson's] additions, distinguished by reference in Arabic numerals to his initial G. at the bottom of each page, are retained, except a very few, which were either uninteresting or erroneous, and most of them are enlarged and new modelled. A few mis-translations, instances of false English, trite observations, and false facts, are freely noticed at the bottom of the page.

'Even Holland's additions, though decried by Mr. Camden, are retained. Mr. Camden's marginal notes are marked by *, †, ‡. Among these must not be forgotten those marked *MS. n. Gale*, being made by the late Mr. Samuel Gale in the margin of his copy of the author's last edition, which has fallen into my hands.'

However, for *additions* in this passage read *notes* and for *Arabic numerals* read *letters of the alphabet*.

After Gough's *Preface* is placed the *Contents of the First Volume* and then follows 'The Life of Mr. Camden' by Gough, running to twenty-two folio pages (i–xxii), with extensive footnotes and specimens of the handwriting of Camden, Cotton and the French scholar Peiresc as a tailpiece.

The next page reproduces the title-page to the 1607 edition which was the original of Gough's translation:

BRITANNIA:

OR, A

CHOROGRAPHICAL DESCRIPTION

and so on as in the title-page to the 1789 edition; followed by Camden's dedication: 'To the most serene and most potent prince James, King of Great Britain, France, and Ireland; Defender of the Faith; born for the eternity of the British name and Empire; founder of lasting peace; author of public security; this work is dedicated by His Majesty's most devoted servant, William Camden'.

Mr. Camden's Preface to the Reader of three pages (i–iii) comes next. Then pp. iv–vii are taken up with Latin quotations, of which pp. v–vii are *Ad Lectorem*, 'To the Reader'. Page viii consists of twenty-six lines of Latin verse headed *Britannia*; and thereafter the real business of the book begins with the introductory chapters. In the present edition, which strictly follows the original spelling and punctuation, early forms of names are given in roman characters and appear in single quotes.

As may be seen from an earlier paragraph, Camden organized his material in rough conformity with the tribal divisions of Britain at the time of the Claudian conquest in A.D. 43, his information being derived from classical writers and not at all from archaeological writers, for none existed until at least two centuries later; and this is not inconsistent with Professor Douglas's statement (*English Scholars*, p. 25): 'His *Britannia* is essentially Roman Britain as seen in relation to its later growth.' Camden himself says that within the chapter devoted to each county he described as exactly as he could 'the bounds and qualities of soil, the places memorable in antiquity, the dukes, earls, barons, and the most antient and illustrious families; for it is impossible to mention them all'. His motive, like Leland's and Gough's, was 'the love of my country'. He claims to 'have omitted nothing that tended to discover the truth in matters of antiquity; to which purpose I have called in the assistance of a smattering of the antient British and Saxon languages. I have travelled over almost all England, and consulted the most experienced and learned persons in each county. I have carefully read over our own writers, and those among the Greek and Roman authors who made the least mention of Britain. I have consulted the public records, ecclesiastical registers, many libraries, the archives of cities and churches, monuments, and old deeds, and have made use of them as of irrefragable evidence, and when necessary quoted their very words however barbarous, that truth may have its full weight.'

In conclusion I would echo Gough's words from his *Preface* (p. viii): 'After all that has been, or can be, collected towards forming a complete edition of the BRITANNIA, much must be left to be corrected and supplied by attentive inspection of judicious travellers, or natives in the several counties. Increase of wealth renders property so fluctuating that it can hardly be ascertained for a succession of years. . . . Increase of cultivation makes rapid alterations in the face of the country. Old stations [sites] are levelled by the plough; old mansion-houses by modern refinement; and old titles revive in new families. Others may trace out many things barely hinted at here, and settle many points which are unavoidably left dubious.' Much of this is as true of the 1970s as it was of 1789.

Gough continues: 'The errors of former editors serve but to awaken a stronger apprehension in the present: and if the great author could not satisfy himself in his last and completest edition, what security is there for another editor's promise? If, in pointing out such errors, those of other Antiquaries are also animadverted on, this it is hoped is done with the candour due to respectable names.

'Far from presuming on an ability to correct the mistakes of preceding editors, it is not without the utmost diffidence I submit to the public eye the result of twenty years journeying, and a longer term of reading and enquiry. . . . I will not blush to acknowledge the secret satisfaction I feel in having attempted to publish a new edition of CAMDEN'S BRITANNIA. . . : I may hope there is some merit in uniting in one comprehensive view the various parts of BRITISH TOPOGRAPHY.'

The point of view of the twentieth-century editor could hardly be better expressed than by these words uttered as the French Revolution was smouldering into flame.

xvi

WILLIAM CAMDEN *was born in London in 1551, the son
of a painter. Educated at Christ's Hospital and St Paul's
School, he proceeded to Oxford in 1566, and it was on
leaving the University in 1571 that he began his antiquarian
travels. He was usher of Westminster School from 1575 to
1593, becoming its Headmaster in the latter year. Between
1578 and 1600 he continued his travels, but did so less extensively in later years. The first edition of the* BRITANNIA
*appeared in 1586. He held the post of Clarencieux
King of Arms from 1597 until his
death in 1623.*

INTRODUCTION

ALMOST all that Camden undertook in the early and middle years of his life contributed towards the *Britannia* and he continued his studies right down to his last years with the purpose of correcting and amplifying it. His early years as a pupil at Christ's Hospital and at St Paul's School in London afforded him opportunities to become well acquainted with the City and Westminster and with their immediate neighbourhoods; and his five years as a student at Oxford (1566–71) enabled him to acquire knowledge of that very different part of the Thames Valley. We know from his Berkshire chapter (Gough edn, p. 148) that he made excursions to Wallingford at this time, and it is likely that he ventured in other directions as well. It was at Christ Church, Oxford, that he came to know Sir Philip Sidney, who encouraged him in his antiquarian investigations; and he continued them on his return to London in 1571, supplementing them by much journeying about the country.

His appointment as usher at Westminster School in 1575 and as Headmaster from 1593 to 1598 established him in a profession that maintained his classical scholarship in continuous active use, albeit at a lowly level in much of his teaching; and it gave him leisure even in term time to extend his reading and in vacations to make further excursions into the shires. In 1578 he had been in Norfolk and Suffolk and four years later he was again in Suffolk, continuing from there into Yorkshire and returning by way of Lancaster. He went into Devon in 1589, going as far west as Ilfracombe, where he held a prebend of Salisbury Cathedral; and in the following year he journeyed to Wales. He returned there in about 1593, going out by way of Salisbury and returning through Oxford. In 1600 he went on an even more momentous journey to Carlisle in Cumberland, making a survey of the northern counties in the company of that other great Elizabethan antiquary, Sir Robert Bruce Cotton. The plague of 1603 caused him to take refuge at Cotton's country seat at Conington in Huntingdonshire, though it may well be that this was not the first visit to his friend's house.

John Aubrey (*Brief Lives*, ed. O. L. Dick, 1962, p. 150) preserved the memory of another of Camden's journeys into Wiltshire: 'When my grandfather went to schoole at Yatton-Keynell (neer Easton-Piers) Mr Camden came to see the church, and particularly tooke notice of a little painted-glasse-windowe in the chancell, which (ever since my remembrance) haz been walled-up, to save the parson the chardge of glazing it.'

Throughout his adult life he was probably exploring the counties nearest London. Even after the publication of the edition of 1607, Camden remained engrossed in amassing further material for the correction and enlargement of the *Britannia*. Gough recorded the fact that Thomas Hearne (d. 1735) had bequeathed to the Bodleian Library a copy of the 1607 edition 'with notes and emendations by Mr. Camden himself in the margin and on little pieces of paper fixed in their proper places'. And it was Aubrey, too, who recorded that Camden 'had bad Eies (I guesse Lippitude) which was a great inconvenience to an Antiquary'; and Aubrey's guess implies that the lippitude, which is soreness and blearedness, was the result of study, for he goes on: 'Mr Camden much studied the Welch language, and kept a Welsh servant to improve him in that language, for the better understanding of our Antiquities.'

But it was to more scholarly teachers, such as Lawrence Nowell (d. 1576), Lambarde (d. 1601), Joscelin (d. 1603) and Francis Tate (d. 1616), that he owed his knowledge of Old English. To Nowell, whose library he inherited, more than to the others, must go the credit for the new interest in Old English that developed in the 1560s and 1570s. He had produced a dictionary of Old English, still surviving in manuscript in the Bodleian Library. No such work of reference appeared in print before 1659; but it is most probable that Nowell's dictionary was in Camden's possession, at least from 1603. It was not only Camden who sat at Nowell's feet, for Archbishop Parker, Lambarde and Joscelin counted themselves his pupils in the years around 1565. Joscelin, too, compiled an Anglo-Saxon dictionary which, with other manuscripts and transcripts, were to pass into Cotton's collection where they were ready to Camden's hand. We know something of Cotton's loans to his antiquarian friends, to Bowyer, Agarde, Tate, Spelman and others in 1606; to Agarde, Tate and Camden in 1612, when Camden borrowed a collection of the lives of the saints (BM, Cotton Otho BX) and a 'Saxon Grammar that was Mr Gocelin' – which is further evidence that Camden continued his studies after 1607.

His appointment as Clarencieux King of Arms in 1597 was to be a cause of controversy with the jealous Ralph Brooke, York Herald, who no doubt believed he had more fitting experience for the post; and his venomous squib, *A Discoverie of certaine Errours . . . in the much commended Britannia 1594*, exposed mistakes in Camden's genealogical paragraphs which he acknowledged only ungraciously in the edition of 1600. But he had defenders even in the College of Arms itself, including Augustine Vincent who in reprisal attacked Brooke's *Catalogue of English kings, princes, and peers* of 1619. Yet the appointment as Clarencieux was probably intended to free Camden, now a well-loved and revered public figure, from the routine of a schoolmaster, so that in pursuance of his new duties he might travel the more.

Towards the end of his life, at any rate, he was employing deputies to make his visitations, for he was by then severely ill from time to time. But in his heyday these journeys would have enabled him to pursue his life's task with ease and without neglect of his official duties.

A further advantage of this appointment was that it brought him more frequently into the company of the other heralds, several of whom were enthusiastic antiquaries. The College of Arms of his time was a repository of antiquarian as well as of genealogical knowledge, readily put at Camden's disposal. In his Berkshire chapter (Gough edn, p. 152), he pays tribute to Robert Glover, Somerset Herald (d. 1588), as 'a person excellently well verst in the heraldic art'; and a little earlier he speaks of William Dethick, Garter King of Arms (d. 1612), as 'a person perfectly acquainted with all that relates to honor and nobility'. William Smith, Rouge Dragon (d. 1618), wrote *A Particular Description of England*, published in 1588, with town-profiles in colour, a picture of Stonehenge and a description of Cheshire with a bird's-eye view of Chester. Lastly, Sampson Lennard, Bluemantle Pursuivant (d. 1633), is characterized as 'a gentleman of singular virtue and politeness' in the Sussex chapter (Gough edn, p. 189). Clearly in these remarks Camden is repaying a debt of gratitude to his colleagues of the College.

The list of his friends includes many of the greatest minds of the Age. Sir Fulke Greville, Lord Brooke (d. 1628), a favourite of Elizabeth, was a patron and intimate friend whose influence with the Queen secured his place as a herald. To Sir Fulke was dedicated Camden's edition of the chronicles in 1603 and to him Camden bequeathed a piece of plate worth £10. Their friend in common, Sir Philip Sidney (d. 1586), already mentioned as a companion at Oxford, is paid far more than a conventional tribute in the account of Penshurst (Gough edn, p. 212). A third poet, Edmund Spenser (d. 1599), with strong antiquarian leanings, devoted to him a stanza of his *Ruines of Time*:

Camden the nourice [nurse] of antiquity
And lantern unto late succeeding age,
To see the light of simple verity,
Buried in ruins, through the great outrage
Of her own people, led with warlike rage.
Camden, though time all monuments obscure,
Yet thy just labours ever shall endure.

Ben Jonson, his pupil at Westminster School, poet and dramatist (d. 1637), wrote thus in heartfelt tribute to him:

Camden, most reverend head, to whom I owe
All that I am in arts, all that I know,
(How nothing's that?) to whom thy country owes
The great renown and name wherewith she goes;

and in dedicating to him the play *Every Man in his Humour* (1598) addressed him as 'the Most Learned, and My Honoured Friend Master Camden, Clarencieux'.

And there were many lesser men who had been his scholars, among them the bishops of London, Oxford, Durham, St Asaph and Rochester; but the greatest antiquarian of them all was his friend Sir Robert Bruce Cotton (d. 1631), whose library was open to Camden, Stow, Speed, Ussher and others with similar interests. It was to Cotton that Camden dedicated his *Remaines of a Greater Worke, Concerning Britain* of 1605, which consists of material collected with the *Britannia* in mind, but not included in it. The chapter headings are sufficient as an indication of its contents: Inhabitants, Languages, English Tongue, Christian Names, Surnames, Allusions, Rebus, Anagrams, Money, Apparel, Artillery, Armouries, Wise Speeches, Proverbs, Poems, Epigrams, Rhymes, Impresses [emblems], Epitaphs and Impossibilities. Cotton inherited the greater part of Camden's library.

Of an older generation, Lambarde (d. 1601) held several legal posts in London during the later part of his life when he could have been frequently in Camden's company. They had exchanged compliments in their major writings, Lambarde in his *Perambulation of Kent* (1570, edn of 1970, pp. 2–3) referring to 'Master Camden, the most

lightsome [elegant] antiquarie of this age'; and Camden returned the compliment, acknowledging his indebtedness to Lambarde in the introductory paragraph to his chapter on Kent (Gough edn, p. 209).

The *Perambulation* was intended to be the first of a series of county descriptions by Lambarde; but as he pointed out (pp. 474–5) – '*Britannia*, wherein . . . he hath not only farre exceeded whatsoever hath been attempted in that kynd, but hath also passed the expectation of other men and even his [Camden's] hope' – the *Britannia* forestalled Lambarde's larger intention and was better than he could hope to achieve. Yet this praise of Camden's work is somewhat offset by Lambarde's suggestion that the historical topography of a county could best be studied by one who dwelt within its borders. 'Nevertheless,' he says, 'being assured that the Inwardes of each place may best be knowen by such as reside therein, I can not but still encourage some one able man in each Shyre to undertake his owne [shire], whereby both many good particularities will come to discoverie every where, and Master Camden him selfe may yet have greater choice wherewith to amplifie and enlarge the whole.' Lambarde knew well the vivid 'particularities' in the disordered notes of Leland and perhaps unreasonably regretted their absence from the *Britannia*. He could hardly have foreseen that his wish for county volumes would be largely fulfilled in later decades, though not in time for Camden to use most of them.

Besides his indebtedness to the *Perambulation*, Camden had access to Lambarde's unpublished *Dictionarium Angliae Topographicum et Historicum*, which was not printed until 1730. It was a topographical dictionary with valuable guidance on place-names. That Lambarde was a good scholar of Old English is evident in the *Perambulation*; and his completion of the paraphrase of the Anglo-Saxon laws, begun by Laurence Nowell, reveals the depth of his knowledge of our early language.

Of a still earlier generation was John Twyne (d. 1581), who like Camden was a schoolmaster. Like Cotton later in the century, he collected

Roman coins and pottery and took an interest in megalithic monuments and in earthworks, all of which were to be found in the neighbourhood of Canterbury where he lived. Camden cites 'the learned John Twine' as an authority for the former existence of a land-bridge between England and the Continent (Gough edn, p. 220).

Richard Carew (d. 1620), whose *Survey of Cornwall* was published in 1602, was Camden's fellow undergraduate at Oxford and they had further opportunities for meeting during Carew's membership of Clement's Inn and of the Middle Temple over a period of about four years until 1577. There is a possibility that it was Camden who persuaded Carew in 1585 to revise his manuscript of the *Survey* and bring it up to date. In his opening address 'To the Reader', Carew says: 'When I first composed this treatise, not minding that it should be published in print, I caused only certain written copies to be given to some of my friends, and put Prosopopeia [an imaginary speaker] into the book's mouth. But since that time, Master Camden's often mentioning this work, and my friends' persuasions have caused my determination to alter, and to embrace a pleasing hope that charity and good construction [favourable interpretation] resteth now generally in all readers', etc. Camden referred to this forthcoming work in the earlier editions of the *Britannia*; in the fifth edition of 1594 he says that he cannot withhold the acknowledgement of his own indebtedness to Carew's work. In the 1607 edition (Gough edn, p. 6), having referred to Edgecombe, he continues: 'Near this is *Anthony*, remarkable for its neatness and for a pool ..., but much more remarkable for it[s] lord, Richard *Carew*, who not only maintains the dignity of this family, but reflects additional lustre to it by his virtues.' Carew returned the compliment, referring to Camden eight times in the body of the *Survey*. On Carew's death in 1620 his old friend wrote his epitaph (edn of 1969, p. 318) and made three errors of fact in a total of sixty-eight words. The inscription actually placed near Carew's grave was by another hand.

The topographic arrangement of the *Survey of Cornwall* is by hundredal divisions; Lambarde's *Perambulation of Kent* winds about that county with some measure of continuity: neighbouring places are described in sequence with few breaks. The *Britannia* follows the coasts and the major rivers, filling in between them in a fairly orderly fashion, but missing not a few things on the way for no apparent reason other than the necessity for brevity in a work covering the whole of Britain as opposed to the description of one shire. In Sussex, for instance, he omits Halnaker, Parham and Danny Park, all great houses; Boxgrove Priory, Bayham Abbey and Horsham town; in Surrey he ignores Newark Priory and Haslemere town; and in Kent, the castles of Hever, Sissinghurst and Scotney, houses such as Knole and Ightham Mote, as well as West Malling Abbey. The lists for each of these counties could be further extended to include places significant in Camden's day and comparable with places that he does mention.

Another antiquary to whom he acknowledges his indebtedness was Thomas Talbot, clerk of the records in the Tower and compiler of manuscript collections, some of which found their way into the Cottonian library. 'In the succession of earls,' says Camden, 'not to conceal my obligations to any, I must acknowledge myself under very great ones to Thomas Talbot, a diligent examiner of records, and perfect master of our antiquities' (Gough edn, p. cxlviii).

Among the many who corresponded with Camden and provided him with information was George Owen (d. 1613), who in 1603 published his *Description of Pembrokeshire*; and another was Sampson Erdeswicke (d. 1613) whose *Survey of Staffordshire* was completed in the year of his death. But he was more interested in the county families and their residences than in general topography. A third local antiquary, Mr St Loe Kniveton of Derbyshire, was left £3 by Camden, who expressly recorded his gratitude to him for material used in the Derbyshire chapter of the *Britannia* (Gough edn, II, p. 301).

John Selden (d. 1654), the jurist and antiquary of the Middle Temple; Sir Henry Savile (d. 1622), translator of Tacitus' *Histories*, and his brother Thomas (d. 1593), an antiquary who corresponded with Camden; Sir Henry Spelman (d. 1641), student of Old English and church historian; Sir Henry Wotton (d. 1639), the scholarly ambassador; Sir Edward Hobey (d. 1617), 'my particular friend' (Gough edn, p. 214), translator from French and Spanish, who became a favourite of James I – these and other distinguished men were content to regard the old schoolmaster as a familiar acquaintance.

Closest of all to him was Cotton; but John Stow the tailor (d. 1605), antiquary and collector of chronicles, 'the most accurate and businesslike of the historians of the century' (*D.N.B.*), must also have spent much time in Camden's company. Like Cotton, Stow had collected a library and made its contents available to his friends – and this in spite of poverty. In his chapter on the Danes (Gough edn, p. cxx), Camden cites the work of 'Dudo de St. Quintin a very antient author in the library of John Stowe, the industrious London antiquary, to which I have always free access'. There Camden was able to make use of a transcript of Leland's *Itinerary* and of a large collection of other important topographical works.

Yet even more valuable was the library of Archbishop Parker (d. 1575), one of Camden's early patrons. In it were to be had many precious Old English manuscripts rescued from destruction at the dissolution of the monasteries; and not a few of these texts were otherwise unknown. It formed a complement to Cotton's library, which was collected later, after the greater part of the Parker collection had passed to Corpus Christi College, Cambridge. Parker was also responsible, mainly through his amanuenses, for the earliest editions of several Saxon and medieval texts important to Camden in his work preparatory to the *Britannia*; and Parker's Latin secretary, John Joscelin (d. 1603), was an Anglo-Saxon scholar perhaps second only to Laurence Nowell (d. 1576), whose work was also to be of much benefit

to the Elizabethan antiquaries. Stow was another of those who was employed by Parker as an editor.

John Selden of the Inner Temple was one of the London antiquaries who possessed a library of more than ordinary antiquarian interest. The studies underlying his *Analecton Anglo-Britannicon* [British and English Literary Gleanings] of 1606, a chronological collection of records down to 1066, were probably available to Camden, at least in discussion, during the years preceding his edition of 1607. The antiquary Francis Tate (d. 1616), also of the Inner Temple, collected manuscripts in a more limited way. We know from Camden himself that the important document known as the *Tribal Hidage*, the original of which was probably compiled in the seventh century, was given to him by Tate (Gough edn, p. cxxx). It had once belonged to William Fleetwood and at some time had been copied by Lambarde.

Lord Lumley (d. 1609), a member of the Society of Antiquaries, had a considerable library, including a number of manuscripts from the monasteries. Some of these, especially those of antiquarian interest, were eventually acquired by Cotton. And Lord William Howard (d. 1640), although a baron of the Scottish border, formed a library composed mainly of works of history and heraldry. He was a friend of Cotton and Camden and in 1592 published an edition of the chronicle of Florence of Worcester which was of more than ordinary importance to the student of early medieval history. Camden called him 'an attentive and learned searcher into venerable antiquity'.

Besides the informal and intimate conversations that Camden could enjoy in the company of these many scholarly acquaintances, he took part in the more formal meetings of the Society of Antiquaries, of which many of his friends were members. Besides Cotton, at whose house they met, and Francis Tate, the secretary, there were Stow, the Spelmans (Sir Henry and Sir John), Lord Lumley, the heralds William Dethick and

Francis Thynne, lawyers such as Sir John Dodderidge, the Solicitor-General, and William Fleetwood, the Recorder of London, George Hakewill (d. 1649), the Archdeacon of Surrey and Arthur Agarde (d. 1615), an exchequer official who presented papers to the Society on such topics as the antiquity of the shires, of Parliament and of the Inns of Court. He also did something to elucidate the Domesday Book. Occasional visitors included Lambarde, Carew and Erdeswicke. In his revisions for the later editions of the *Britannia* Camden must have benefited much from the learned discussions that occupied the meetings of the Society. At the end of his life he was shown honour by some of the highest in the land, for his funeral procession included such old friends as Cotton and the members of the College of Arms, as well as some of the greater prelates and nobles.

Through his many friends and acquaintances the total range of manuscripts and printed books to which Camden had access is very remarkable and amply made up for the lack of a national collection. The library accumulated by Parker down to the time of his death and that amassed later by Cotton, together concentrated in and near London a wealth of material within easy reach. Parker's collection was at Lambeth, where Archbishop Bancroft began to form a permanent library in 1610; Cotton's was at his house in Westminster. Stow's library, too, was near by and there were smaller collections at the Middle Temple, as well as the greater libraries of the Inns of Court. Moreover, the muniments at the Guildhall have a bearing on the history of England as well as of London.

The magnitude of Camden's task can best be appreciated by a rather more detailed consideration of the range of sources available to a London antiquary in the late sixteenth century, making some realization possible of how vast were the studies preliminary to the writing of the *Britannia*. Of course, some of Camden's other works – those projected as well as those completed – made a contribution to the introductory chapters and to local detail in the main body of the work, especially where, as often happens, he relates local events to national history. His own edition of the chronicles of Thomas of Walsingham, of William of Jumièges, with part of that of Geoffrey Baker (though then wrongly attributed to Sir Thomas de la More), Asser's *Life of Alfred* and the Giraldus Cambrensis, all published in one book in 1603 at Frankfurt, gave him an intimate knowledge of these texts.

As mentioned in the preface Professor Douglas has said that the 'Britannia is essentially Roman Britain as seen in relation to its later growth'; and indeed the whole plan of the work is determined by the tribal organization in being at the time of the Claudian conquest. Classical texts were therefore crucial to Camden, and not merely those that were familiar to him as a schoolmaster. Caesar's *Commentaries* he knew well, but the printed editions of 1585 and later provided a convenient new text. There had been continental editions of Tacitus in the earlier part of the sixteenth century; later there was sufficient popular interest in his works in England for translations of the *Histories* and *Agricola* to appear in 1581, and the *Annals* and *Germania* in 1598, though, of course, Camden himself had no need of them in English. Printed editions of the elder Pliny's *Natural History* had been published on the Continent at varying intervals from 1473 onwards and Philemon Holland, translator in 1610 of the *Britannia*, produced an English rendering of Pliny in 1601. Diodorus Siculus, mentioned by Camden perhaps more often than his relevance justified, had appeared in print at Basel in 1548 and Strabo's *Geography* was presented in the original Greek four years earlier. Erasmus himself produced an edition of Ptolemy's *Geography* in 1533 and there were several other editions preceding that by Mercator in 1578. The *Antonine Itinerary*, a work fundamental to Camden's method, had been twice published abroad in the early sixteenth century; in England, Robert Talbot's manuscript notes on the British section is known to have been available to Leland, Lambarde and Camden. As Sir Thomas Kendrick has pointed out (*British Antiquity*, p. 135), this work afforded scholars what was essentially a skeletal map of Roman Britain. Also available, though less valuable for Camden's purpose, was the Peutinger Table, which had been discovered in 1507. Camden had learned of its details long before its publication. And the last of the essential classical sources that he used was the *Notitia Dignitatum*, printed at Basel in 1552. He refers to later works such as the *Panegyrici Latini*, the largely fictional *Historia Augusta*, *Ammianus Marcellinus* and the *Historia* of Orosius, but they are of no great consequence as his sources and all but the *Panegyrici* were available to him in sixteenth-century printed editions or in manuscripts. He could, however, have taken what he wanted of them from secondary sources.

The raw material for writing the history of fifth-century Britain was to hand in Polydore Vergil's edition of Gildas's *de Excidio* of 1525 and there was a manuscript copy of Nennius' *Historia Brittonum* in Cotton's library in 1617 which may well have been there a decade earlier. Cotton also possessed a number of the works fundamental to a reconstruction of the history of the Anglo-Saxons, including seven of the principal recensions of the Old English Chronicle, namely the manuscripts now usually known as Ā, A, B, C, D, E and F, the last of which is in English and Latin. This bilingual text had formerly been in Camden's own possession and the manuscript included Robert de Monte's Chronicle. The manuscript closest to the archetype of the Old English Chronicle, manuscript Ā, had been one of Archbishop Parker's treasured possessions and on his death in 1575 it passed, with much else from his library, to Corpus Christi College, Cambridge, in a binding that included texts of the laws of kings Ine and Alfred of Wessex, a list of popes and of archbishops to whom they had sent the pallium, as well as lists of English bishops and archbishops. Cotton also had one of the versions of the genealogy of the West Saxon kings down to Edward the Martyr (d. 978). Equally important for the Anglo-Saxon period was Bede's *Ecclesias-*

tical History. Cotton had two of the earliest and least corrupt texts and besides these Camden probably had access to one or more of the ten or so editions of Bede printed on the Continent. They range in date from 1475 to 1601. The version printed at Antwerp in 1550 was especially valuable in that it was a critical revision of the text based on good manuscripts.

Copies of the laws of the kings of Kent and Wessex were at one time or another in the possession of men known to Camden, some of them well known to him. Apart from Archbishop Parker and his Latin secretary John Joscelin (d. 1603), Selden had owned several of these texts. Some of the Parker copies of the laws are known to have been studied by Talbot, Nowell and Lambarde, as well as by Joscelin; and the *Textus Roffensis*, used by Parker and Lambarde, and probably known to Camden, comprised laws of the early Kentish kings, the laws of Alfred and the later West Saxon kings, genealogies of the Saxon and Anglian royal houses, lists of popes and emperors and of English bishops and archbishops, most of which were useful at least for preserving a relative chronology. There are also in the *Textus* binding the laws of the Conqueror and the *Institutiones henrici regis* (i.e. Henry I), besides a cartulary of the priory of Rochester Cathedral.

Other basic texts which Camden knew at first hand or in transcripts were the *Burghal Hidage*, bound in with manuscript A of the *Anglo-Saxon Chronicle*, which was in Cotton's library; and a manuscript of the *Tribal Hidage* which had belonged to William Fleetwood. Yet another Cottonian text that Camden refers to is that which recounts the revival of monasticism in tenth-century England; but the ownership of the manuscript of King Alfred's will, referred to several times in the *Britannia*, cannot be traced back before the early eighteenth century. Obviously, however, he had access to an original or a transcript of it, probably through the good offices of one of the London antiquaries.

Lastly among important documents of the Anglo-Saxon period, mention should be made of the land charters, which throw some light on several aspects of Anglo-Saxon history. It is doubtful, however, whether much of the indirect evidence that they afford to modern scholars was derivable from them by Camden and his contemporaries, however learned. Certainly there is little in the *Britannia* to suggest it. Yet scores of charters were to be found in Cotton's library (Sawyer, *Anglo-Saxon Charters*, pp. 50–54) and Parker had possessed many too (ibid., pp. 44–5). There were others at the College of Arms, at Lambeth Palace, at the Guildhall (ibid., pp. 57–8), St Paul's (ibid., p. 61), Westminster Abbey (ibid., p. 62), and above all in the royal records, of which Domesday Book was an important item. This latter source was not printed until 1783, but the original was easily accessible to Camden and he cites it from time to time, especially in his remarks on the earlier history of the towns.

About two hundred manuscripts of Geoffrey of Monmouth's *History of the Kings of Britain* are known to exist and some no doubt have been lost. Printed editions appeared in Paris in 1508 and 1517 and in Heidelberg in 1587. A text of one kind or another was to be had in Elizabethan London, for Camden and his contemporaries obviously used one; but he, unlike Leland, largely rejected it and it is of little significance in relation to the *Britannia*.

Of the other numerous medieval sources only a few of the main ones need to be noticed here. As was said earlier, Camden himself had edited Asser's *Life of Alfred*, the chronicles of Walsingham and Jumièges and some of the works of Baker and Cambrensis. It was natural that he should cite these most familiar works rather more often than their relevance warranted. The works of William of Malmesbury, or at least some of them, could be consulted in Lord Lumley's library and Matthew Paris was readily accessible in Stow's edition of 1571. Stow's other editions, such as his Matthew of Westminster of 1567 and his *Chronicles of England* of 1580 were also easily available. Henry of Huntingdon's *History of the English* came later, in 1597, among Savile's *Rerum Angli-*

carum Scriptores post Bedam, but in good time for the expanded editions of the *Britannia*. Higden's *Polychronicon* was to be had in a transcript by Nowell as well as in Caxton's edition of 1480. The fact that William Howard was able to translate Florence of Worcester's *Chronicon ex Chronicis* in 1592 makes it likely that a manuscript was available to the London antiquaries, of which Howard was one. Similarly, Camden's use of one of Walter Map's works, those of John of Salisbury and of others, was made possible either by the accessibility of the original manuscripts or by transcripts of them.

The number of printed works on topographical subjects was few and apart from Lambarde's *Perambulation of Kent*, which Camden acknowledged that he used extensively, of no great help; but there was Leland's unpublished and invaluable *Itinerary* to be drawn on copiously, probably in John Stow's transcript of it. The extent of Camden's debt to Leland was amply demonstrated by Gough in his 'Additions' to the edition of 1789, in which he cites the *Itinerary* often at considerable length. This has been done also in the present edition not simply to reveal the sometimes frequent dependence of the one topographer upon the other, but because of the intrinsic interest of Leland's observations and their illumination of Camden's text.

Leland's was an unfinished work that would probably have remained unfinished even had he retained his sanity and lived long enough to have been able to complete it. Its merit, even where it consists only of rough jottings, is the immediacy of his descriptions: the notes seem often to have been made on the spot as he stood, or sat his horse, viewing a building. Camden, on the other hand, generalizes and seldom gives the reader an impression of first-hand witness. One of the very few instances of his deliberate showing of first-hand knowledge occurs in his paragraph on Wallingford (Gough edn, p. 148). Speaking of the castle, he confesses: 'Its size and magnificence used to strike me with astonishment when I came thither a lad from Oxford, it being a retreat for the students of Christ Church.' But there was little room in the *Britannia* for such things. In order to keep it within manageable compass, he was forced to eschew detail and to compress his descriptions, so much so that many of them are lacking in the kind of particularity that serves to make memorable distinctions. Occasionally, his reference to places is so perfunctory as to be hardly worth the space they occupy in the text.

But the point in which he differs most essentially from Leland is in his constantly associating places with people, whereas Leland is interested in a place for its own sake, rather than for its antiquarian or human associations. He was primarily interested in the England of his own day; Camden was mainly concerned with the contemporary appearance of things only in so far as they illustrated the past, and preferably the distant past. As Kendrick so rightly says (*British Antiquity*, p. 150): 'There is no sense of joyous exploration in Camden's work. . . . In his slow-moving dignified description of Britain he found little room to record the erratic enthusiasms of his famous predecessor.' Nevertheless, he showed 'how great was the unexplored wealth of valid antiquarian evidence to be found by going to look for it'; and in this he set an example of research in the field – or rather along the highways and byways – that even today continues to influence topographical studies. And a further debt was owed to Leland, whose journeys between 1534 and 1543 had as their ostensible purpose the search for manuscripts to be included in Henry VIII's library, and although topography soon came to dominate his mind, he was not altogether unmindful of the King's commission to him. His *Itinerary* and even more the *Collectanea* contain numerous extracts from medieval chronicles that provided Camden with source material not otherwise available to

him, though he does not acknowledge his intermediate source. But he does cite and acknowledge Leland's poem *Cygnea Cantio* of 1545 (Gough edn, p. 211, and see also p. 117); and his *Assertio . . . Arthurii* of the previous year is the origin of some other of Camden's statements. This work of Leland's was intended as a counterblast to Polydore Vergil's assertions that Geoffrey of Monmouth had mingled fact with fiction in his *History* and particularly in his account of King Arthur. Leland admitted that Geoffrey made some mistakes, but sought to rebut the charge that parts of the work were fictional. Leland's fanatical patriotism stifled any critical sense he might have brought to bear on Geoffrey's work; yet already in the first edition of the *Britannia* in 1586, Camden leaned towards Polydore Vergil's view.

But Camden himself was certainly not scrupulous in his use of evidence. In the notes to the present edition a number of instances will be found where he has altered an early form of a place-name in order that it should the better fit into some preconceived notion that he had of its origin. Professor Douglas (*English Scholars*, p. 23) says of seventeenth-century scholars that 'sometimes they allowed the intensity of their beliefs to distort their use of evidence' and (ibid., p. 165): 'Neither Commelin nor Camden displayed a sufficient regard for accuracy or a nice discrimination in their choice of materials.' Yet with all his faults, in genealogy, in the handling of evidence and, if indeed it can be called a fault, in his omissions of significant places comparable with those he includes, Camden's achievement in the *Britannia* remains among the greatest in sixteenth-century scholarship. His work is of enduring value to all who seek to explain the detailed features of the face of Britain.

ABBREVIATIONS USED IN THE NOTES

Additions	Gough's Additions to his translation of 1789
Ant. Journ.	Antiquaries Journal
Arch. Cant.	Archaeologia Cantiana
Arch. Journ.	Archaeological Journal
Arch. Kent	The County Archaeologies: Kent
A.S. Charters	Anglo-Saxon Charters
A.S. Chron.	The Anglo-Saxon Chronicle
Bede (E.H. or *H.E.)*	Ecclesiastical History of the English People (Plummer)
B. of E.	The Buildings of England series
Brit.	Britannia, a History of Roman Britain
Camb. Hist. Eng. Lit.	Cambridge History of English Literature
Cinque Ports	The Constitutional History of the Cinque Ports
Coastline	The Coastline of England and Wales
Dic.	The Concise Oxford Dictionary of English Place-Names
D.N.B.	Dictionary of National Biography
Domesday Geog. S.E. Eng.	The Domesday Geography of South-East England
E.H.D.	English Historical Documents
Elements	English Place-Name Elements
Eng. River N.	English River-Names
E.P.D.	English Pronouncing Dictionary
E.P.N.S.	English Place-Name Society
Etym. Dic.	The Oxford Dictionary of English Etymology
Hist. Geog. Eng.	An Historical Geography of England before A.D. 1800
K.P.N.	Kentish Place-Names
Lamb.	A Perambulation of Kent (Lambarde)
Lang. & Hist.	Language and History in Early Britain
Lost Villages	The Lost Villages of England
L.T.S.	Itinerary in England and Wales in or about the Years 1535–1543
Med. Arch.	Medieval Archaeology
Med. Eng.	Medieval England: an aerial survey
New Towns	New Towns of the Middle Ages: Town Plantations in England, Wales and Gascony
Norman Conquest	The Norman Conquest: its Setting and Impact
The Normans	The Normans and the Norman Conquest
Orig. E.P.N.	The Origin of English Place-Names
Oxf. Hist.	Oxford History of England
P.N. Kent	The Place-Names of Kent
Public Records	An Introduction to the Use of the Public Records
S.E. Eng.	An Archaeology of South-East England
Surnames	The Penguin Dictionary of Surnames
Two Saxon Chrons.	Two of the Saxon Chronicles Parallel
V.C.H.	Victoria County Histories

CANTIUM · KENT

SELECT BIBLIOGRAPHY

References to the companion volume on Surrey and
Sussex are given as *Surrey* or *Sussex*

Antiquaries Journal, VIII, 1928; XIX, 1939

Archaeologia Cantiana (Publications of the Kent Archaeological Society), LIII, 1940: 'Stonar and the Wantsum Channel', F. W. Hardman and W. P. D. Stebbing; LIV, 1941; LV, 1942; LXV, 1952

Archaeological Journal, LXXXVI, 1929; XCVII, 1940; CXXV, 1968; CXXVI, 1969: 'The Anglo-Saxon Cathedral Church at Canterbury', H. M. Taylor, 101f.; 'The Roman Haven of Dover', S. E. Rigold, 78f.; 'The Summer Meeting at Canterbury', A. D. Saunders et al., 181f.

Buildings of England, The: North-East and East Kent; West Kent and The Weald, J. Newman, 1969

Canterbury under the Angevin Kings, W. Urry, 1967

Coastline of England and Wales, The, J. A. Steers, 1946, 318f.

Constitutional History of the Cinque Ports, The, K. M. E. Murray, 1935

County Archaeologies, The: Kent, R. F. Jessup, 1930

Domesday Geography of South-East England, The, H. C. Darby and E. M. J. Campbell (eds.), 1962, 483f.

Dover Castle (Official Guide), R. A. Brown, 1966

Excavations at Faversham, 1965, B. Philp, 1968

History of Kent, F. W. Jessup, 1958

Hundred of Hoo, The, R. Arnold, 1947

Invaders' Shore, The, W. P. D. Stebbing, 1937 (Deal and Walmer)

Kentish Place-Names, J. K. Wallenberg, 1931

Little Guides, The: Kent, R. F. Jessup, 1950

Lullingstone Roman Villa, The, G. W. Meates, 1955

Medieval Archaeology, II, 1958; III, 1959; V, 1961; VI–VII, 1943; VIII, 1964; IX, 1965: 'Early Kentish Churches', E. Fletcher, 16f.; X, 1966; XIII, 1969; XIV, 1970; XVI, 1972

New Towns of the Middle Ages, M. Beresford, 1967, 456f. (Hythe, Queenborough and New Romney)

Perambulation of Kent, A, W. Lambarde, 1570, edn of 1826, rep. 1970

Place-Names of Kent, The, J. K. Wallenberg, 1934

Richborough: Fourth Report on the Roman Excavations, J. P. Bushe-Fox, 1949; *Fifth Report on the Roman Excavations*, B. W. Cunliffe, 1968

Roman Canterbury, S. Frere, 4th edn, 1965

Roman Folkestone, S. E. Winbolt, 1925

St Augustine's Abbey, Canterbury (Official Guide), A. Clapham, 1955

Victoria County History, The: Kent, vols. II and III, 1932

The General Bibliography is on p. 91.

CANTIUM

I COME now to Kent; which county, though so exactly described in a work expressly on the subject by WILLIAM LAMBARDE,[01] a person of great learning and character, and so happy in his researches that he has left very little for others,[a] yet the method of my design requires that I should survey this as well as the rest; and that I may not be suspected of unfair dealing, as the Comedian[b] says, I gladly embrace this opportunity to acknowledge this work for the foundation and source of my knowledge here.

Time has not yet stripped this county of its antient name, but, as Cæsar, Strabo, Diodorus Siculus,[c] Ptolomy, and others, called it CANTIUM,[05] so the Saxons, according to Ninnius, called it 'Cant-guar-lantd',[06] q.d. *the country of the people inhabiting Cantium*, and we at present KENT. Mr. Lambarde derives this name from *Cainc*, which in British signifies, a Leaf,[d] because the country was antiently covered with woods.[08] If I might be allowed to hazard a conjecture, as I observe Britain runs out here with a large corner eastward, and find the like

a. Lambarde returns Camden's compliment by calling him the most *lightsome* Antiquary of this age, p. 9. Ed, 1596. 4to.[02]

b. *Sublesta fide*. Plaut. Pers. 3.1.20.[03]

c. Some copies of Diodorus read corruptly *Carion*. C. One MS. reads Κατιον by an obvious omission of the *ν*. Lib. V. p. 346.[04]

d. Bowghes or woody. Lamb. p. 9.[07]

01 William Lambarde (1536–1601) produced a collection of Anglo-Saxon laws (1568) and wrote other legal works of great authority. He finished the draught of his *Perambulation of Kent* in 1570 and it was first printed in 1574. A second edition of 1596 was reprinted in 1826 and again in 1970. It was the first of the county histories to be published and it afforded a model in arrangement and style for later works of the kind. Lambarde had embarked on research to cover the whole of England, but abandoned it after hearing of Camden's project for the *Britannia*, a work which treated each of the counties more summarily than Lambarde had treated Kent. He died at Greenwich and was first buried there, but later his body was removed to Sevenoaks where his monument may be seen. For it see *B. of E., W. Kent*, p. 491. Camden's indebtedness to Lambarde is evident in almost every paragraph of this volume and the more obvious instances of this borrowing have been indicated in the following notes by *Lamb*. with page references to the reprint of the *Perambulation* of 1970.

02 'lightsome' here means 'illuminating'.

03 Plautus (c. 254–184 B.C.), the Roman comic poet. The phrase cited is from the *Persa*.

04 Diodorus Siculus, a Sicilian of CI B.C., not a trustworthy authority.

05 Caesar did indeed call it *Cantium*, and Diodorus, Ptolemy and Strabo give its Greek equivalent Καντιον (*Dic.*, p. 259). Jackson, *Journal of Roman Studies* XXXVIII, 55, suggests that the name of the region is probably a derivative from the tribal name, meaning 'land of the Cantii', and that the name of the people might mean 'the hosts or armies' or possibly 'the people of the borderland'.

06 Nennius was a Welshman of C8 and accommodated English names to his own language. The more usual Old English forms are *Cent(land)* or *Kent(land)*. *Cantguar* is a rendering of Old English *Cantware*, 'people of Kent'. See Canterbury, p. 42, n. 70.

07 *Bowghes* means 'boughs, limbs of trees'; *Lamb*. refers to *Perambulation of Kent*, which is, in this matter, more correct than Camden. The etymology occurs on p. 2 of the reprint of 1970.

08 This is an overstatement; the Weald, which name itself means forest, was probably almost continuous forest, as were much of the chalk lands, wherever they are overlaid by clay-with-flints; but the higher chalk regions were probably unwooded.

09 Kintyre or Cantyre, a peninsula in the south of Argyllshire. In the Dark Ages it was called *Cendtire*. See O.S. *Map of Britain in the Dark Ages*. The *Decantae* inhabited the more southerly parts of what is now Ross and Cromarty, mainly Wester Ross. See O.S. *Map of Roman Britain*, p. 20.

10 This is probably a mistake for *Gangani*, a tribe located by Ptolemy (O.S. *Map of Roman Britain*, p. 20) on the north side of the River Shannon, near its estuary. There may well have been a confusion between initial 'C' and 'G' in Camden's source.

11 A people of northern Spain conquered by the Romans 25–19 B.C.

12 A people of central Spain who for many decades down to 72 B.C. succeeded in resisting the Romans.

13 The Celtiberians were partly Celtic, as their name suggests, and the *Gangani* probably wholly so. Hence they originally had a 'common language with our Britans', though this, in itself, does not go far in proving an identity of word-root in the tribal and place-names cited by Camden.

14 It was borrowed into English with this meaning in c16.

15 The etymology of the word-root *cant-* is obscure. The Helvetii was a tribe occupying at one time part of modern Switzerland. Here the Swiss are meant. Herodotus (c. 480–425 B.C.), the Greek historian, is an authority of value whenever he writes from personal knowledge. The *Kynetai* may have been the same people as the *Cynetes* of what is now southern Portugal.

16 Larousse derives it from Italian *cantone*; *Etym. Dic.*, p. 142, merely indicates that the French and Italian words are equivalent. However, see n. 05 above.

corners in Scotland called *Cantir*,[09] and the inhabitants of another corner in that part of the island called by Ptolemy *Cantæ*, and another in Wales occupied by the *Cangani*[10] (not to mention the *Cantabri*,[11] who possessed an angle among the Celtiberians[12]); who, as they had one common origin, so had also one common language with our Britans,[13] I should suppose the name given it from its situation, and the rather, because the French our neighbours use *Canton*[14] for a *Corner*,[e] and probably from the old Gaulish language, it not being deduced from the German or Latin,[16] which, together with the antient language, have contributed to form the modern French, and because this country is called a *Corner* by all the antient geographers. For it faces France with a great angle, surrounded on every side by the Thames' mouth and the ocean, except where bounded on the west by Surrey, and on the south by part of Sussex.

KENT

THE country at present called KENT is much diversified, being more level and woody to the west,[17] and to the east rising with gentle hills.[18] The inhabitants divide the south part along the Thames[19] into three parts, or, as they call them, *degrees*,[a] of which the uppermost[21] on the Thames they

e. Whence *Canton* in heraldry for a *corner*, and the districts of the Helvetii are called by the French *Cantones*, q.d. *Corners* (C.) rather *divisions* or *cantonments*. Concerning the Κυνηται of Herodotus mistaken by some for the Cantii of Cæsar and introduced here again by bishop Gibson, see before.[15]

a. Which do not appear in Lambarde or Hasted.[20]

17 The Weald Clay region from around Appledore to the neighbourhood of Edenbridge with a WNW trend.

18 The Lower Greensand line of hills and the North Downs. Like most such brief statements, this of Camden's is only very roughly true, for there is higher land to the south and west of the Weald Clay and lower to the east of the hills.

19 This must mean along the southern shore of the Thames estuary.

20 On Lambarde see n. 01 (*Lamb.*,

pp. 7, 74). Edward Hasted (1732–1812) spent 40 years on the compilation of his *History and Topographical Survey of Kent*, which was published in four volumes from 1778 to 1799. Only the earlier ones were available to Gough towards the very end of the long period of study for his edition of the *Britannia* in 1789.

21 Presumably around Greenwich, Charlton and Woolwich, which are situated on well-drained soils. The second 'part' would then be the Greenhithe and Gravesend area.

2

account most healthy and rich; the lowermost rich but un-healthy, being for the most part marshy,* but producing most luxurious herbage. Almost the whole county abounds with meadows, pastures, and corn fields, is wonderfully fruitful in apples, as also cherries, which were brought from Pontus into Italy in the year of Rome 680†,[23] and about 120 years after into Britain.[24] They thrive here exceedingly, and cover large tracts of ground, and the trees being planted in the quincunx[25] exhibit an agreeable view. It has many cities and towns, toler-ably safe harbours, and some iron mines,[26] but the air is some-what thick from the vapours rising from the waters. The inhabitants still deserve that reputation for humanity [27] which Cæsar formerly gave them: not to mention their courage, which a certain monk [28] says the Kentishmen possessed in so eminent a degree, that in the disposition of the English army, the front was assigned to them as the flower of the English troops.[b] Johannes Sarisburiensis [30] proves the same in his Poly-craticon.[c] "In reward for that illustrious valour which our Kent displayed with vigour and perseverance against the Danes, it has still the honour of the foremost rank and the first charge[32] in all battles." Malmesbury [d] also celebrates them to this effect:

*Rumney Marsh.[22]　　　　　　　　　　†Plin. 15, c. 25.
b. *Tanquam triariis*.[29]
c. The Triarii were always in the rear, whence Livy VIII. 8. describing a desperate push says, *Ad triarios res rediit*,[31] but as they were the men on whom the greatest confidence was placed, the comparison holds equally true of our Kentishmen, whatever part of the battle was assigned them.
d. De gest. Pont. prol. lib. I.[33]

22 As Thames-side marshes are clearly intended here, they must be those of the Hundred of Hoo and of the Isle of Sheppey. Camden's afterthought here is a slip.

23 According to legend, Rome was founded in 753 B.C. and on that reckoning, according to Camden, the cherry arrived here in about A.D. 47.

24 Pliny in his *Natural History*, XV, 25, put the introduction of the cherry to Britain after c. A.D. 50. But there were cherries in northern England before the Roman Conquest. See R. E. M. Wheeler,

The Stanwick Fortifications, 1954, p. 60 and n. In Wales, the stones of wild cherry have been found in late Neolithic context. See W. F. Grimes, *Prehistory of Wales*, 1951, p. 28. Pontus was a state on the Black Sea in the north-east of Asia Minor. John Aubrey in C17 believed that 'Cherries were first brought into Kent tempore H. viii, who being in Flanders, and likeing the Cherries, ordered his Gardener, brought them hence and propagated them in England.' *Aubrey's Brief Lives*, ed. O. L. Dick, 1962, p. 28. Aubrey probably had this from Lambarde (*Lamb.*, pp. 222–3).

25 The spatial arrangement of 5 on a dice.

26 The Wealden iron industry was mainly in Sussex, but there were certainly ironworks round Lamberhurst, Bayham, Brenchley and Horsmonden in which region surviving hammer-ponds and place-names such as Furnace Wood, Furnace Mill, Furnace Pond and Cinderhill are memorials. A Lamberhurst forge produced the iron railings for St Paul's Cathedral. For the blooming process, see *Med. Eng.*, p. 237; for the industry in Sussex, see p. 30, n. 15, *Sussex*.

27 'By far the most civilized inhabitants are those living in Kent... whose way of life differs little from that of the Gauls.' Caesar, *Conquest of Gaul*, p. 136, n.

28 Leland (*L.T.S.* IV, 57) cites Gervase, the monk of Canterbury (fl. 1188) as saying this.

29 The *triarios* were soldiers of the third rank in the Roman army and were commonly used as reserves. See Gough's note c.

30 John of Salisbury (d. 1180) studied under Abelard in Paris, where he met Theobald, archbishop of Canterbury, whose service he entered. Having offended Henry II, he retired to Rheims. He later entered Thomas à Becket's service, was with him in Canterbury in 1170 at the time of the martyrdom, and wrote Becket's life. He became bishop of Chartres. He was 'the most learned classical writer of the middle ages' (*D.N.B.*, p. 694). See also *Camb. Hist. Eng. Lit.* I, 187; *Oxf. Hist.* III, 3, 195, 235–6 etc.; *Wandering Scholars*, passim.

31 The attack reached the *triarii*.

32 'major responsibility'.

33 Book I of *Gesta Pontificum Anglorum* (History of the English Bishops) finished 1125. William of Malmesbury's *History of the Kings of England* and his *Modern History*

3

range from A.D. 449 to 1142, which was probably the year before his death. Like his contemporary chroniclers, he wrote in Latin. On his fine quality as an historian see the brief account of him in the *Camb. Hist. Eng. Lit.* I, 164–6.

34 The Camden reading was restored by Gough to the English translation. *Acrior* in the passage would mean 'the more vehement in resenting insults'.

35 Gough's edition of the *Britannia*, pp. xxvi–lxiv. On p. xlvi, note Z, he observes that Camden 'seems to have taken his account chiefly [of the civil and military organization of Britain] from the *Notitia*'. The *Notitia Dignitatum* is an official list of the disposition of the Roman forces in the Empire in c4. See O.S. *Map of Roman Britain*, text p. 17.

36 Segovax.

37 For a recent discussion of Caesar's two British expeditions see *Brit.*, p. 27f.

38 On the organization of the province see *Brit.*, p. 194f., and on its re-organization in early c4, p. 210f.

39 The location of forts of the Saxon Shore from west to east was Porchester, Hants. (much of it surviving), Pevensey, Sussex (impressive remains), Lympne, Kent (only a few shattered fragments), Dover, Kent (much surviving), Reculver, Kent (parts of the ramparts remain after heavy erosion by the sea), Bradwell, Essex (also eroded by the sea, a small fragment of wall still visible), Burgh, Suffolk (much surviving), and Brancaster, Norfolk (little visible). The fort at Walton, near Felixstowe, has been entirely destroyed by the sea. The fort at Bitterne, Hants. (completely destroyed) replaced that at Porchester in about A.D. 370. On the last point see B. Cunliffe, *The Regni*, 1973,

"The rustic yet civilized people of Kent more than the rest of the English still breathe a consciousness of their antient nobility, being the foremost to exercise acts of respect and hospitality, and the last[e] to resent injuries."

But to premise a few particulars before I come to the places themselves: Cæsar, on his first approach to our island, made a descent, and as the Kentish Britans opposed his landing, he could not make himself master of the shore without a sharp dispute. In his second expedition to our island, he landed his army here, and the Britans gave him a warm reception with their horse and chariots at the river Sture; but were soon repulsed by the Romans, and retired into the woods. From thence they made frequent sallies, skirmishing with the Roman horse on their march, but the latter had always the advantage. Some time after they made a fresh attack on the Romans, forced their way through the centre of their army, and having slain Laberius Durus a military tribune, retreated with safety, and the next day annoyed the foragers, &c. as I have before[*] related from Cæsar. At this time Kent was governed by Cyngetorix, Carvilius, Taximagulus, and Segonax,[36] whom Cæsar, to make it seem that he had subdued kings, honours with that title,[37] though they were in fact only petty princes, or noblemen of the first rank. When the Roman empire was established here Kent was put under the governor of Britannia Prima.[38] The sea coast called the *Saxon Shore*,[39] as was also the opposite coast from the Rhine to Xainctoigne[40] had an officer from the time of Diocletian[41] called by Marcellinus[42] *Count of the sea coast*, and in the Notitia *a respectable*[43] *person*,[f] *Count*

e. Camden reads, ad propulsandas injurias *serior*. The printed Ed. Lond. 1596. & Francf. 1601. *acrior*.[34]   *Romans in Britain.[35]

f. *Vir spectabilis.* He had under him 2200 foot and horse. G.[44]

p. 127, and for the forts of the Saxon Shore in general see *Roman Britain*, pp. 60–61; *Roman Forts of the Saxon Shore*; *Brit.*, pp. 338–9.

40 Now the name of a former province, Saintonge, immediately to the north of the Gironde estuary. For the location of the Gaulish forts, none of which occurs between Boulogne and the Rhine, see *Roman Forts*, map p. 4.

41 Roman Emperor A.D. 284–304.

42 Ammianus Marcellinus wrote a history of the Roman Empire covering the period from A.D. 96 to 378. Only the sections from the year 353 survive.

43 i.e. 'worthy of respect by virtue of his office'.

44 On this and the following military units see *Arch. Journ.* XCVII, 144.

of the Saxon shore in Britain, whose office was by disposing garrisons at proper places along the coast to restrain the inroads of the barbarous nations, but especially the Saxons, who grievously harrassed Britain. He was under the direction of *the illustrious officer of foot*[g] called *Præsentalis*,[h] who, besides garrisons at ports, assigned him for greater emergencies the cohorts called *Victores Juniores Britanniciani*, *Primani*[46] *Juniores*, & *Secundani*[47] *Juniores*. His officers were a commander in chief of foot under the Præsental, two accountants, a secretary, a register[48] of sentences, an adjutant or assistant, a deputy adjutant, a register, receivers of the revenue, shorthand writers, and other inferior officers.[i] Nor do I doubt but our ancestors imitated this plan of the Romans in appointing a warden or governor of the ports along this coast, commonly called *Warden of the cinque ports* from his presiding over five ports as the Count of the Saxon shore did over nine.[50]

When the Romans quitted Britain,[51] Vortigern,[52] who had the supreme command over the greatest part of Britain, appointed over Kent a *Guorong*,[53] that is a *Viceroy*, or *Freed-*

g. *Illustris magister peditum.*

h. From his constant attendance.[45]

i. *Princeps ex officio magistri præsentalium a parte peditum: numerarii duo, commentariensis, cornicularius, adjutor, subadjuva, regendarius, exceptores, singulares, & reliqui officiales.* Bishop Gibson translates *commentariensis* a goaler, which is certainly the more common meaning in later writers; but as Du Cange gives instances wherein it means *notarius*, I adopt that, and the rather as he shews that *Cornicularius* was a writer derived from his *ink horn*, and not from a horn to sound. *Singularis* is by Cujacius rendered a shorthand writer.[49]

45 i.e. 'present, at hand'.

46 Soldiers of the First Legion.

47 Soldiers of the Second Legion. This unit was in Britain from the time of Hadrian, and from c. A.D. 70 was at Caerleon. Later, in C4, it was at Richborough.

48 In the English of C16 this could mean 'registrar'.

49 On Bishop Gibson, see Appendix. Du Cange (1610–88) was a French scholar who produced a valuable dictionary of medieval Latin, *Glossaire de la moyenne et de la basse latinité*, in 1678; and Cujacius is presumably the Latinized form of

the surname of another Frenchman, Jacques Cujas (1522–90), who was an authority on Roman Law.

50 From A.D. 1012 'every English king had possessed a permanent naval force ... manned by professional crews'. By 1051 this force had been abolished and in its stead Edward the Confessor made agreements with the men of Sandwich, Dover, Fordwich and Romney and probably with Hythe and Hastings, to provide a fleet in emergencies. Rye, Winchelsea and several 'members' were added later (*Oxf. Hist.*II, 424–6). In this is seen the origin of the Cinque Ports,

which received charters in the reign of Henry II (*Oxf. Hist.*III, 433–4). Edward I tightened their organization and made them the nucleus of a naval command under an admiral (*Oxf. Hist.*IV, 655). On the Warden of the Cinque Ports see *Cinque Ports*, p. 77f. This office evolved during C13, culminating in the Wardenship of Sir Stephen de Pencestre (Penshurst) with whom the link between the offices of Warden and of Constable of Dover Castle became permanent (ibid., p. 80). Camden's analogy, then, with the system of defence of the Saxon Shore is not inapposite and there was indeed some topographical correspondence between the two systems: *Anderita* and Pevensey; *Lemanis* (Stutfall Castle) and Hythe; *Dubris* and Dover; *Rutupiae* (Richborough) and Sandwich. For a list of the Wardens see *Lamb.*, p. 114f.

51 On 'the controversy concerning a Roman re-occupation of Britain after 410' see *Oxf. Hist.*I, 292–301; *Roman Britain* (Britain in Pictures), p. 48; and cp. *Arch. Journ.* XCVII, 125f.

52 On Vortigern see *Oxf. Hist.*I, 314f., 357f. The use of Germanic mercenary soldiers, comparable with the band of Hengist and Horsa, in late Roman Britain is increasingly confirmed by archaeological finds and studies. See 'Romano-Saxon Pottery' in *Dark Age Britain*. The evidence of coins for this period is reviewed in the same volume, p. 3f., by C. H. V. Sutherland. The mercenaries' accoutrements are studied by S. C. Hawkes and G. C. Dunning in *Med. Arch.* V; J. Morris *The Age of Arthur*, revised edn, 1975.

53 This story is from Nennius, a Welshman, editor of a *History of the Britons* of early C9, who, though he used his sources quite uncritically, provides some useful scraps of information about the coming of the Anglo-Saxons to Britain. In

Geoffrey of Monmouth (VI, 12) he becomes (Earl) Gorangonus (*Lamb.*, p. 12).

54 For a modern edition of the Benedictine *acta* see *Oxf. Hist.* IV, 737.

55 On Ninnius (Nennius) see n. 53 above.

56 On William of Malmesbury and his *Gesta Regum Anglorum*, see p. 3, n. 33. The *Anglo-Saxon Chronicle* ignores the Rowena story perhaps because in the earlier annals it relies only on English sources. For Vortigern (Wyrtgeorn) see the next note (annals for 449 and 455).

57 It may have been the first kingdom, but it was probably not the first Saxon settlement in Britain. See J. N. L. Myres, 'The Adventus Saxonum' in *Aspects of Archaeology in Britain and Beyond*, ed. W. F. Grimes, 1951, p. 221f.

The annals of the *Anglo-Saxon Chronicle* (MS 'A') that enshrine the traditions of the conquest of Kent are:

449 – In this year Mauricius [corrected to 'Martianus'] and Valentinian became Roman emperors and reigned for VII years. And in their days Hengest and Horsa, having been invited by Wyrtgeorn [Vortigern] king of the Britons, arrived in Britain [at the place] on the shore which is called *Ypwines fleot* [Ebbsfleet], at first to aid the Britons, but they fought against them later. [Then follows an addition by a Canterbury scribe of C12, *E.H.D.* I, 142, n. 3]: The king commanded them to fight against the Picts and they did so and were victorious wherever they went. Then they sent to Angel [their homeland] and commanded them to send reinforcements and to inform them of the worthlessness of the Welsh and of the excellence of the land. They [of the homeland] then sent them reinforcements. These men came from three German tribes: the Old Saxons, the Angles, [and] the Jutes. From the Jutes sprang the people of Kent and of Wight, [and] that is the tribe which still dwells in Wight and the people among the West Saxons that is still called the

man,[k] without whose knowledge he presently after freely gave up Kent, according to Ninnius[1] and Malmesbury,[m] to Hengist the Saxon, to oblige his daughter Rowenna, of whom he was violently enamoured. Thus was founded the first Saxon kingdom in Britain, A.D. 456,[57] called in their language 'Cant-wara-ric',[58] *the kingdom of the Kentishmen*, which, 320 years after, by the defeat of Baldred the last king, came into the power of the West Saxons,[n] to whom it remained subject to

k. Acta Bened. sec. 4ti. in Marcwardo, p. 608. MS. n. Gale.[54]

l. *c*. 36. He calls him *King Guoirangon*.[55]

m. De gest. reg. I. p. 4. The Saxon chronicle takes no notice of Rouenna, but says that Hengist won Kent by force of arms, having defeated Vortigern in two battles at Aylesford and Crayford, where he killed four companies of the Britans, and put the rest to flight, A.D. 455. 457. Saxon Chron. p. 13.[56]

n. Sax. Chroh. Flor. Wig. A.D. 823. not 830. as Gibson. Chron. Mailros, A.D. 824. M. Westm. 827. I do not find his authority for saying that Baldred left his kingdom to his son Athelstan.[59]

people of the Jutes. From the Old Saxons came East Saxons and South Saxons and West Saxons. From Angel, which has ever since remained waste between the Jutes and Saxons, came the East Angles, Middle Angles, Mercians and all the Northumbrians.

455 – In this year Hengest and Horsa fought against king Wyrtgeorn in the place that is called *Āgæles threp* [probably near Aylesford], and his brother Horsa was killed. And after that Hengest succeeded to the kingdom and Æsc his son.

457 – In this year Hengest and Æsc fought with the Britons at the place that is called *Crecgan ford* [probably Crayford] and there slew four bands [4000 men], and the Britons then departed from Kent and with great fear fled to *Lunden byrg* [London].

465 – In this year Hengest and Æsc fought against the Britons near *Wippedes fleot* [unidentified] and slew twelve Welsh noblemen there; and one of their thanes whose name was Wipped was slain there.

473 – In this year Hengest and Æsc fought against the Welsh and seized countless booty, and the Welsh fled from the English as [from] fire.

58 See p. 1, n. 06.

59 The *Anglo-Saxon Chronicle*, MS 'A', for the year 823 (correctly 825) reports the battle of *Ellendun* (at Wroughton, Wilts.), where Egbert of Wessex defeated Beornwulf of Mercia, and continues:

Then he [Egbert] sent Æthelwulf his son from his [Egbert's] army, and Ealhstan his bishop [of Sherborne] and Wulf heard his ealdorman [chief officer of a shire] with a large force to Kent; and they drove Baldred the king [of Kent] northward across the Thames; and the men of Kent submitted to him [Æthelwulf] and those of Surrey, Sussex and Essex because they had formerly been wrongfully forced away from [their allegiance to] him.

The annal goes on to record that East Anglia also turned to Egbert for protection against Mercia. As Baldred had been set up as an underking of Kent by the Mercians (*History of the Anglo-Saxons* II, 397), the battle at *Ellendun* and the campaign in Kent may be seen to be interrelated politically.

The other sources cited by Gough, Florence of Worcester (see p. 23, n. 09), the *Chronicle of Melrose Abbey*, Scotland (on which see *Oxf. Hist.* IV, 752), and Matthew

6

the coming of the Normans.[o] Then, if we may believe Thomas Spott[p] the monk (for no older writer mentions it), the Kentish men at *Svanescomb* (a little village where Suene the Dane is said to have antiently had a camp)[62] carrying boughs before them submitted to William the Conqueror, on condition they might enjoy their original privileges inviolate, and especially that which they called *Gavelkind*.[63] By this the lands subject to it are equally divided among the heirs male, or for want of such, among the females. By this persons take possession of an estate at 15 years of age, and may alienate by gift or sale without consent of the lord. By this children whose parents suffer for robberies succeed to these estates, &c. as it is expressed in an old record more exactly than elegantly. "The county of Kent saith that in the said county every one shall be free of this grievance; for it saith that this county was never conquered like the rest of England, but submitted by treaty to the Conqueror's dominion, reserving all its liberties and free customs antiently held and used."[q] Afterwards William the Conqueror, in order to ensure his possession of Kent, which is accounted the key of England, appointed a constable in Dover castle, making the same person, according to the old Roman custom, guardian of the shore, with its five ports, and styling him Warden of the cinque ports.[64] These are Hastings, Dover, Hith, Rumney, and Sandwich, to which are added Winchelsey and Rie as chief towns, and other lesser ones as members.†

o. Malmsb. de gest. reg. I. p. 5. says Baldred reigned 18 years, and that the kingdom of Kent subsisted 375 years from A.D. 449. Lamb. p. 22. 368 years, also Sprot Chron. p. 97.[60]

p. This story cited by Lambarde, p. 28. from Sprott is in Thorne's Chron. inter x Script. p. 1786.[61]

q. Mr. Somner, in his treatise on Gavelkind, præf. & p. 63. confutes this story; in which he is followed by others: yet it must be confessed to have some remains in the present constitution, and it remains to be proved how this county alone came to retain a custom which antiently obtained all over Britain, as now in some parts of Wales. G. Robinson on Gavelkind, pp. 28, 29.[65]

† See in Sussex, p. 203. [Gough's note should refer to his p. 204 where he refers to Winchelsea in his additions to Camden.]

of Westminster (see p. 23, n. 15) are derived either from the *Anglo-Saxon Chronicle* or, in part, from the imaginations of their authors. The interval between the foundation of the kingdom of Kent, traditionally 455, and the expulsion of Baldred is 370 years.

60 The only information from nearly contemporary sources, the *Anglo-Saxon Chronicle*, merely records Baldred's expulsion from Kent. On William of Malmesbury see p. 3, n. 33 and on Lambarde see p. 1, n. 01. Thomas Sprott (or Spott), who flourished in late C13, wrote a history of St Augustine's Abbey, Canterbury, of which he was a monk. It was edited as *T. Sprotti Chronica* by T. Hearne in 1719.

61 Like Sprott (previous n.), William Thorne, who flourished in late C14, was a monk of St Augustine's. His history of its monks was printed by Sir Roger Twysden in 1652 in the collection *Historiae Anglicanae Scriptores Decem* (Ten Writers on English History). Gough consulted the edition of 1786. Thorne's work is entitled *Chronica de rebus gestis abbatum Sancti Augustini Cantuariae, 578–1397*. There is a translation of it ed. A. H. Davis, 1934.

62 Swanscombe is a place-name that probably antedates *Swein* by several centuries. Although the charter of C7 (*A.S. Charters*, no. 1246, pp. 362–3) may be spurious, spellings of the place-name from 1086 onwards make it probable that its meaning was '*Swān*'s or the swineherd's (*swān*) field (*camp*)'. *K.P.N.*, p. 17.

63 On gavelkind see *Oxf. Hist.* III, 49, n. 2, and p. 38; also *Pre-Feudal England*, p. 19f. Camden no doubt had his information on gavelkind from *Lamb.*, p. 478f.

64 Odo, Bishop of Bayeux, the Conqueror's half-brother, 'was set in Dover castle in order to guard the Kentish ports' (*Oxf. Hist.* II, 591). The most famous castellan of Dover and in effect Warden of the Cinque Ports was the Lord Edward (later Edward I) who was given these duties in 1266. See p. 5, n. 50.

65 William Somner (1598–1669) was a Kentish antiquary who published a work on Anglo-Saxon

Greenwich in 16[

laws that had been compiled by Lambarde (n. 01), a *Saxo-Latin-English Dictionary*, 1659, and *A Treatise of Gavelkind*, 1647. As Gibson's note *q* suggests, Kentish custom had something in common, superficially at least, with the custom of the Celtic fringe. On the Celtic field-system in England see *English Field Systems*, p. 227f., and on partibility of inheritance, which had much in common with gavelkind, p. 268. For Gray's conclusions on the Kentish system see his ch. VII and especially pp. 303–4.

66 Subsidies were taxes levied for special royal needs.

67 'Wards' in this context does not refer to minors, but to 'guards', which is a cognate word. The meaning is that the barons of the Cinque Ports were free from the service of castle-guard in person ('as to bodily service'). On castle-guard see *Domesday Book & Beyond*, pp. 190, 234. The service 'was generally commuted at an early date for money rents' (*Oxf. Hist.* III, 18).

68 Brought before a court of law.

69 The indirect course of the Thames is 210 miles, but the Severn has a comparable length of only 180 miles.

70 Deptford dockyard was estab-

These being bound to serve in war by sea enjoy many great privileges, being free from payment of subsidies,[66] and the law of wards[67] as to bodily service, nor can they be impleaded[68] except in their own towns; and those of the inhabitants who have the style of baron, bear the canopy over the kings and queens of England at their coronation, and have a table for them at the king's right hand on that day, &c. The warden also, who is always one of our most approved noblemen, has the authority of admiral and other rights within his jurisdiction. I proceed now to the survey of places.

The north part of this county, as I before observed, is washed by the Thames, the largest river in Britain,[69] which leaving Surrey, and, by a winding course almost returning back on itself again, first visits *Deptford*,[70] a noted dock where the king's ships are built and repaired, and where is a noble storehouse, and a kind of college ‡ for the use of the navy. This place was antiently called *West Greenwich*, and upon the conquest of England fell to the share of Gilbert de *Mamignot*,[72] a

‡ Holy Trinitie House.[71]

lished by the Creek in the time of Henry VIII, though royal ships had been built there by Henry V (*Hist. Geog. Eng.*, p. 273, n. 3). Of the buildings of 1513 only two walls remain (*B. of E. London* II, 107; *Lamb.*, p. 386).

71 Founded in 1514 by Sir Thomas

Spert and incorporated by Henry VIII in 1529, it was in effect the headquarters of the merchant navy, entrusted with the provision of lighthouses, buoys and so on.

72 Gilbert Maminot, friend and physician of the Conqueror and Bishop of Lisieux, attended William

I.

Wenceslaus Hollar

Norman, whose son's son Walkelyn defended Dover castle against king Stephen,[73] and left an only daughter, who, on the death of her brother, carried by marriage the fine estate called the *honour of Mamignot* into the family of the *Says*.[74]

From hence the Thames runs to *Greenwich*, q.d. the Green bay (*Wic* being the German for a bay),[75] antiently famous for the Danish fleet lying here, and for the cruelty of that people to Ealphege, archbishop of Canterbury, whom they put to death here by the most horrid torments, A.D. 1012.[76] The occasion of his death is thus related by Ditmar of Merspurg, a contemporary writer[r] in the eighth book of his chronicle. "I have heard from Sewald that lamentable and therefore remarkable account how a base band of Northmen[s] still under the conduct of Thurkil[78] having taken the excellent prelate of Canterbury

r. He died 1018. Hoffm.[77]   s. *Normanni* signifying the Danes. C.

on his deathbed in 1087. Deptford was later held by Hugh de Maminot whose castle was in ruins in Gough's day (1789) (*Additions*, p. 225).

73 Gough (*Additions*, p. 225) cites Ordericus Vitalis to the effect that Hugh de Maminot's son Walkelyn held Dover castle in 1138 for the Empress Matilda. On the campaign of which this was a part, see *Oxf. Hist.* III, 135–6. Ordericus Vitalis (1075–1143?) was born in England of Norman parents, but spent most

of his life as a monk of St Evroult in Normandy. His *Historia Ecclesiastica*, which goes down to 1141, is valuable for its account of events after 1066, as seen from the cloister. See *Camb. Hist. Eng. Lit.* I, 163–4; *E.H.D.* II, 281f.

74 Their manor house, in existence since CII at least, is now entirely gone. It took its name from the family of Saye as a result of the marriage of Geoffrey de Saye with the daughter of Walkelyn de Maminot in CI2

(*Additions*, p. 225, citing Dugdale's *Baronage*). Later Sayes Court was a home of the Evelyn family.

75 The name Greenwich first occurs in CI0 as *Grenewic*, the second syllable, *wic*, probably meaning 'port (in a green place)'. The Old Norse word *vík* meaning 'bay, small creek', is found only in the regions of Scandinavian settlement in northern England. See *Names of Towns and Cities*, p. 205.

76 Archbishop Ælfheah (St Alphege) was captured after a siege of Canterbury in September 1011. MS 'E' of the *Anglo-Saxon Chronicle* for the year 1012 tells much the same story as Thietmar, which is available in translation in *E.H.D.* I, 320, §42. Neither account gives Greenwich as the scene of the martyrdom (*Lamb.*, p. 387f.). See also *Two Saxon Chrons.* II, 189–90.

77 Hoffman was editor of a Lexicon or encyclopedia.

78 Thurkil, according to the *Chronicle*, was harrying the southern and eastern counties between the years 1009 and 1013. He was 'the Thorkell the Tall of Scandinavian history . . . and the brother of jarl Sigvaldi, the commander of the pirates of Jómsborg' (*A.S. Chron.*, p. 138, n. 6).

79 'greedy gulf' is a curious usage in this context, but Gibson was probably aware of the use of the word 'gulf' in the sense 'voracious appetite' (*S.O.E.D.* s.n. gulf, 3b, 1566). The translation in *E.H.D.* I, 320, reads: 'the voracious Charybdis of thieving magpies summoned the servant of God'.

80 Humphrey, Duke of Gloucester (1391–1447), youngest son of Henry IV, was created duke in 1414. He was a patron of writers and donated books for a library which became a nucleus of the Bodleian at Oxford.

81 The Roman name for Piacenza; in Middle English 'pleasaunce' (a pleasing place). Duke Humphrey bought the manor in 1423. Of the present visible structures, only the Queen's House, by Inigo Jones, was begun in Camden's lifetime, but not completed until later. Of the original Placentia an undercroft in brick of early C16 survives. See *B. of E. London* II, 141f., pl. 12(b); plan in *Architecture in Britain*, fig. 14, p. 69, pl. 39(A), (B). See also *Lamb.*, pp. 389–90.

82 Henry VII founded houses for the Friars Observant not only at Greenwich (its site covered by College Approach and Nelson Road), but at Richmond (Surrey), Canterbury, Southampton and Newcastle. *Oxf. Hist.* VII, 229.

83 Wren's Observatory stands, with later buildings, on the site of Duke Humphrey's tower.

84 The Thames.

85 He was the first Earl of Northampton (1540–1614), created earl in 1604, a catholic and a man of learning. He had a hand in the building of Audley End, Essex, and the long-lost Northumberland House, Charing Cross. See *Architecture in Britain*, pp. 42–3. In Greenwich he built the Trinity Hospital (1613), now much altered. In its chapel there is a fragmentary monument to him, taken from Dover Castle. *B. of E. London* II, 155–6.

86 In 1533.

named Ealphegus with other persons, made him undergo a close imprisonment, hunger, and inexpressible torments, according to their cursed practice. He through human frailty proffered them money, requesting a suspension of his sufferings till he could raise it, that if he could not by a handsome ransom redeem himself from instant death, he might at least have time for confession to qualify himself to be offered up a living sacrifice to the Lord. When the time allowed was expired, the greedy gulf [79] of pirates ordered out the servant of the lord, and with threats demanded the instant payment of the promised money. He replied, like an innocent lamb, I am ready for all you dare to inflict on me, through the love of Christ, that I should be thought worthy to be made an example to his servants. I fear you not this day. Wretched poverty, not my inclination, makes me seem to you false to my word. This guilty body, which I cherished too much in this pilgrimage, I offer to you, knowing you have it in your power to do what you please with it. As to my sinful soul, over which you have no power, I humbly commit that into the hands of the Creator of all. While he was speaking a troop of profane wretches surrounded him, collecting various weapons to dispatch him. Their captain Thurkill seeing this at a distance ran up presently, calling out and beseeching them not to do so, and offering all the gold and silver, and every thing else that he had except his ship, rather than they should sin thus against the Lord's anointed. This mild address could not check the fury of his comrades harder than iron and stone, nor would any thing satisfy them but the shedding innocent blood, which they all united to do with ox heads and showers of sticks and stones.''

The place is now famous for the royal palace built by Humphry duke of Gloucester, [80] and called *Placentia*, [81] enlarged in a magnificent manner by Henry VII. who added a small house of friars mendicants, [82] and finished the tower that duke Humphrey began on a high hill, [83] which commands an extensive and beautiful prospect over the meandering river [84] and the verdant meads. This place is greatly indebted for additional handsome buildings to its new inhabitant Henry Howard earl of Northampton. [85] But the greatest glory of Greenwich is our sovereign Elizabeth, who was born here [86] under a most fortunate planet, and diffused so much lustre of royal virtue all over Britain, as well as over the whole world, that words are wanting to express her surpassing praise. Take, however, these lines of Leland[87] the antiquary on Greenwich.[t]

> *Ecce ut jam niteat locus petitus,*
> *Tanquam sydereæ domus cathedræ.*
> *Quæ fastigia picta? quæ fenestræ?*
> *Quæ turres vel ad astra se efferentes?*
> *Quæ porro viridaria, ac perennes*
> *Fontes? Flora sinum occupat venusta,*
> *Fundens delicias nitentis horti.*
> *Rerum commodus estimator ille,*
> *Ripæ qui variis modis amœnæ*
> *Nomen contulit eleganter aptum.*

> Behold the glories of the place,
> Bedeckt with each celestial grace,
> Fit seat of Gods! the roofs how gay
> The painted windows' rich array,
> The lofty tow'rs that kiss the skies;
> The bow'rs a ceaseless spring supplies,
> The gardens trim, that Flora court
> To make this spot her lov'd resort,
> And willing yield their royal lords
> The richest bounties she affords.
> What skill these varied beauties plann'd
> That thus adorn old Thames's Strand,
> And, conscious of its future fame,
> Devis'd *Placentia* for its name.

I shall only add (that I may not suffer the memory of munificent deeds to be lost), that William Lambarde,[89] a person alike eminent for learning and piety, built here a house for poor persons, which he called *the college of queen Elizabeth's poor*.[90] Behind this place lies *Eltham*, another royal retreat,[91] scarce three miles out of the road, built by Anthony Bec, bishop of Durham, and patriarch of Jerusalem,[92] who presented it to queen Eleanor, consort of Edward I. having embezzled the estate of the Vescys,[93] to whom this place at first belonged. For this bishop, whom the last baron Vescy appointed to hold his estate in trust[94] for his bastard son William de Vescy then an infant, is said to have not dealt fairly by his ward.[*]

Below Greenwich the Thames bursting its banks has covered many acres of land, where for these many years certain persons have at immense expence by throwing up vast banks with great difficulty hardly been able to defend the adjoining fields

t. Cygnea Cantio, in Itin. IX. 16.[88]   *Liber Dunelm.[95]

87 On Leland see Appendix.

88 The *Cygnea Cantio*, completed by Leland in 1545, is a long descriptive poem that opens with a description of the Thames from Oxford to Greenwich as seen by a swan. It concludes with a lengthy recital of the history of the palace of Greenwich and the virtues of Henry VIII. Gough in his note refers to its inclusion in Leland's ninth Itinerary.

89 See p. 1, n. 01 above.

90 In Greenwich High Road, founded by Lambarde in 1576 and rebuilt in 1819. *B. of E. London* II, 153.

91 Of Eltham Palace, royal residence from the time of Edward II to that of Henry VIII, the main survivals are the Great Hall of c. 1479, the bridge over the moat and the so-called Lord Chancellor's House of C16, but externally of C18 (*B. of E. London* II, 458–9 and pl. 5). From the time of Henry VIII, Greenwich Palace replaced it. See *Lamb.*, p. 470f.

92 Antony Bek held the bishopric of Durham from 1284 until his death at Eltham in 1311. He was not Patriarch of Jerusalem.

93 According to Leland (*L.T.S.*1, 28) the family of Vesci were lords of Caythorpe Castle and held part of the manor of Ancaster, both in Lincs.

94 Gough notes (his edn, p. 226): 'On William the bastard being slain in the battle of Bannocburn 1314, his kinsman Gilbert de Aton lord Vesci inherited by his disposition', i.e. by William's arrangement of his affairs, presumably by a will. The most famous of the family was probably Eustace (1170?–1216), lord of Alnwick, a leader among the barons who secured John's assent to the Great Charter. *Oxf. Hist.* III, 470, 481.

95 Presumably *Liber Vitae Ecclesiae Dunelmensis*. This is a register of the Cathedral Church of Durham listing the deaths of persons connected with it, including laymen who had made benefactions to it. Its earlier entries were written at Lindisfarne monastery before A.D. 825.

96 The depression of the land-levels of the South-East, relative to that of the sea since Roman times, is about 15 feet. On the marshes of north Kent see *Coastline*, pp. 399–400. See also p. 16, n. 07, *Surrey*, and references there; and p. 42, n. 70 below. Gough (p. 226) citing Hasted, says that the Woolwich marshes were first inundated in 1236 and again in James I's time. *Lamb.*, p. 396, speaks of an inundation here in c. 1527.

97 Not a grass but a broad-leaved plant of the family *Cruciferae*. English Scurvy Grass (*Cochlearia anglica*) and Scurvy Grass (*C. officinalis*) are both found on muddy sea-shores and tidal estuaries. They were valued by early navigators as a remedy for scurvy, a disease consequent on a deficiency of vitamin C in the diet. See e.g. *British Plants*, p. 51.

98 Pliny the Elder (A.D. 23–79), administrator, soldier and admiral, died during the eruption of Vesuvius when Pompeii and Herculaneum were overwhelmed. Of his writings only the encyclopedic *On Natural History* has survived. Pliny claimed that its 37 books contained 20,000 noteworthy facts drawn from over 470 authors. Medieval writers relied on it extensively and it would have been known to Camden in one of the several editions published on the Continent from 1473 onwards.

99 Pliny's *Historia Naturalis*, bk 22, ch. 2. Hardouin (1646–1729) was a French scholar with eccentric ideas.

01 Germanicus (15 B.C.–A.D. 19), was a general successful in campaigns against the German tribes.

02 These are some of the signs of scurvy (*scorbutus*) and were probably thought to be a result of drinking from the spring.

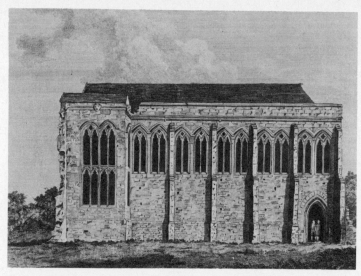

Eltham Palace, engraved by J. Basire, published in 1782

from the innundations.[96] Hereabouts grows plenty of *Cochlearia*, or as we call it *Scurvy grass*,[97] which some physicians will have to be the *Britannica* of Pliny,[98] by which name I have already mentioned it. But let us hear Pliny himself:[u] "Cæsar Germanicus[01] having pushed his camp on the other side of the Rhine in Germany, they found on the sea coast a single spring of fresh water, which made the teeth of all who drank of it drop out within two years, and loosened the joints of their knees.[02] Physicians call these complaints *Stomacacè & Sceletyrbè*.[03] The herb called *Britannica* was discovered to be a remedy for it, being good not only for the nerves and jaws, but for quinsies, the bite of serpents, and in other cases. The Frisians,[04] among whom our troops were encamped, informed them of it. I cannot account for the name, unless the inhabitants of the sea coast gave it out of compliment to their

u. H.N. XXII. c.2. see Harduin's notes.[99]

03 Terms no longer in use: quinsy is tonsillitis.

04 A people of the islands and coastlands of modern Holland and Germany from the Zuider Zee to the Elbe, the Frisians were closely related to the Saxons in culture and

language, probably crossing over with them to Britain in some numbers in c5. See *Oxf. Hist.* I, 337, 412, and J. N. L. Myres, 'The Adventus Saxonum', p. 239 in *Aspects of Archaeology in Britain and Beyond*, ed. W. F. Grimes, 1951.

neighbours of Britain." The learned Hadrian Junius[05] gives another and more probable derivation of the name in his Nomenclator, which the reader may consult at his leisure; for the mention of *Britannica* has already carried me too far out of my way.

The Thames after this confined within its banks meets the river *Darent*, which coming down from Surrey[06] flows gently not far from *Seven-oke*,[07] said to take its name from seven very large oaks, to 'Ottan-ford', now *Otford*,[08] witness of the slaughter of the Danes in 1016,[09] and boasting a royal palace[10] built by Warham, archbishop of Canterbury,[11] for himself and successors, on so magnificent a plan that his immediate successor Cranmer[12] to avoid envy thought it adviseable[u] to exchange it with Henry VIII. *Lullingston*, where was a castle[14] formerly the seat of a noble family of the same name, stands lower on the Darent, which at its mouth gives name to *Darentford*, commonly called *Dartford*,[15] a large and populous market-town, below which the little river *Crecc* falls into it. On a ford

u. [sic] *necesse habuerit*.[13]

battle was probably disastrous for King Offa of Mercia (*Oxf. Hist.* II, 206). Plummer notes (*Two Saxon Chrons.* II, 53) that 'Many skeletons with weapons lying near them have been discovered in the neighbourhood'. But there is still a further report of a battle here. John Weever in *Ancient Funerall Monuments*, 1631, p. 345 (quoted in *Little Guide, Kent*, p. 11), speaks of a victory over the Danes here in 904. But the *Chronicle* makes it clear that the army of Wessex, with a Kentish contingent, was fighting in East Anglia at that time. *Lamb.* (pp. 459–60) mentions battles here in 773 and 1016.

10 The tower and part of the hall survive. They are on the site of an earlier manor-house used by Becket. Archbishop Henry Dene (d. 1503) rebuilt the tower in 1501 and Wareham (next note) enlarged the rest. *Lamb.*, pp. 462–3.

11 William Wareham (1450?–1532) was archbishop from 1504.

12 Thomas Cranmer (1489–1556) became archbishop in 1553 and was burned at the stake in 1556.

13 This is not a normal usage in classical Latin. It implies that Cranmer had to make the exchange of necessity. Gibson: 'he was forced to exchange it with Henry VIII'.

14 The house is of Tudor origin with later additions. The Tudor gatehouse is a pleasing survival. The castle (site c. NG 527637) was in ruins in Leland's time and no remains of it are now visible. The place is now remembered best for the post-war excavation of a Roman house with strong Christian associations. See *The Lullingstone Roman Villa*. I can find no mention of a family of this name, nor could Gough. See his *Additions*, p. 227.

15 Dartford, the point at which the Roman Watling Street crosses the Darent, has little beauty to relieve its industrial nastiness. *Lamb.* (p. 402f.) retails a few historical anecdotes of the place.

05 Hadrianus Junius (1511–75), a Dutch poet and historian, published *Nomenclator omnium rerum* in 1567.

06 The source of the Darent at NG 423547 is just inside Surrey.

07 Sevenoaks was *Sevenak, Sevenok* and later Snooks, in pronunciation, though later again the fuller spelling influenced the pronunciation, giving the modern form of the name. In Old English *āc*, 'oak', did not add '-s' in the nominative plural; its plural was formed like goose/geese, mouse/mice. Although Camden's *Sevenoke* does not show the mutated vowel, it is without the final '-s'. Camden omits Knole (*B. of E., W. Kent*, p. 342f.) probably because *Lambarde* (pp. 469–70) omitted it at this point.

08 The earliest surviving spelling of Otford is *Otteford* in a charter of A.D. 883 which may be authentic (see *A.S. Charters*, no. 1414, p. 398). Camden may well have taken the form *ottan ford(a)* from charter no.

382, which refers to an estate in Surrey (*P.N. Surrey*, p. 165). However, the early spelling of the Kentish place-name would have been the same. It meant 'ford of a man called Otta' (*P.N. Kent*, pp. 58–9).

09 This is reported in the *Chronicon ex Chronicis* of Florence of Worcester (on whom see p. 23, n. 09) but not in the *Anglo-Saxon Chronicle* for 1016. There, only Sheppey and Aylesford are mentioned in connection with the campaign in Kent waged by King Edmund against his Danish successor Cnut. On these events see *Oxf. Hist.* II, 385–7. Earlier, in the *Anglo-Saxon Chronicle* under the year 773 (which should be 776), we are told that a red crucifix appeared in the sky after sunset, 'and in the same year the Mercians and the men of Kent fought at Otford; and wonderful adders were seen in the land of the South Saxons'. The effect of this

16 Crayford. Here the Watling Street crosses the river Cray. Today the place is merely an unpleasant extension of dirty Dartford and the Wen. It is probably the *Crecganford* of the *Chronicle. Lamb.* (p. 400f.) describes marling-pits (dene-holes) in the chalk here. See p. 6, n. 57, under the year 457. The annal makes no mention of the slaying of the Britons' leaders, though *Lamb.* (p. 400) does. See p. 18, n. 64; and on the place-name, *P.N. Kent*, p. 29.

17 Gravesend. In a flurry of fort-building in about 1539, coastal defences were constructed from Hull to Milton Haven and as far away as the Scilly Isles. For a short account see *Regional Guides to Ancient Monuments*, vol. II, Southern England, H.M.S.O., 1952, pp. 48–9. The major Kentish examples of Henry VIII castles are: Deal, Walmer, Sandown (N. of Deal), Sandgate near Folkestone, Camber (Sussex). See *Arch. Journ.* CXXVI, 201f., map fig. 5 on p. 202; p. 215f. (Walmer), and p. 217f. (Deal). The place-name meant 'at the end of the grove'. *Lamb.* (p. 435) confuses the etymology of the name, but enlarges on Gravesend's function as a port and recounts some incidents in its history. See *P.N. Kent*, p. 100.

18 Cobham. On Cobham Hall, the family seat, see *Arch. Journ.* CXXVI, 274f., and *B. of E., W. Kent*, pp. 221–2, pl. 47, 48. The college, a chantry, was founded by John, third Lord Cobham (d. 1408) in 1362 for five, later seven, chaplains to serve in the parish church. The mason was Henry de Yevele, master-mason also for the rebuilding of the nave of Westminster Abbey. The College became an almshouse for which buildings were completed in 1598 on three sides of a quad-rangle, of which the fourth is enclosed by the original college hall. See G. H. Cooke, *Medieval Chantries and Chantry Chapels*, 1963, p. 65, and see p. 31 n. 78.

View of Gravesend, published in 1784

of this *Creccanford*, now *Creyford*,[16] Hengist the Saxon, eight years after his arrival in Britain, fought a battle with the Britans, slew their leaders, and made such havock of them as to destroy all future apprehensions from them, so that he estab-lished his kingdom in Kent with perfect security.

From the Darent to the mouth of the Medway Thames visits only a few small towns, which I might pass over without derogating from their fame or properties. Among them, how-ever, the principal is *Graves-end*,[17] as remarkable a place as any in England, being the port between Kent and London, where Henry VIII. fortified both sides of the river. Behind it a little more inland lies *Cobham*,[18] long the seat of the barons *Cob-ham*,[19] of whom the last John founded here a college, and built a castle at *Couling*,[20] and left an only daughter wife of Sir

19 The family first came into prominence in C14 and the third baron (previous note) gave distinguished service during the Hundred Years' War. Froissart mentions him and Sir Reginald de Cobham, the latter frequently. The family is commemorated in the parish church by a series of fine brasses and monuments of which the earliest is to Sir John de Cobham (d. 1299). See *B. of E., W. Kent*,

p. 219f.; *Brass Rubbings*, pl. 5,3; 6,3; 14,1; 14,3; 30,2; 32,2; and *Monumental Brasses*, pl. 10, 14. At Lingfield, Surrey, are further brasses and monuments of Cobhams of C14 and C15 (*B. of E. Surrey*, pp. 297–8). Five members of the family held the Wardenship of the Cinque Ports (*Lamb.*, pp. 115–16).

20 Cooling Castle was begun soon after 1381 by Sir John Cobham

14

John de *la Pole*,[21] who had also an only daughter, who had several husbands, but children only by Reginald *Braybrook*.[22] Her third husband John *Oldcastle* attempting innovations in religion was hanged and burnt.[23] Joan, only daughter [24] of Reginald Braybrook, was married to Thomas *Brooke* of Somersetshire,[25] from whom the sixth in descent is the present Henry Brooke,[26] baron Cobham, who because fortune did not answer all his expectations, in the transports of his passion rebelled against his most gracious sovereign, and was condemned to suffer capital punishment, but lives a monument of the royal clemency.

From Graves end a little tract called *Ho*,[27] a kind of Chersonesus, runs out between the rivers Thames and Medway, a great way to the east in an unhealthy situation.[28] On it is *Cliffe*, a tolerably large town, so called from the cliff it stands on.[29] Whether it be the *Clives at Ho*, famous for the council in

(n. 18 above) ostensibly to protect the area against French raids, but perhaps with an eye to cowing Kentish peasants too ready to rebel. On the right-hand tower of the entrance gate is fixed an original copper plaque that reads:

> Knouwyth that beth and schul be
> That i am mad in help of the cuntre
> In knowyng of whyche thyng
> Thys is chartre and wytnessing;

which may be modernized as '(Whoever reads this) should know that I have been made for the protection of this region now and in the future. This document is evidence of the same.'

There had certainly been French incursions in 1379 into this region, but no doubt the rural unrest that culminated in the Peasants' Revolt of 1381 was an additional motive for building a castle rather than a defensible manor-house such as Penshurst (p. 16, n. 33). Bodiam (p. 66, n. 29, *Sussex*) is an example similar to Cooling of a castle built with the French in mind. At Cooling the architect was again (n. 18 above) Henry Yevele. See *The Hundred of Hoo*, p. 24f., for Sir John, his buildings and his architect.

Much work of C14 and somewhat later survives and it is worth a diversion north of Rochester into the Hundred of Hoo if only to see the fine entrance gateway at Cooling. *Arch. Journ.* CXXVI, 201; *B. of E., W. Kent*, pp. 231–2.

21 Joan de la Pole died in fact c. 1388, her father Sir John in 1408. Her daughter Joan was five times married. Her first husband was Sir Robert Hemendale, her second Sir Reginald Braybrooke (d. 1405), her third Sir Nicholas Hawberk (d. 1407), the fourth Sir John Oldcastle who died in 1417 at the stake for heresy. He was the original of Falstaff in Shakespeare's *Henry IV* and *Henry V*. Her fifth husband was Sir John Harpeden, whose brass is in Westminster Abbey (*Brass Rubbings*, pl. 21). Joan de Cobham's brass (1433) depicts her with the five husbands, six sons and four daughters. There are brasses to Braybrooke and Hawberk in Cobham church. See also n. 19 above.

22 See previous note.

23 See n. 21 above.

24 If Joan de Cobham had 'children only by Reginald Braybrook' and (a later) Joan was the 'only daughter of Reginald Braybrook', it is at first difficult to understand why the first Joan's brass represents four daughters. In fact, Braybrooke's daughter was the only one of the offspring to survive.

25 He became, as a result of the marriage, the seventh Baron Cobham.

26 Henry Brooke (1564–1619), the eighth baron, was arrested in 1603 for complicity in a plot to place Arabella Stuart on the throne and he implicated Sir Walter Raleigh. The latter was eventually executed in 1618. Brooke died in the Tower in the following year.

27 Cooling (n. 20 above) is within the Hundred of Hoo. The meaning of Hoo (Old English *hōh*, 'a heel') in this instance is probably 'promontory' (*Chersonesus*, as Camden puts it), for the Hundred projects into the North Sea between the Thames and Medway estuaries. Yet *hōh* in place-names could also mean 'ridge' or 'the end of a ridge', which is equally apt as describing the high ground running south-westwards from All Hallows. See *Elements* I, 256–7.

28 The extensive marshes of the region provided a habitat for mosquitoes which spread the parasites that cause malaria (ague). 'In the Fenland and low-lying coastal areas from Suffolk to Kent, malaria once used to undermine the health of the people. Between 1860 and 1870 it began to die out...' as a result of improvements in living conditions. See A. D. Imms, *Insect Natural History*, 1947, pp. 137–8.

29 Cliffe-at-Hoo has never been more than a village. Camden is here using the word 'town' in one of its older senses, probably 'collection of houses, village'. See *Elements* II, 190 (6). The village is not named from a 'cliff' in the usual modern sense, but from the steep slope down to the marshes. See ibid. I, 98.

30 Councils of the Church were held at a place called *Cloveshoh* in c8 and early c9, but the locality is unidentified (*Oxf. Hist.* II, 133). In his edition of Bede, *E.H.* II, 214, Plummer says: 'It was almost certainly in Mercia, and probably near London.' *Lamb.*, pp. 439, 440–41.

31 The river-name Medway is probably British, but beyond that it is wise not to speculate. See *Orig. E.P.N.*, p. 76, and cp. *K.P.N.*, pp. 49–50. *Lamb.*, pp. 197–8, gives an OE derivation.

32 See p. 52, n. 12, *Sussex. Lamb.*, p. 189.

33 The present house is of very considerable archaeological and historical interest and is set in a park and beside a village of some beauty. The house is of mid C14, C15 and later and it came into the possession of Sir William Sidney in 1552. He died in 1554 and his tomb is to be seen in the parish church, wrongly inscribed 'firste of that name'. *B. of E., W. Kent*, pp. 435–6.

34 Gough (*Additions*, p. 229) says: 'The Sidney family originate from Anjou, whence Sir William came with Henry II.'

35 Sir Henry Sidney (1529–86) was knighted in 1550. His major work was in Ireland, where he was three times Lord Deputy. He was buried in Penshurst Church, but has no monument.

36 John Dudley (1502?–53) was made Viscount Lisle and in 1547 Earl of Warwick. He became Duke of Northumberland in 1551. On the accession of Mary Tudor he was executed for having sought to put his daughter-in-law, Lady Jane Dudley (née Grey) on the throne. See *Oxf. Hist.* VII, 526–30.

37 Robert Sidney (1563–1626), second son of Sir Henry (n. 35 above), was with Sir Philip at his death in Arnhem. He became Viscount Lisle in 1605 and Earl of Leicester in 1618.

the infant state of the English church,[30] as some think, I do not presume to affirm; its situation not being favourable for such an assembly, and that Clives at Ho seems to have been in the kingdom of Mercia. The river *Medwege*, now *Medway*, called in British, if I mistake not, *Vag*, (to which the Saxons added *Med*)[31] has its source in the *Anderida Sylva*, called the *Wealde* or *woodland*,[32] occupying the south part of this county for a great extent. While but a small stream it passes by *Penshurst*, the seat[33] of the antient family of the *Sidneys*, descended from William de *Sidney* chamberlain to king Henry II.[34] Of this family was Henry Sidney,[35] the famous lieutenant of Ireland, who by a daughter of John Dudley duke of Northumberland and earl of Warwick,[36] had Philip and Robert. Robert was enobled by king James with the title of baron *Sidney of Penshurst*, and afterwards of viscount *Lisle*.[x][37] It would be highly unpardonable to omit Philip,[38] the glory of the family, the hope of mankind, the most lively pattern of virtue and the delight of the learned world, who lost his life at Zutphen in Guelderland fighting against the enemy.[39] This is that Sidney whom Providence raised up as an example of our ancestors to our age, and as suddenly recalled to himself, and took from us as more worthy of heaven than earth. Thus does perfect virtue suddenly withdraw itself, and the best men are the shortest lived. Rest in peace, Sidney, if I may be allowed thus to address thee; we will not lament thy memory with our tears but our admiration. Whatever, as that excellent writer[y] says of that excellent governor of Britain, whatever in thee was the object of our love and admiration, remains and will remain in the minds of men through endless ages on immortal record. Many have sunk inglorious and ignoble into oblivion. Sidney will survive to the latest posterity. For as the Greek poet says, *Virtue is beyond the reach of Fate.*

x. See in Berks.   y. Tacitus, of Agricola.[40]

38 Sir Philip (1554–86) numbered among his friends Camden, the poets Sir Fulke Greville and Edmund Spenser and many of the most cultured men of the age. He was knighted in 1583.

39 The Spaniards.

40 Cornelius Tacitus (b. circa A.D. 55) held high office in Rome and the provinces. Agricola (A.D. 37–93) served in Britain in A.D. 60 and as Governor of this province from 75 to 85. His daughter became Tacitus' wife and the historian probably gives an unduly favourable account of his son-in-law's life, hence Camden's use of the word 'excellent'.

From hence the Medway flows by *Tunbridge*,[41] where is an old castle built by Richard de *Clare*,[42] who had it in exchange for *Brionne* in Normandy. His grandfather Godfrey, natural son of Richard I. duke of Normandy,[43] was earl of Ewe and Brionne.[44] After a long dispute about Brionne, Richard, as William Gemeticensis[z] writes, "had Tunbridge castle in England given him for recompence[a] of the said castle. They say the Lowy[53] of Brionne being measured round with a cord, the said cord was carried into England and Tunbridge was found to answer to the measure." The manor, as it is called, of Tunbridge was holden of the archbishops of Canterbury by his successors earls of Gloucester[54] on condition they should act as stewards at the archbishops' installation, and grant them the wardship of their children. The Medway glides thence not far from *Mereworth*,[55] where is a house like a little castle, which came from the earls of Arundel to the *Nevilles* lords of Abergavenny[56] and *le Despenser*,[57] whose lineal heir is Mary *Fane*,[58] to whom and her heirs king James in his first parliament

z. P. 300.[45]

a. *pro repetione*. Gibson[46] translates it *recompence*, sed q.[47] *Repecio* from *repeciare* (Du Cange[48]) may signify *repair*, or may stand for *reparatione*[49] abridged. In Mon. Ang. I. 724.[50] it is said *in excambium*.[51] *Repane* in Old French writers 1250, signified a measure of land. La Combe Dict.[52]

41 Tonbridge Castle was begun by Richard FitzGilbert (d. 1090?) soon after 1070. The great motte is of this time and the fragmentary shell keep surmounting it is of a generation later. The fine gatehouse is of c. 1220–40. 'The town was simply part of the outer defences of the castle.' *New Towns*, p. 457; *Lamb.*, p. 380f.; *B. of E., W. Kent*, p. 547f. The architectural and aesthetic interest of the High Street diminishes almost annually as the 'developers' have their way.

42 Richard FitzGilbert was son of Gilbert, Count of Brionne (d. 1039), a kinsman of the Conqueror. Richard was made Lord of Clare (Suffolk) and Tonbridge. On him see *Oxf. Hist.* II, 622–5, and on the barony of Clare, *E.H.D.* II, 446.

43 Richard I (942–96) was the third Duke of Normandy.

44 Eu is near the coast at Le Tréport; Brionne is on the river Risle south-west of Rouen.

45 William of Jumièges (fl. 1060) produced 'a sober and interesting chronicle' at the Norman monastery of that name. This work, entitled *Gesta Normannorum Ducum* (the exploits of the Norman Dukes), was published by La Société de l'histoire de Normandie. See *E.H.D.* II, 215–16, for a translation of the passage describing the invasion of England in 1066.

46 Bishop Gibson, Camden's second translator, on whom see Appendix.

47 '...but query...'

48 On Du Cange see p. 5, n. 49.

49 The verb *reparo* could mean 'acquire by exchange' in classical Latin.

50 Sir William Dugdale's *Monasticon Anglicanum* (3 vols., 1655, 1661, 1673), an account of English monasteries, compiled in collaboration with Roger Dodsworth. Dugdale (1605–86), one of the great antiquaries of C17, held appointments in the College of Arms. He became Garter King of Arms and a Knight in 1677. His other published works include the *Antiquities of Warwickshire*, 1656; a *History of St Paul's Cathedral*, 1658, and the *Baronage of England*, 1675–6.

51 'in exchange'.

52 Jacques Lacombe (1724–1811), lawyer and encyclopedist.

53 A 'lowy' was an area of jurisdiction extending for about a league outside a town. The word is from Latin *leucata*, a derivative of Latin *leuca*, 'a league'. *Lamb.*, pp. 383–4.

54 The Clare family held this title c. 1218 until the death of Gilbert de Clare at Bannockburn in 1314. See p. 68, n. 60, *Sussex*; p. 14, n. 89 and p. 25, n. 95, *Surrey*.

55 Mereworth Castle existed at least as early as the reign of Edward II. It came into the hands of the Fiennes family (p. 55, n. 31, *Sussex*) in the 1440s. The present 'castle' is a most splendid Palladian villa built 1720–30. *B. of E., W. Kent*, p. 403f.

56 The first of the Nevilles to be Baron of Bergavenny (Abergavenny from 1730) was Edward (d. 1476), a privy councillor and commissioner of array for Kent. There is a brass to Sir Thomas Nevell (d. 1542) in the rebuilt church of Mereworth. See *Brass Rubbings*, pl. 43, no. 6.

57 A family chiefly notable in C13 and C14, few of whom died peacefully in their beds. See p. 65, n. 23, *Sussex*.

58 Monuments to members of the Fane family are to be seen in the churches at Hunton, Tudeley, Brenchley and Mereworth. *B. of E., W. Kent*, pp. 326, 552, 169, 407.

59 Maidstone. Camden's *Medwegston* is not a good form, if indeed it ever existed. Forms such as *Mæidesstana* and *Mægthan stan*, cited by Ekwall (*Dic.*, p. 297) suggest a first element *mægth*. This, however, might be *mæg(e)th*, 'maiden', *mægthu*, 'family, kindred, folk or tribe', or *mægthe*, 'mayweed', the last perhaps affording the least likely meaning. The second meaning is the most probable, giving 'tribe's or folk's stone'. *P.N. Kent*, p. 140. Maidstone was the meeting-place for a hundred court and the precise location of the moot was perhaps a stone, which came to be referred to as 'the folk's or tribe's stone'. Many hundreds met at stones and the actual stone survives at Hurstingstone, Hunts., and Kinwardstone, Wilts. (See plate II of my *Conquest of Wessex*.) A conspicuous location was commonly chosen so that the hundred court could not easily be surprised and the course of justice perverted by violence; and the spot was usually accessible by means of several converging tracks leading from as many as possible of the villages within the hundred. The hundred-moot (meeting) came together every four weeks for the settlement of local disputes. On its origin and functions see *Oxf. Hist.* II, 295–8. Leland (*L.T.S.* IV, 37) says:

Maideston . . . is a market town of one long streat wel builded and ful of ynnes. The ruler of the town ther is cawlled Port Rive. Ther is yn the town a fair college of prestes. The castel standeth abowt the myddes of the town, being well maynteynid by the Archebisshop of Cant. There is the commune gayle or prison of Kent, as yn the shire town.

See also n. 67 below; *Lamb.*, p. 195ᶠ.

60 *Vagniacae* should probably be located at Springhead on the Watling Street, where traces of a Roman settlement have been found. See *Arch. Kent*, pp. 173, 213, pl. IX; *Arch. Journ.* CXXVI, 185; *B. of E., W. Kent*, p. 292.

"restored, gave and granted the style, honour and rank of baroness le Despenser, and that her heirs should be successively barons le Despenser for ever." And now the Medway hastes to *Maidston*,[59] which being called by the Saxons *Medwegston* and 'Medweagston', I am apt to think it the VAGNIACÆ[60] mentioned by Antoninus[61] and called by Ninnius[62] in his catalogue of cities *Caer Megwad* for *Medwag*.[63] Nor is the distance from hence to *Noviomagus*[64] one way, and to *Durobrovis*[65] the other, of which hereafter, against this supposition. Under the later emperors, as appears by the Peutinger table[66] lately published by Velser, it is called MADUS. Thus names gradually alter in a course of years. This is a populous and neat town and of great length.[67] In the centre is a palace[68] of the archbishops of Canter-

61 See p. 28, n. 46, and O.S. *Map of Roman Britain*, pp. 17, 18, 21.

62 On Nennius see p. 5, n. 53.

63 See Jackson, 'Nennius . . .' in *Antiquity* XII. *Cair Meguaid* (ibid., p. 51) has not been identified.

64 *Noviomagus* was probably at Crayford. Chichester was also a *Noviomagus* ('new city'), but of the *Regnenses*, whose capital it was.

65 *Durobrivæ* is now considered the correct form. Rochester is built over the site of this Roman town. See p. 27, n. 28.

66 The Peutinger Table, so called from a sixteenth-century owner, is a strip map about 21 feet long by a foot wide. The end of it that included Spain and most of Britain is lost. It shows Roman routes, places and mileages, affording a useful check on the *Antonine Itinerary* (p. 28, n. 46) for southern and eastern Britain. It is probably a thirteenth-century copy of a fourth-century original. For editions later than Velser see *Antiquity* I, 195. See there also, opposite p. 189, a photograph of the surviving damaged British portion of the Table. *Madus* seems to refer to a place marked on the map as 'xvi or xvii [Roman miles]' from somewhere not evident from the

map; but it does not seem likely from this evidence that *Madus* should be identified with Maidstone. In any case, the Table is better regarded as an authoritative document only when it confirms or expands another reliable source. There was, nevertheless, a major Roman settlement on the site of Maidstone, but we have no good clue to its name in Roman times. See *Arch. Kent*, p. 259.

67 It now sprawls on all but the south-east side, but the medieval core of the town is of much historical interest and, from a few vantage points, aesthetically satisfying. Leland (*L.T.S.* IV, 37) records that

Courtenay [Archbishop of Canterbury 1381–96] was fowndar of the college of Maydestone, where the master is a prebendarie. The residwe be ministars to synge devyne service. Courtney buildyd muche in the towne selfe of Maydestone, and also at the palace ther.

68 This manor-house of the archbishops was begun by Ufford, who demolished the Norman house on the site, and the new building was by Islip. It was much renovated by Archbishop Morton (1486–1500) and later owners. There are some fragments of the Norman building to the south of the banqueting hall. See *Arch. Journ.* CXXVI, 253; *B. of E., W. Kent*, pp. 389–90; *Lamb.*, p. 197.

Maidstone, the Bishop's Palace, engraved by B. Winkles
after G. Shepherd

bury, begun by archbishop John Ufford,[69] and finished by Simon Islip.[70] The other common goal of this county is here, and the town[71] owes many of its privileges to queen Elizabeth,[72] who appointed a mayor for its chief magistrate instead of the Portgreve[73] which it had before: which I mention because this is an old Saxon word, and signifies still in Germany a *governor*, as *Markgrave, Reingrave, Landgrave*, &c.[74]

Here below Maidston a little river[75] from the east falls into the Medway, rising at *Leneham*[76] probably the DUROLENUM[77] of Antoninus,[78] corruptly written in some copies DUROLEVUM. For *Durolenum* signifies in Britain the *water of Lenum*,[79]

69 John de Offord or Ufford (d. 1349) became archbishop-elect only a year before his death, so preventing his rebuilding the manor-house.

70 Simon Islip was archbishop from 1349 to 1366.

71 One has to remember that in C16 'Maidstone [was] twice the size of Manchester'. *The England of Elizabeth*, p. 187.

72 Maidstone, which was incorporated by Edward VI, forfeited its privileges for Wyatt's Rebellion [1554] under Mary. On her accession Elizabeth immediately restored them, adding further privileges, along with that of sending two burgesses to Parliament.

Ibid., p. 196, citing Hasted's *History of Kent*, ed. 1798, IV, 272; *Lamb.*, p. 196. On Wyatt's rebellion see *Oxf. Hist.* VII, 538–9.

73 A 'port-reeve' was chief officer (OE *ge-rēfa*) of a town (OE *port*); a sheriff was chief officer of a shire (*scīr*). Camden's form 'Portgreve' preserves a vestige of the first syllable of *ge-rēfa*, which survives as 'grieve' (farm manager) in the North. *Lamb.*, pp. 435–7.

74 The *graf* of Markgrave and so on is matched by another northern English form, 'grave' (steward of property), which is cognate with OE *ge-rēfa* and the Old German

graf. A Mar(k)grave was a count (*graf*) of a border territory; a Rhinegrave was one whose territory bordered the river Rhine; and a Landgrave was a count having under him several counts of lower rank.

75 The river-name is Len and it was first used by Camden in his edition of the *Britannia* of 1607. Len is a back-formation from the place-name Lenham. For its original name see p. 20, n. 90 and *Eng. River N.*, p. 247.

76 Lenham. This place-name is of a type common in Kent but unusual elsewhere in that a personal name, probably *Lēana*, is compounded with *hām*, 'homestead, village', without a genitive inflexion. *K.P.N.*, p. 223, and see *Elements* I, 229; *Dic.*, p. 281. This is a place not to be missed by the modern itinerant. See *B. of E.*, *W. Kent*, p. 361f.; *Lamb.*, p. 292.

77 The Peutinger Table (see n. 66 above) has *Durolevo*, locative case; and *Durolevum* is the accepted spelling of the name of this Romano-British place. It may have been situated at the place later called Ospringe, where an extensive Romano-British cemetery has been found dating from near the beginning to near the end of the Roman occupation of Britain. There were also vestiges of habitation in the vicinity. It is estimated that the cemetery originally contained over 750 burials. The first part of the place-name *Durolevum* meant 'stronghold'. At Syndale House, in the near vicinity of the cemetery, is a pre-Roman hill-fort to which this word could have been applied. On the cemetery see the *Society of Antiquaries Report* No. VIII, 1931, on the 'Excavation of the Roman Cemetery at Ospringe, Kent'. See also O.S. *Map of Roman Britain*, p. 21; *Arch. Journ.* CXXVI, 248.

78 See p. 28, n. 46.

79 This is a further illustration of Camden's practice of modifying a place-name to suit his theories.

80 The Romano-British name for Canterbury.

81 The Romano-British name for Rochester. If *Durolevum* is to be placed between these two towns, an obvious spot would be at Ospringe on the Roman Watling Street. See n. 77 above.

82 The main Roman route from Dover, the Watling Street, runs via Canterbury and Rochester to London. However, there is a lesser Roman road to the south, roughly parallel with it, which ran from Lympne via Maidstone to Rochester, but it passes four and a half miles to the south of Lenham. See *Roman Ways in the Weald*, p. 228f.

83 Ranulph Higden (d. 1364) was a Benedictine monk of St Werburgh's, Chester. His *Polychronicon* was translated into English by John of Trevisa c. 1387. It covers the period of human history from the Creation to 1340 and was the favourite universal history in C14 and C15.

84 Boughton Malherbe, where the early C16 house of the Wottons was deliberately gutted in 1923. *B. of E., W. Kent*, pp. 167–8.

85 Brasses in the viciously restored church include those to Nicholas Wotton (d. 1499) and Edward (d. 1529). The most celebrated member of the family, Sir Henry (1568–1639) was a friend of Camden and, like the later Nicholas (see next note), a diplomat. He is, however, best remembered as a poet. His provostship of Eton is commemorated in the name of one of its boarding-houses.

86 Nicholas Wotton (1497?–1567) was employed, among other embassies, in negotiating Henry VIII's marriage with Anne of Cleves in 1539.

87 Edward Wotton (1521–87) was yet another diplomat. He was knighted in 1591 and became a Privy Councillor and Comptroller of the Household in 1602, being created Baron Wotton of Marley in 1603.

and besides the traces of the name, the distance from *Durovernum*[80] and *Durobrovis*[81] proves this to be *Durolenum*, not to mention its situation on the Roman consular way which formerly led from Dover,[82] as Higden of Chester[83] says, through the middle of Kent.

In the neighbourhood at *Bocton Malherb*[84] has long resided the noble family of the *Wottons*,[85] of which in my time flourished Nicholas Wotton,[86] LL.D. privy councellor to Henry VIII, Edward VI, Mary and Elizabeth, who having been nine times embassador to foreign princes, thrice appointed to treat of peace between England, France, and Scotland, closed a long life with reputation of great devotion and prudence; and Edward Wotton,[87] his brother's grandson, whom from his great experience queen Elizabeth created comptroller of the houshold,* and king James baron *Wotton* of *Merlay*.

This river[89] has nothing else in its way remarkable except *Leedes* castle,[90] the work of the noble *Crevequers*, called in old deeds *Crevecuer* and *Crepito corde*. Afterwards it became the unfortunate residence of Bartholomew baron *Badlesmer*,[91]

* *Aulæ censor.*[88]

88 *Censor* here implies one of the main functions of the ancient Roman *censor*, namely the superintendence of the collection and expenditure of money. *Aula* means 'palace'.

89 The Len, for which see p. 19, n. 75.

90 Leeds Castle. This place-name is not of similar origin to that of Leeds, Yorks., but comes from Old English *hlȳde*, 'the loud or noisy (stream)', the old name of the Len. See p. 19, n. 75 and *Dic.*, p. 280. The Castle stands on islands in a lake and what is visible dates from C13 to C14 and from 1822. *Arch. Journ.* CXXVI, 254–5; *B. of E., W. Kent*, p. 355f. The probable founder was Robert de Crèvecoeur, who in 1119 founded also the priory at Leeds, of which scanty fragments remain. Hamo de Crèvecoeur became one of the *Custodes* of the Cinque Ports in 1235. The family died out in 1265.

The Castle and its surroundings (landscaped by Capability Brown in C18) is a place of great beauty. It was captured by Stephen in 1138. Leland records (*L.T.S.* IV, 43): 'Ther ly buried at Leedes Priory 3. Crevicure, Robert, Robert, and Thomas, that be likelihod had the landes here in descent.'

91 Bartholomew, Lord Badlesmere, was a Kentish tenant of the Archbishop of Canterbury and in 1368 became steward of the royal household. He became Warden of the Cinque Ports, Constable of Dover Castle and of Leeds Castle. In 1321, in his absence, his wife refused Isabella, queen of Edward II, admittance to Leeds Castle, which the king quickly seized. For his involvement in the rebellion that culminated at Boroughbridge in 1322, Badlesmere was beheaded at Canterbury. The family took its name from the village whose old

Leeds Castle in 1762, engraved by Godfrey after Francis Grose

who treacherously fortified it against Edward II, who had given it to him; but afterwards suffered the punishment due to his perfidy, being hanged. Take the whole story from the short history of Thomas de la More[92] a nobleman, who lived at the time, lately published by me.[b] "A.D. 1321 queen Isabella came to the castle of Leedes about Michaelmas[94] and wanted to lodge there; but she was refused admittance. The king resenting this as an affront offered to him, summoned some of the neighbourhood from Essex and London, and ordered the castle to be besieged. It was then held by Bartholomew Badilsmer, who had left in it his wife and children, while himself was gone with the rest of the barons to spoil the estate of Hugh le Despencer.[95] The besieged despairing of relief, the barons with their troops came to Kingston[96] praying the king by the bishops of Canterbury and London, and the earl of Pembroke[97] to raise the siege, promising after the next parliament to put the castle into his hands. The king knowing the besieged could not hold out long, and exasperated at their obstinacy refused to hear the request of the barons, and upon their departure, with some difficulty made himself master of the place. He hanged all that were in it except Badilsmer's wife and children whom he sent to the Tower of London."

The Medway increased by the little river *Len*[98] flows through rich grounds,[99] and falling down by[01] *Allington*

b. Angl. & Norm. p. 595.[93]

nucleus lies at NG 014550. There was intermarriage between the Badlesmere and Burghersh (p. 65, n. 21, *Sussex*) families. See *Oxf. Hist.* v, 52, 55, 58, 64, 73, 80; see also p. 33, n. 05.

92 Sir Thomas de la More (fl. 1327–51) was for long believed to be the author of the Latin *Life and Death of Edward II*. This passage in Camden is in fact an extract from the chronicle of Geoffrey Baker (fl. 1350), of which the first part runs from the Creation to 1336 and the second from 1303 to 1356. More was Baker's patron. But see *Oxf. Hist.* v, 547, where the *Life* is considered to be the work of another, but anonymous, author.

93 The full title of this work of Camden's is *Anglica, Hibernica, Normannica, Cambrica a veteribus scripta*. It is a collection of chronicles 'marred by faults' (*English Scholars*, p. 165) published in 1605 (1603 according to *D.N.B.*) at Frankfurt. In a sense it was work undertaken in preparation for the *Britannia*.

94 The Feast of St Michael, 29 September.

95 Favourite of Edward II. See p. 65, n. 23, *Sussex*.

96 Kingston upon Thames, Surrey, an important river crossing above London. There are about two dozen Kingstons in England.

97 Aymer de Valence (c. 1270–1324) became Earl of Pembroke in 1308. *Oxf. Hist.* v, 1, n. 1; not as *D.N.B.*

98 See n. 90 above.

99 Now largely orchards. 'Grounds' probably has the meaning here of 'outlying fields'. See *Elements* I, 210.

01 The Len actually joins the Medway in the heart of Maidstone. Allington Castle is situated about 1½ miles downstream from this confluence.

02 The manor of Allington passed through the hands of Odo, Bishop of Bayeux (p. 30, n. 62), and William de Warrenne (p. 24, n. 78, *Surrey*), who probably built a motte-and-bailey castle which was partly destroyed in 1175 following a rebellion against Henry II (*Oxf. Hist.* III, 332f.). A little to the north of the surviving motte was built (1281–9) a large manor-house of which the brickwork is among the earliest surviving in England from the Middle Ages. In Saxon times Roman brick was sometimes the commonest and most readily available building material, especially in the vicinity of Roman towns, and it was re-used in the construction of many Saxon and medieval churches. Both Leland and Camden refer to 'Britan' or 'British' bricks that we know to have been of Roman manufacture. Construction in newly-made bricks probably began again in C12. The builder was Sir Stephen de Penchester (Penhurst) who died in 1299. He appears as Warden of the Cinque Ports after 1271 and had a hand in planning and building New Winchelsea (see p. 62, n. 99, *Sussex*). See *B. of E., W. Kent*, p. 124f. for a description of the Castle.

03 'restored, renewed'.

04 Sir Thomas Wyatt (1503?–42) was sheriff and knight of the shire for Kent. He had been a lover of Anne Boleyn before she became queen. He is best remembered as the poet who introduced the sonnet from Italy. Leland (*L. T. S.* IV, 47): 'Ailington, sometyme the Graies Castle, as in Henry 3. and Edward the third's dayes: sence the Savels and Wiats.'

05 The first syllable of the place-name Aylesford is the personal name *Ægel*, one which recurs in a number of counties. See *P.N. Glos.*, 1964, I, 199–200. 'Eaglesford' may be Camden's attempt at an etymology, revealing his quite natural misunderstanding of the first element

Allington Castle in 1760, engraved by Sparrow after Francis Grose

castle,[02] where is a beautiful house rebuilt[c] by Thomas Wiat the elder,[04] a learned knight, comes to *Ailesford*,[05] Saxon 'Eaglesford', by Henry of Huntingdon *Elstre*,[d] by Ninnius

c. *restauravit*.[03]

d. II. 178. *Aielsstreu*. Bede and Sax. Chron. at end of Wheloc's edition of Bede.[06] Aillesford, M. West.[07]

of Aylesford. Huntingdon's *Elstre* and Nennius' *Episford* may be safely ignored. See p. 6, n. 57 under the years 455 and 465. The *Ægæles threp* of 455 may well have been the name of a settlement (*throp*, 'hamlet', misread by the scribe) adjacent to the ford of Aylesford. This possibility is strengthened by the fact that one of the early meanings of *throp/thorp* was 'a place of assembly' (*Elements* II, 207 (4); 214–15) and that Aylesford gave its name to one of the lathes of Kent, an administrative region which had its regular assemblies at the place from which it took its name. (On the 'lathe' see *Pre-Feudal England*, p. 152f.) The substitution of *-ford* for *-throp* may be explained as a change from an unfamiliar to a familiar word; for *throp* is otherwise unknown in Kent and Sussex. But perhaps an equally strong cause for

the change was that, of the two Kentish places bearing *Ægel*'s name, the ford as an important means of communication was of greater significance to neighbouring communities than the nearby hamlet. Eventually the ford-name ousted the other completely, at some time before C10. *Lamb.*, p. 368, probably misled Camden in this etymology.

06 Wheloc's transcription of MS A2 of the *Chronicle* was published in 1643 as *Chronologia Anglo-Saxonica*. This work included Bede's *Ecclesiastical History* and other matter relevant to his title. MS A2 was almost destroyed in a fire in 1731, so that Wheloc's transcription has especial importance. See *Parker Chronicle*, p. 4.

07 Matthew of Westminster, on whom see n. 15 below.

Episford, who adds that it was called in the British language *Saissenaeg-habail*,[e] from the defeat of the Saxons there, as others named it *Anglesford*[16] to the same purport. For Vortimer[17] the Briton, son of Vortigern, here attacked Hengist and the Saxons unawares, unable to resist the shock and routed them so completely that they would have been ruined had not Hengist, who knew how to extricate himself from the danger, retired into the isle of Tanet, till that invincible ardor of the Britans had subsided, and fresh supplies came over from Germany. In this battle two generals fell on each side, Catigern[18] the Briton and Horsa the Saxon, of whom the latter was buried at *Horsted*[19] not far from hence, and left his name to the place:

e. *Sathenegabail*, c. 46.[08] He only gives the two first names without explaining either. *Egelesthrep*, Flor. Worc.[09] Ethelward,[10] p. 475. *Epiford* or *Aglisthrop*, Hollinsh.[11] p. 80. Query if Holinshed does not confound it with *Wipedfleet*,[12] where Aur. Ambrosius,[13] A.D. 473, defeated Hengist and *Oslac* his son;[14] the last the same with *Horsa*. M. Westm.[15] p. 171.

08 This is either a misreading for the accepted *Rit hergabail* or a form from a variant MS. The relevant chapter of Nennius' *Historia Brittonum* is 44. Chadwick, *Origin of the English Nation*, p. 39, and other later and authoritative commentators offer no explanation of the phrase. However, *Rit* may be from British *ritu-*, 'a ford'. *E.P.N. Journ.* I, 50.

09 Florence of Worcester (d. 1118), the author of *Chronicon ex Chronicis* which goes down to 1117. This work was continued by other chroniclers to 1295. It was first edited by Lord William Howard in 1592. Florence is original only where he interpolates contemporary matter of his own lifetime. His main sources are Bede and the *Anglo-Saxon Chronicle*. See *Camb. Hist. Eng. Lit.* I, 161–2; *Oxf. Hist.* II, 682; and for a translation of select passages, *E.H.D.* II, 204f.

10 On Æthelweard (Ethelward) see p. 81, n. 71.

11 Raphael Holinshed (d. 1580) whose Chronicles of England go down to 1575. It was a source-book for Shakespeare and others.

12 See p. 6, n. 57 under the year 465. This annal, and the *Anglo-Saxon Chronicle* as a whole, make no mention of Ambrosius.

13 Ambrosius Aurelianus is mentioned by Gildas (a British writer of C6 whose book, *The Destruction and Conquest of Britain*, is not a historical work but rather a homiletic diatribe against the evil priests and rulers of his day) and Nennius (on whom see p. 5, n. 53), though the latter speaks simply of Ambrosius. On him see *Oxf. Hist.* I, 314, 381–2; and 328–9 on Gildas.

14 Hengest's son was *Æsc*, who succeeded to the kingdom of Kent in 488, according to the *Chronicle*. An Oslac is mentioned in the *Chronicle* under the year 568 (MSS 'E' and 'F') and another of that name was King Alfred's maternal grandfather. See *Asser's Life of King Alfred*, p. 163.

15 The *Anglo-Saxon Chronicle* couples Hengest with Horsa in the annal for 455. Matthew of Westminster is the name of an imaginary chronicler to whom was attributed a *Flores Historiarium* which was in fact the work of several chroniclers at St Alban's and Westminster Abbeys. Camden knew it from the edition of 1567, published by Stow.

16 Who the 'others' were matters little; the 'Anglesford' is on a par with Camden's 'Eaglesford' (see note 05). This is a pleasing and much-photographed place, with a medieval bridge and a Carmelite Priory. Leland (*L.T.S.* IV, 45) speaks of its 'faire bridg of ston' and later (V, 219) tells how the lordship of Aylesford and Hoo Hundred passes by way of a daughter of Lord Grey of Codnor to the Wyatts. 'There were some of the Lord Grayes of Codnor byried at Aylesford Freres [i.e. the Priory].' *Lamb.*, p. 369f., connects the place with events in national history.

17 The *Anglo-Saxon Chronicle*, under the year 455, makes this a battle between the forces of Hengest and Horsa on the one side and Wyrtgeorn (Vortigern) on the other. Vortimer is from Nennius, ch. 44, a highly suspect source.

18 Catigern (Catigirn) is made the son of Vortigern in ch. 44 of Nennius. Geoffrey of Monmouth (VI, 15) repeats Nennius' story.

19 Plummer, *Two Saxon Chrons.* II, 11, probably following the Kentish historian Hasted, speaks of the 'flint-heap' at Horsted 'which seems to preserve Horsa's name, and this is probably the monument mentioned by Bede', who (*H.E.* I, 15) reports a tradition that Horsa had been killed in a battle with the Britons (its location unnamed) and that a monument still bearing his name existed in the eastern parts of Kent. The earliest recorded form of this place-name, *Horsum stydæ*, of C9, may well be corrupt (*Dic.*, p. 240) although it occurs in a probably genuine charter (*A.S. Charters*, pp. 151–2, no. 327). However, like other Horste(a)ds, it

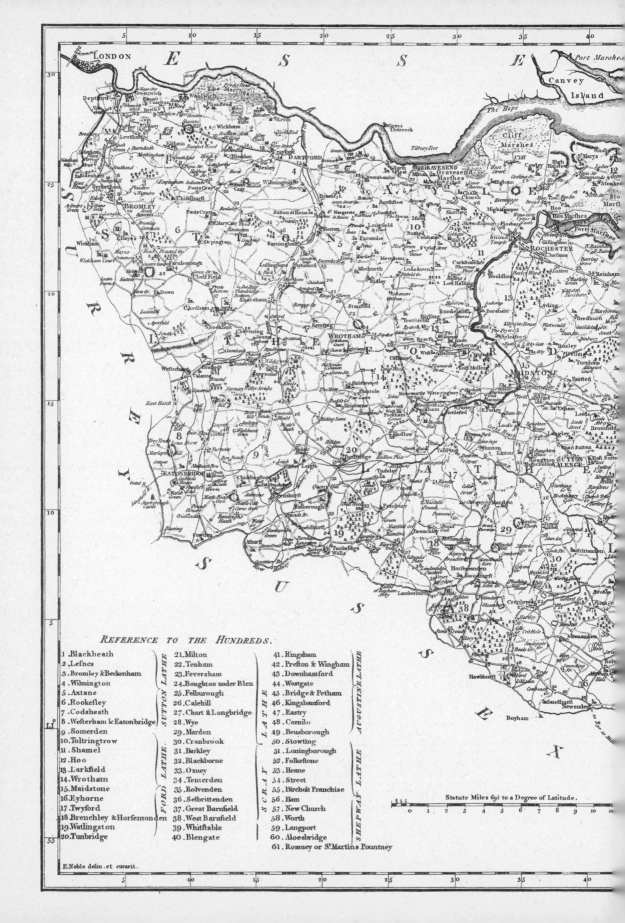

probably meant 'place of horses, a stud-farm' (*Hors-stede*), rather than 'Horsa's place' (*Horsanstede*). A personal name compounded with *stede* is rare and exceptional (*Elements* II, 149, and see also *K.P.N.*, p. 206). On the matter of this supposed monument to Horsa see Gordon Ward, *Hengest*, 1949, pp. 36–7. A possible genesis of the tradition might be a defective Roman monumental inscription (of which there must have been many in such a highly Romanized district) in which the word '(co-)hors' was misunderstood. See *Oxf. Hist.* I, 358, n. 1; *Lamb.*, p. 327; *Arch. Cant.* LXV, 101f.

20 Catigern has almost certainly no connection with this name. Kit's Coty House is the most spectacular of Kentish prehistoric tombs. It now has only one great stone slab laid across the three uprights. This burial chamber was originally enclosed in a rectangular mound of earth and was one of a group of long barrows of which other imperfect instances survive at Addington and the Coldrum. They have affinities with tombs in Scandinavia and Holland, unlike all other British long barrows so far examined. See, however, Jessup, *South-East England*, pp. 95–112 and pl. 19–29. The name 'Kit's Coty' perhaps commemorates a shepherd who habitually sheltered in the 'little house' (*cot*) formed by the stones. However, the word 'House' in addition to 'Coty' is redundant.

21 Boxley Abbey was founded in 1146 directly from the Cistercian mother-house of Clairvaux (*Monastic Order in England*, p. 247, n. 2; and see also *Lamb.*, p. 203f.; *B. of E., E. Kent*, p. 149 for the very slight remains of this abbey). William de Ypres (d. 1165?) was not Earl of Kent. He came to England in 1133 and fought for King Stephen, being rewarded with the revenues of some Kentish Crown lands.

Kit's Coty House in 1760, engraved by Godfrey after Francis Grose

the other is supposed to have been interred in a magnificent manner near Ailesford, where stand those four great stones with others laid across their tops in the form of that British monument called Stonehenge. This is still called by the ignorant vulgar from Catigern *Keith coty house*.[20] Nor must I forget *Boxley* in this neighbourhood, where William de *Ipre*, a Fleming, earl of Kent, founded A.D. 1145, a monastery for monks, which he brought over from Clarevalle in Burgundy:[21] and not far from it on the opposite bank is *Birling*,[22] formerly the barony of the *Maminots*, afterwards of the *Says*,[23] whose estate came at length by females to the families of *Clinton*,[24] *Fienes*,[25] and *Aulton*.[26]

On the east bank of the Medway (after it has passed by *Halling* where Hamo de Heath bishop of Rochester built a house for his successors)[27] somewhat higher up is an antient

22 Birling Place is now a farmhouse. Leland (*L.T.S.* II, 14) refers to the Sayes family, but not in relation to Birling. See *B. of E., W. Kent*, p. 166, for a description of the house.

23 On the Maminots and the Sayes see p. 8–9, nn. 72, 73, 74.

24 Edward Fiennes de Clinton (1512–85), ninth Baron Clinton and Saye, was created Earl of Lincoln in 1572.

25 On the Fiennes family see p. 55, n. 31, *Sussex*.

26 The Aultons seem to have made no mark in national history.

27 Halling is a village mercifully abandoned by the cement industry. Only a fragment of wall of the Bishop of Rochester's palace survives. See *Lamb.*, pp. 363, 366–7; *B. of E., W. Kent*, p. 301.

Halling House in 1759, engraved by Godfrey after Francis Grose

city called by Antoninus DURO-BRVS, DUROBRIVÆ, and elsewhere more correctly DUROPROVÆ or DURO-BROVÆ,[28] by Bede[f] *Durobrevis*, and in the decline of the Roman empire,

f. P. 2, 3. Durobrabis, Durobrisin.[29] Horsl.[30] Index. *Durobrius, Durebrivis, Durobrivis*, &c. See Wesseling.[31] 472. See Camden's derivation of *Brivæ*, Herts.[32] castrum Roffi, i.e. Ruffaine, Roman: see in Devon.[33] Dorman ceaster,[34] see in Northamptonsh. A like mistake about Tunnocelum in Northumberland.[35] *Breviodurum* is a town of Gallia Lugdunensis.[36] 'Rofibrevi' in Ethelbert's charter in Textus Roffensis,[37] and elsewhere

28 The accepted form of this name is *Durobrivæ*. It recurs as the Romano-British name of a small walled town at The Castles, Chesterton, Hunts. It has been thought to mean 'bridges of the stronghold' (*Orig. E.P.N.*, p. 80) or 'town at the bridges' (*Elements* I, 140). As the Roman town was preceded by a Belgic oppidum (*Brit.*, p. 48) the name could have come into use then; but it was equally applicable to the Roman town.

29 Bede (*H.E.* II, 3) has *Durobrevi* and there, and in IV, 5, he has *Hrofescæster* (with variations from one MS to another). See Plummer, *H.E.* II, 85, 215. *Lamb.*, p. 332, differs somewhat from Camden in the forms he cites.

30 John Horsley (1685–1732) published *Britannia Romana* in 1732. It 'may be regarded as the first and in many ways still the best book on Roman Britain as a whole'. *Oxf. Hist.* I, 466.

31 On Wesseling's edition (1735) of the *Antonine Itinerary* see *Antiquity* I, 195.

32 In Gough's edition this occurs on p. 339:

The termination *Briva* added to many names of places I think signifies among the antient Britans and Gauls a *bridge* or *passage*, it being only found in names of places near rivers. In this island were one or two places of the name of *Durobrivæ* [see n. 28 above], i.e. if I mistake not, *the passage of the water*. In France *Briva Isaræ*, now Pontoise,

where they crossed the Isere, as at *Briva Oderæ*, the Oder and at *Samarobrivæ* (for that is the true name) the Some.

This is an instance of Camden's scholarly approach to place-names, although he confuses the British word-roots *dubro-*, 'water' and *duro-*, 'stronghold'. It is, nevertheless, a natural inference since 'bridges' and 'waters' (rivers) are in collocation in all his instances.

33 Camden (in Gough's edn, p. 27) gives a list of British names of cities all of which are prefixed by *Caer*. For '*Caer*, to observe once for all, signifies among the Britans a city; whence they called Jerusalem *Caer Salem*, Paris *Caer Paris*, Rome *Caer Ruffayne*'.

34 This is probably from Henry of Huntingdon (1084?–1154), author of *Historia Anglorum*, who states that Castor, Northants. (near *Durobrivæ*, n. 28 above), was formerly called *Kair Dom*, id est *Dormeceastre*. John of Tynemouth (fl. 1366) in his *Splendid History from the Creation to the time of Edward III*, calls it *Dormundescastre*, which suggests that the place was once in the possession of a Middle Anglian landowner called *Dĕormund*. *P.N. Northants*, 1933, p. 232.

35 This is probably the Romano-British name for a fort on the Cumberland coast near Moresby. (So the O.S. *Map of Roman Britain*). In *P.N. Cumberland*, 1952, pp. 430, 510, it is located at St Bees Head; but see the same work, p. 512, under the name '(?)Itunocelum'.

36 No town of this name seems to occur in the region. See e.g. Vidal-Lablache, *Atlas Classique*, (n.d.), p. 18, 'Gaule au temps de César'.

37 There are at least two grants answering to this description in the *Textus Roffensis*, one by Æthelbert of Kent in A.D. 604, doubtfully genuine, and another by Æthelbert of Wessex (and Kent) in 781. For references see *A.S. Charters*, nos. 1 and

266. The *Textus Roffensis* is the cartulary of the cathedral church of Rochester and was edited by the antiquary Thomas Hearne (1678–1735) in 1720. He was the editor also of Leland's *Itinerary* (1710–12) and *Collectanea* (1715).

38 *Fraw* is from British *Frāmā* from which comes also the river-name Frome in English-speaking areas of Britain. See *Lang. & Hist.*, p.294; *Eng. River N.*, pp.166–8; *P.N. Glos.* 1964, I, 7. 'Aberfraw' means 'mouth of the (river) Fraw'.

39 Thomas Gale (1635?–1702), Dean of York, produced a series of volumes in Latin which were editions of chronicles and early historians. His younger son Samuel Gale (1682–1754) annotated a copy of Gibson's edition of Camden's *Britannia*, which Gough acquired. He added Samuel's annotations as footnotes to the edition of 1789, distinguishing them as *MS. n. Gale.*

40 This seems to be a Middle English spelling for Rockingham, Northants. See *P.N. Northants*, 1933, p.171.

41 The Peutinger Table. See p.18, n.66.

42 See p.27, n.30.

43 John Smith (1659–1715) spent many years working on an edition of Bede's *Ecclesiastical History* which was completed and published by his son George in 1722. See Plummer's edition of *E.H.* I, lxxx–lxxxii, on the great value of Smith's work.

44 *Justum ... Augustinus episcopum ordinavit in civitate Durobrevi* 'Augustine consecrated Justus bishop in the city of Durobrevi'. (*H.E.* II, 3.)

45 The evolution of this name from *Durobrivæ* to Rochester is curious. The associated ideas of bridges and a stronghold no doubt were formed from structures spanning the Medway from either the Belgic oppidum (p.27, n.28) or the Roman town. The Jutes of Kent, failing to

length of time had so contracted the name that it was called ROIBIS,[g] whence by the addition of 'Ceaster' (which our ancestors corrupted from the Roman *Castrum*, and put for a *city, town,* or *castle*) it came to be called 'Hroveceaster', by contraction at present *Rochester*, and in Latin *Roffa* from one *Rhoffus* as Bede[h] conjectures; though it seems to me to preserve something of its antient name *Duro-brovis*.[45] We can have no doubt of the name; since besides the distance in the Itinerary[46] and the authority of Bede, it is expressly called *Durobrovis* in the foundation charter of the cathedral. I would just observe, that in the printed copies of Bede it is spelt *Darvervum*,[i] whereas in the MSS. it is *Durobrovis*.[49] It lies in a valley, surrounded on one side with weak walls,[50] in a

civitas HRobi, alias Durobrevia, Rofi, Dorofi, Dorofraw, from a river as in Aber fraw.[38] MS. n. Gale.[39]

g. Rochester, Rocingham,[40] MS. n. Gale. Peuting. table.[41] Camden seems to have mistaken this for *Raribis*. See also Horsl. 517.[42] Text Roff. calls it *Hrofbrevi, Civitas Roibi*. Smith in Bede, II, 3.[43]

h. P. 2, 3, 14. in which places he calls it *civitas*.[44]

i. In Smith *Dorubrevi*, p. 2, 3.[47] In Wheloc[48] *Doruverni*, a plain mistake for Canterbury, which follows immediately under that name.

understand the name, called the remains of the Roman town *Hrofesceaster*, and according to Bede (as Camden notes) this Saxon name commemorated a former chief man of the place called *Hrof* (Bede, *H.E.* II, 3). This chief was almost certainly an imaginary person, invented to explain an otherwise inexplicable place-name. As so many English place-names have personal names as the first element, this attempted etymology was not nonsensical; and there are early analogies for the similar invention of etymologies (see my *Conquest of Wessex*, pp. 145–6, 151–2, 167). *Dic.*, p. 371, gives a series of early spellings of the place-name which go some way in making clear its transmutation.

46 The *Antonine Itinerary* is a route-book for the Roman Empire, with distances between places stated route by route. It was probably compiled during the reign of the Emperor Caracalla (A.D. 211–17), whose proper name was Marcus

Aurelius Antoninus. The Itinerary was amended and added to later. The British Section is given as a map in the O.S. *Map of Roman Britain*, p. 21.

47 On Smith's edition of Bede see n. 43.

48 On Wheloc's Bede see p. 22, n. 06.

49 Plummer, who based his edition of the *Ecclesiastical History* on a collation of the four oldest manuscripts, gives *Durobrevi* without variants in the footnotes. Where they occur in the MSS, he gives variant readings. See his edition, I, p. 85 and *Lamb.*, pp. 332–3.

50 Of five surviving lengths of wall, that on the Esplanade is the most informative. The Roman foundation has had its facing removed, but the Norman wall above it survives more completely and crowned with blocked openings of c13. Recent excavation has produced information about the East Gate. See *Med. Arch.*

very narrow situation, as William of Malmesbury[k] expresses it, on which account it was antiently considered rather as a castle than a city, and Bede[l] calls it a castle of the Kentishmen.[53] At present it is enlarged with great suburbs to the west, east, and south.[54] It has experienced a variety of fortunes. A.D. 676, it was ruined by Ethelred[m] the Mercian, and afterwards frequently plundered by the Danes.[57] Ethelbert king of Kent[58] built a noble church which he made the see of a bishop, appointing Justus the first bishop;[59] but this decaying by time Gundulphus[60] repaired it about 1080, and turning out the priests introduced monks, who being afterwards turned out were succeeded by a dean, six prebendaries

k. Gest. Pont. I. 132. *situ minime angustum sed in edito locatum.*[51]
l. P. 4, 5.[52]
m. Lothare the usurper of Kent.[55] Hist. of Rochest. p. 8. Ethelred came 686. unless confounded with Ceadwalla, Ib. p. 9.[56]

XIV, 182–3. The walls were probably no weaker than those of most medieval towns, but the impression of their ineffectiveness may have arisen from King John's seizure of the town in 1215 as a preliminary to besieging the castle. The same sequence occurred in 1264 during Simon de Montfort's rebellion, but its occupation by Kentishmen during the rebellion led by Wat Tyler in 1381 is perhaps not relevant, for many of the townspeople were no doubt in sympathy with the rebels. See *B. of E., W. Kent*, p. 451. Leland (*L.T.S.*IV, 45–6):

Going out of Rochester to Cantewarbyri remainith the most parte of a mervelus strong gate. Gates no mo [more] appere there but be communely usid. In the waulles yet remaine a vi. or vii. toures. There be in the toune ... paroche chirches. The cathedral chirch and the palace with other buildings there occupiith half the space of the cumpace within the walles of Rofecestre.

51 *Gesta Pontificum Anglorum* (Lives (or Deeds) of the English Bishops), I, 132. 'On a very confined but elevated site.' On Malmesbury see p. 3, n. 33.

52 See next note.

53 Bede, *H.E.*IV, 5, in retailing the decisions of the Council at Hertford of A.D. 672, refers to *Putta, episcopus castelli Cantuariorum, quod dicitur Hrofescæstir* (Putta, bishop of the Kentishmen's fortress, which is called Rochester). It was only from about 1050 that Latin *castellum* (Old English *castel*) came to mean 'castle'. The implication in the passage is that the town was defensively strong. See *Elements* I, 81–2; *Etym. Dic.*, p. 151.

54 Strood ('marshy land') to the west; Chatham ('homestead or village (*hām*) by the forest (British *cēto-*)') to the east; the extension to the south appears to have had no early name. Chatham, which Camden refers to but does not name at the end of this same paragraph, became a noteworthy place only in his own lifetime.

55 Hlothhere (reigned 673–85) was a great-grandson of the Æthelberht who received Augustine. There is no early evidence of his being a usurper; Bede (IV, 6) merely says that he succeeded his brother

Ecgberht. He was killed in a battle with the South Saxons. For his Laws see *E.H.D.* I, 360f.

56 The *Anglo-Saxon Chronicle*, MS 'E', under the year 686 reads: 'In this year Ceadwalla and Mul his brother ravaged Kent and Wight. This Cædwalla gave to St Peter's monastery, at Medeshamstede [Peterborough], Hoo, on an island called Heabureahg.' Hoo is on what must have been, even in C7, a peninsula. Its old name is preserved in Avery (Farm) at NG 841785 (*K.P.N.*, pp. 19–21). 'Ethelred' king of the Mercians (675–704) laid waste Kent in 676, according to MSS 'A' and 'E'.

57 For example, in 839, when there was much slaughter; and the Danes were there in 885, 894 and 999, according to the annals of the *Anglo-Saxon Chronicle*. It is likely that Camden was here thinking of Leland (*L.T.S.*IV, 57) where he cites Roger Hoveden's Chronicle for the years 884 and 946. Leland also records (*L.T.S.*IV, 125) that 'in the yere of our Lorde 1137. Rofecestre with the chirch was burnid by mischaunce of fier'. See also *Lamb.*, p. 334f.

58 Æthelberht (560?–616) was the first English king to accept Christianity. He was baptized by St Augustine in 597. See Bede, *H.E.* I, 26, for details, and p. 48, n. 16.

59 Bede, *H.E.* II, 3. See n. 44 opposite. For a plan of this first church at Rochester see *Med. Arch.* IX, fig. 9, p. 23 and references there.

60 Gundulf (1024?–1108) was a monk of Bec who became Bishop of Rochester in 1077. He reorganized the monastery and rebuilt the cathedral. He was also in charge of the building of the White Tower in London. See later in this paragraph Camden's reference to the *Textus Roffensis*. For a description of the cathedral, see *B. of E., W. Kent*, p. 451.

61 The site of an early, temporary castle, of which the motte survives, is said to exist in the grounds of Satis House immediately to the south of the present one. The permanent castle was begun by Bishop Gundulf c. 1087–9, but of this period only a part of the riverside wall survives. The fine keep was the work of William of Corbeuil, Archbishop of Canterbury, between 1125 and 1139. Some parts of the outer defences were remodelled in c14. See *Lamb.*, p. 355f.; *B. of E., W. Kent*, p. 470f.; *Oxf. Hist.* III, 101.

62 Odo (d. 1097) was half-brother of the Conqueror and fought at Hastings. He was given Dover Castle and the earldom of Kent in 1066 and was, next to the king, the most powerful man in England, having acquired vast wealth. The Conqueror finally imprisoned him at Rouen and he was a main conspirator against Rufus. After being besieged at Pevensey and Rochester, he had to leave England in 1088. His one known virtue was his patronage of learning. He did not build the surviving Rochester Castle. See the previous note. *Lamb.*, pp. 335–6, misled Camden in this.

63 William de Corbeuil, presumably. See n. 61 above.

64 Aylesford. See p. 22, n. 05.

65 This passage, on Folio 2b of Domesday, reads: 'the bishop held land there [Aylesford] valued at 17s. 4d. in exchange for the land on which the castle [of Rochester] stands'.

66 See n. 62 above.

67 See p. 27, n. 37.

68 Haddenham near Aylesbury.

69 A hundred pounds weight in money. The initial letter of *libra* gives us the abbreviation '£' for pound sterling, and 'lb' for a pound weight is from the same Latin word.

and scholars. Near the church the castle[61] overhangs the river, strong by nature and art, said to have been built by Odo bishop of Bayeux and earl of Kent.[62] But William was certainly the builder of it:[63] for we find in Domesday book,[n] "the bishop of Rochester holds lands in Elesforde[64] in exchange for the ground on which the castle stands."[65] It is clear, however, that bishop Odo in the then uncertainty of affairs held out this castle against William Rufus till he was compelled by want of provisions not only to surrender it but to forfeit his rank and quit the kingdom.[66] Of the repair of this castle take this account from the Textus Roffensis.[o] "King William II. refusing to confirm Lanfranc's gift of the manor of Hedenham[68] in the county of Bucks to the church of Rochester, unless Lanfranc and Gundulph bishop of Rochester, would give the king 100lb. of money;[p] at length, by the interposition of Robert Fitz-Haimon[70] and Henry earl of Warwick,[71] the king remitted his demand of the money, which he asked for the conveyance of the maner, upon condition that bishop Gundulph who was experienced and practised in the science of masonry, should build the king a stone castle at Rochester, at his own expence. The bishops with reluctance consenting to this in the king's presence, bishop Gundulph built the castle entirely at his own cost." And a little after king Henry I. "granted[72] to the church of Canterbury and the archbishops, the custody and constableship of it for ever, and leave to build a tower in it for themselves,"[73] as Florence of Worcester[74] relates.[q] Since that time it sustained several sieges,[75] but the greatest when the barons alarmed the whole

n. P. 2. b.

o. An antient MS. record of this church, published by Hearne, 1720. c. 87. p. 144.[67]

p. *centum libras denariorum.*[69]

q. P. 503. A.D. 1126.

70 Robert FitzHamon (d. 1107) supported Rufus during Odo of Bayeux's revolt and was rewarded with grants of land in Glos., Bucks. and Cornwall.

71 Henry de Newburgh or Beaumont (d. 1123) was created the first Earl of Warwick by Rufus.

72 In 1126.

73 The keep. See n. 61. above.

74 On Florence of Worcester see p. 23, n. 09.

75 On the siege of 1088 see n. 62 above, and *Oxf. Hist.* III, 101; on that of 1215 see p. 28, n. 50; and for interesting details of King John's methods of taking the Castle see *King John*, pp. 267–8. The rebuilt corner-tower of the keep is well seen in H. Braun, *The English Castle*, 1948, pl. 42; and see *Lamb.*, pp. 336–8.

Rochester Castle in 1759, engraved after Francis Grose

kingdom with their commotions, and Simon de Montfort[76] attacked it with great vigour, but without success, and cut away the drawbridge. In the room of this was afterwards built with the spoils of France, a magnificent stone bridge on arches,[77] by John Cobham[78] and Robert Knowles,* which last rose from the lowest to the highest rank by his bravery. Under this bridge the Medway foams and rolls with great violence and rapidity, and presently abating both, forms a dock furnished for the finest fleet the sun ever beheld, and ready on a minute's warning, built lately by our most gracious sovereign Elizabeth at great expence for the security of her subjects and the terror of her enemies with a fort on the shore for its defence.[80]

The Medway now broader and gayer with its curling waves, washes most pleasant meadows till it divides at the *isle of Shepey* (which I take to be the TOLIATIS[r] of Ptolemy) and

*Called by the French *Canoles*.[79]
r. or *Toliapis*.[81]

76 On the events leading to this siege see *Oxf. Hist.* IV, 187. Leland (*L.T.S.* IV, 57–8) quotes these events at length from the additions to the Chronicle of Gervase of Canterbury. In the revolt of 1381 the Kentishmen, with some from Essex, forced Sir John Newton to surrender the Castle. *Oxf. Hist.* V, 408; *Lamb.*, p. 338.

77 According to Gough (*Additions*, p. 233) the bridge was rebuilt c. 1387–92 by Knollys, who also built a chapel 'at the end of the bridge'. Cobham contributed much to the new bridge and had built a chapel at the end of the old bridge which Knollys replaced. It was endowed with 52 manors for its maintenance and in the time of

Henry V a corporation was formed to administer the estates and to see to repairs. It was 565 feet long and 14 broad, with eleven arches. It was surpassed only by the bridges of London and Westminster in Gough's day. Leland (*L.T.S.* IV, 44–5) lists the benefactors of the bridge as recorded on a tablet in the bridge chapel. Three archbishops, a cardinal, four bishops and worthies such as Sir Richard Whittington were enrolled there. Later (*L.T.S.* IV, 52) Leland says that 'One John Warner, a marchant of Rochester, made the new coping of Rochestre Bridg, and Bisshop Warham the yren barres.' See also *Lamb.*, pp. 344–56.

78 This is presumably the third Baron Cobham (d. 1408) on whom see p. 14, nn. 18, 19; or a member of the same family.

79 This spelling seems to indicate a French attempt to imitate the English pronunciation of 'kn' in which the 'k' was sounded. Although now silent in standard spoken English, the 'k' of 'kn' is still retained in some dialects. Sir Robert Knollys or Knolles (d. 1407) became immensely wealthy from plunder got in the French campaigns. He was active against the rebels of 1381. Froissart mentions him briefly.

80 This is Chatham; see p. 29, n. 54; *Arch. Journ.* CXXVI, 272. The fort is Upnor Castle built in 1561, of which there are some remains. *Arch. Journ.* CXXVI, 276f.; *B. of E., W. Kent*, p. 565.

81 Leland (*L.T.S.* IV, 58): 'Shepey by likelihod is caullid of Ptoleme Caunos'; *Lamb.*, p. 255, 'Covnos'; but see O.S. *Map of Roman Britain*, fig. 1, p. 20, 'The British Isles according to Ptolemy', where *Toliatis ins(ula)* and *Counus ins.* are placed well to the north-east of the North Foreland. They may represent a vague notion of the positions of the islands we know as Thanet and Sheppey.

82 On Yenlet see next note. On Smith see p. 28, n. 43.

83 Bede, *H.E.* v, 8: '...Berctwald, *qui erat abbas in monasterio, quid iuxta ostium aquilonale fluminis Genladae positum, Racuulfe nuncupatur*' which may be rendered: 'Berhtwald, who was abbot of the monastery, which stands near the north bank of the mouth of the river Genlade, called Reculver'. Confusion has arisen from the recurrence of the same unusual river-name twice in the same region. It seems not to occur outside Kent. An Old English name *gegnlād*, with some such meaning as 'creek, backwater', was given to the watercourse that almost separates the Isle of Grain from the Hoo peninsula, now called Yantlet Creek, and also to a northern arm of the Wantsum river, formerly called Yenlet, near whose mouth, but west of it, stand the ruins of Reculver. (*Eng. River N.*, p. 477.) Camden's reference is inappropriate in the context of the Isle of Sheppey. Moreover he confuses the Yantlet Creek with the Swale. *Lamb.*, p. 232f.

84 The name Sheppey is composed of Old English (Kentish dialect) *scēp*, 'sheep', and *ēg*, 'island'. It is still noted for sheep. *Lamb.*, p. 225, gives the Latin equivalent: '*Insula Ovium*...Ile of Sheepe'.

85 This is roughly its present size although much continues to be lost by marine erosion, especially along the north coast. Along the Swale, however, there has been some reclamation.

86 Minster, ultimately from Latin *monasterium*, meant 'a monastery, a church' (Old English *mynster*). See *Elements* II, 46–7; and *Oxf. Hist.* II, 148–9, 152–6 for *mynsters* as mother-churches of a district. Only the gatehouse and monastic church survive.

87 Various dates between 664 and 675 have been suggested for this foundation. *Sexburg* was daughter

32

The Monastery of Minster in 1759, engraved by T. Morris after Francis Grose

empties itself into the mouth of the Thames at two mouths, the western of which is called *West Swale*, the eastern which seems to have separated Shepey from the main land *East Swale*, and by Bede's *Genlad* and *Yenlett*.[83] This island from the numerous flocks of sheep which it feeds was called by our ancestors *Shepey*,[84] q.d. *Sheep island*, and is about 21 miles in circuit,[85] uncommonly rich in corn, but destitute of wood. On the north side it has a small monastery, now called *Minster*,[86] founded by Sexburga, wife of Ercombert king of Kent A.D. 710;[87] below which lately a certain Brabanter[88] has begun to extract by furnaces brimstone and copperas from stones found on the shore.[89] On the west it has a handsome and strong

s. Bede, V. 8. mentions *Genlada*, which his editor Smith says is now *Inlade*; but I find nothing of *Yenlett*.[82]

of *Anna*, king of the East Angles, and married *Eorconberht*, king of Kent, c. 640. He died in 664 and it was as a widow that she founded the monastery and became its abbess. She later became the second abbess of Ely, c. 679, and died c. 699. See *B. of E., E. Kent*, p. 376f.

88 A man from the region of Brabant, now divided between Holland and Belgium. *Lamb.*, p. 227,

met him at Queenborough in 1579.

89 The Brabanter was Mathias Falconer, 'the stones were pyrites and the copperas a sulphate of iron used as a mordant in dyeing'. They were to be found 'at the foot of the cliffs on the north side of Sheppey'. Mathias established the factory in Queenborough in 1579. See *Hist. Geog. Eng.*, p. 359; *Little Guide, Kent*, p. 233; *Lamb.*, pp. 227–8.

castle,[90] erected by Edward III. as he himself expresses it "in a pleasant situation to the terror of the enemy and the relief of his people," to which he added a town,[91] and in honour of Philippa of Hainault, called it *Queenborough*[92] or *Queen town*. The present constable is Sir Edward *Hobey*,[93] my particular friend,[t] who has improved his noble mind by literary studies. To the east is *Shurland*,[95] formerly belonging to the Cheneys,[96] now to Philip Herbert[97] second son of Henry earl of Pembroke,[98] whom king James created on the same day baron *Herbert of Shurland* and earl of *Montgomery*.

This island belongs to the hundred of *Midleton*, so called from the town of *Midleton* now *Milton*.[99] This was antiently a royal vill,[01] and of much greater note than at present, though the Danish pirate Hastings in order to do all the mischief he could[u] fortified the neighbouring castle A.D. 893.[03] In this neighbourhood are to be seen *Sittingborn*, which has many inns;[04] and the remains of *Tong* castle,[05] the antient seat of

t. *mihi observandus*.[94]

u. *ut officeret*.[02]

90 Demolished c. 1650, its site is now barely perceptible at NG c. 913722. *Lamb.*, p. 227.

91 In 1365 onwards. See *New Towns*, pp. 457–9; *Lamb.*, pp. 226–7.

92 Queenborough has only the Guildhall and some merchants' houses of C16 and early C18 in the High Street that are now worthy of more than passing notice. For an account of this 'unusually late foundation' (of the town) see *New Towns*, pp. 457–9; for its present interest, *B. of E., E. Kent*, p. 404.

93 Sir Edward Hobey (1560–1617) was a Member of Parliament and a favourite of James I whom he entertained at Bisham, Berks.

94 *Observare* had the meanings 'heed, pay attention to, regard, esteem'. Here the gerundive is used with the sense 'esteeming me'.

95 Shurland retains interesting remains of a house and courtyard of early C16. See *B. of E., E. Kent*, pp. 291–2; *Lamb.*, p. 256.

96 Sir Thomas Cheyney (1485?–1558) became Warden of the Cinque Ports in 1536. His tomb is in the church at Minster-in-Sheppey (*B. of E., E. Kent*, p. 378). There is a Cheyney monument at Guestling, Sussex, and a brass at West Hanney, Berks. Chenies, Bucks., is from the family name also, but it may be that several families of this name are so commemorated. Queenborough became the official residence of the Wardens in 1582. There is a Cheyne brass at Hever.

97 Philip (1584–1650) was created Earl of Montgomery in 1605 and, as a favourite of James I, was given several high offices, including that of Lord Lieutenant of Kent in 1624. He became Earl of Pembroke in 1630 in succession to the third earl of the Herbert line, William, his brother. He was a Roundhead in the Civil War.

98 Henry Herbert (1534?–1601) married Lady Jane Grey's sister and held several high offices.

99 Milton next Sittingbourne or Milton Regis is *Middeltun* in the entry of the *Anglo-Saxon Chronicle* for 893. Leland (*L.T.S.* IV, 88): 'Ther cummith a preaty creke to Midleton in Kent a…miles from Sidingburne, and thither cum praty crayers [small trading vessels] and shippleletys [small ships].'

01 In 1052 (*Chronicle*, MS 'E') this place is called *Middeltun thæs cynges*, i.e. king's or royal Milton. See *B. of E., E. Kent*, p. 374f.

02 *Officere* here has a figurative sense 'be harmful or hurtful to'.

03 The *Anglo-Saxon Chronicle*, MS 'A', under the year 893 (which should be 892: all entries from 754 to 845 are dislocated due to a scribal error), has as its final sentence: 'Then soon afterwards *Hæsten* came with 80 ships to the mouth of the Thames and built himself a fort at *Middeltun*.' It is possible that the earthwork called 'Castle Rough' is the remains of the Danish fort (*Lamb.*, p. 215). See p. 59, n. 66, *Sussex*, for possible surviving remains of other Danish forts.

04 Sittingbourne on the main highway from London to Canterbury (the most important English place of pilgrimage in the Middle Ages) and on to Dover and the Continent, was one of the halting-places on the route, hence the number of inns. Some of these remain. Demand was revived by the needs of stage-coach passengers and again, to a smaller extent, of the motorist. Industrialization has not yet destroyed all the quality of this place, but the 'developer' may do so yet. See *B. of E., E. Kent*, p. 444f.; *New Towns*, p. 457. Leland (*L.T.S.* IV, 68): 'Sitingburn, alias Sidingburne, is a pretty thorowgh fare of one paroche, and by the chirch renneth a litle burne or rille, wherof peraventure the towne toke name.'

05 Tonge Castle is thus described by Leland (*L.T.S.* IV, 42): 'The

33

Guncelline de Badilsmer, a man of great rank, whose son *Bartholomew* had a son named *Guncelline*, who by the heiress of Ralph Fitz-Bernard, lord of Kingsdowne, had *Bartholomew* that rebel before mentioned,[06] who by Margery *Clare*[07] had *Giles*, who died without issue, Margery wife of William *Roos* of *Hamlak*,[08] Matilda of John *Vere* earl of Oxford,[09] Elizabeth of William *Bohun* earl of Northampton[10] and afterwards of Edmund *Mortimer*,[11] and Margaret of John *Tiptoft*,[12] from whom descended a fair lineage of princes and nobles.

After this we see *Feversham*[13] in a very convenient situation surrounded by the richest part of this county, and having a bay convenient for importation and exportation, on which account it is now the most flourishing town in this neighbourhood. It seems also to have been formerly considerable; a council of the wise men[x] of the realm having been held here by king Ethelstan, and laws enacted A.D. 903;[15] and Stephen who usurped the crown of England founded here a monastery for Cluniacs,[16]

x. *prudentum conventus*.[14]

diches and the kepe hille of Thonge Castle appere in a litle wood a two flites shotte by south from Thong church.' He later adds (ibid., p. 68): 'Thong castel…was made, as sum say, of Hengist and the Saxons.' Remains of the Norman motte and bailey have been investigated. 'The complex (of buildings on the site) belonged to a small farming community, with extensive farming lands in the neighbouring manor of Tonge' (*Med. Arch.* IX, 202). See also ibid. VIII, 255. The finds were largely of C13. And see *Lamb.*, p. 220f.; *B. of E., E. Kent*, p. 461.

06 See p. 20, n. 90 and references there. In 1086 the manor was held by Hugh de Port, an important landowner in Hampshire. See *Oxf. Hist.* II, 625. It later reverted to the Crown and was given by Edward VI to Sir Ralph Vane (Fane), who was executed in 1552 on a charge of conspiring to murder. *Oxf. Hist.* VII, 492.

07 On the Clare family see p. 17, nn. 41, 42, and references there.

08 This man, the second Baron Roos, died in 1317.

09 The de Veres were among the most powerful of medieval families. This John was a grandson of Edward I and an intimate friend of Edward III. He became Constable of England and was active in every major engagement between 1340 and his death in 1366. He became earl in 1331.

10 William de Bohun (d. 1360) was immensely wealthy with great land holdings in Essex, the Welsh Marches and elsewhere.

11 Presumably Edmund de Mortimer (d. 1331), first Earl of March.

12 John Tiptoft who was, presumably, ancestor of Tiptoft, Earl of Worcester (1375?–1443).

13 Faversham was described by Leland (*L.T.S.* IV, 68) thus:

[It] is a market town franchised with a sanctuary, and hath a great abbey of blake monkes of the fundation of king Stephane. The towne is encluded yn one paroche, but that ys very large. Ther cummeth a creke to the towne that bereth vessels of xx. tunnes, and a myle fro thens north-est is a great key cawled Thorn to discharge bygge vessels.

It is still a flourishing town and retains relics of its earlier prosperity in a number of attractive old buildings. For a brief history and perambulation of the town see *Arch. Journ.* CXXVI, 247f.; for greater detail, *B. of E., E. Kent*, p. 300f. *Lamb.*, p. 228f., gives some historical anecdotes. On sanctuaries see *English Wayfaring Life in the Middle Ages*, p. 77f.

14 'Assembly of wise men'. In Old English, *witena-gemōt*, 'the moot (meeting) of the *witan* or wise men'. See p. 44, n. 94.

15 On Athelstan's councils see *Oxf. Hist.* II, 347–8. The one held at Faversham was c. 930 (ibid., 346). See also *E.H.D.* I, 390, §10.

16 Very little of the Abbey, founded in 1147, remains. *Excavations at Faversham, 1965* is a description of the recovery (pp. 15–17) of the site of the royal mortuary chapel at the east end of the abbey church. The vaults, which had held the remains of King Stephen, his queen and his son Eustace, had been robbed. Gough (*Additions*, p. 234) quotes Stowe to the effect that 'Stephen, his queen, and son, were thrown in the creek for the lead coffins at the dissolution'. Above ground some fragments of the outer gatehouse survive, incorporated into a dwelling, and there are still parts of the precinct walls and barns of C15 to C17 (pp. 30–34). The Cluniacs, so called from their mother-house, founded at Cluny in 910, were a reformed branch of the Benedictine order of monks. Beginning in C10, it reached its zenith in late C11, though by C16 it had 2000 houses in Europe, with 35 in England. Lewes Priory (p. 50, n. 96, *Sussex*) was the first established and chief house in England of the Cluniacs. See *Monastic Order in England*, p. 145f.

Faversham Abbey in 1756, engraved by Sparrow
after Francis Grose

in which himself, his wife Matilda[17] and his son Eustace[18] were buried. Near this town as well as in other parts of the county are here and there found pits of a great depth with narrow mouths, but broad at bottom, divided into rooms, with pillars hewn out of the chalk. Various are the opinions about them: I can only suppose them to have been pits out of which the antient Britans dug chalk to manure their lands, as Pliny tells us.[y] He says "they dug pits 100 feet deep, narrow at the mouth, but spacious at bottom," of which kind are these we have been describing, nor are they found any where but in a chalky soil;[20] unless one should suppose the Saxons made them for the same purposes as their German ancestors, who, as Tacitus[z] informs us, "used to dig caverns under ground, and cover them over with great quantities of dung both as a shelter from the winter and to lodge their corn in; such places abating the intenseness of the cold; and the enemy always ravaging the open country in their inroads, whatever was concealed and buried escaped or was not thought worth their search."[22]

y. N.H, XVII. 8.[19] z. de morib. Germ. c. 16.[21]

17 Matilda of Boulogne (1103?–52), wife of Stephen, was a woman of determined action like her namesake, the daughter of Henry I (1102–67), who had been the wife of Henry V of Germany, Emperor of the Holy Roman Empire (1111–25). The Empress Matilda married Geoffrey of Anjou in 1128; and the Civil War arose mainly from her claim to the throne, based on her recognition by the barons which was exacted from them by her father. Her failure against Stephen was largely due to her being 'a disagreeable woman, haughty, tactless and grasping'. On the confrontation of the two Matildas and on Stephen see *Oxf. Hist.* III, 131f.

18 Eustace took an active part in support of his father during the anarchy, but in 1152 the Pope 'forbade Archbishop Theobald to crown Eustace on the ground that "Stephen appeared to have seized the kingship contrary to his oath" ' (*Oxf. Hist.* III, 163). He died in 1153 shortly before the Treaty of Winchester by which Henry was recognized as Stephen's successor. A contemporary notes (of Eustace): 'wherever he was [he] did more evil than good' (ibid., 164).

19 *Natural History*, bk 17, ch. 8. On Pliny see p. 12, n. 98.

20 Camden's supposition is very probably correct. *Lamb.*, p. 401. The excavated chalk was used for marling fields deficient in lime. See *Archaeology in the Field*, p. 91 and n. 9; p. 234; p. 92, fig. 12 for the plan and section of a dene-hole at Bexley, Kent. On examples at Gravesend, Abbey Wood, Borden, Lenham, and Lydden, see *Arch. Kent*, pp. 161–3. One at Darenth proved to be of C13 (*Med. Arch.* IX, 216).

21 *De Moribus et Populis Germaniae*, i.e. 'On the Customs and Peoples of Germany', often referred to as the *Germania*.

22 Tacitus, in the chapter of the *Germania* which Camden quotes, expressly refers to the houses built of timber and then goes on to describe the underground store-places which

35

Reculver, engraved by Cook after J. Pridden, published in 1809

they used also as winter dwellings. He is describing a feature of an Early Iron Age culture. In the southern Britain of Tacitus' day, and earlier, pits were dug around farmsteads for the storage of corn which had been dried in a kiln. These were identified as 'pit-dwellings' by earlier archaeologists, though as dwellings they would have been wretchedly uncomfortable even in summer; in winter they would have been almost unusable, since a fire could not be lit in them without suffocating the occupants. After a few years the pits could no longer be used for grain storage owing to their being infected by fungi. They then became convenient places for the disposal of refuse. See *Prehistoric Communities of the British Isles*, pp. 195–6. It is quite possible that some pits that had been dug for marl were afterwards used as grain stores.

23 Whitstable has for centuries been the principal place for oyster-fishing. *Lamb.*, p. 236.

24 Reculver, on which see the following notes.

Proceeding along an open shore abounding with shell fish and oysters[23] and plenty of oyster-pits, we come to *Reculver*,[24] called by the Saxons 'Reaculf';[25] but by the Romans and Britons REGULBIUM,[26] as in the Notitia,[27] which places here the Tribune of the first cohort of *Vetasii*,[28] under the Count of the Saxon shore;[29] by which name all this coast went at that time, and this its antiquity appears by the coins of Roman emperors

25 Bede has *Racuulfe* (i.e. Rac-wulf) c. 730; and the Old English translation of his History, c. 890, has *Reaculfe*, the form cited by Camden. In adopting this British word into English it was assumed to be a personal name (cp. Rochester, p. 28, n. 45). As such names with -*wulf* as the second element were very familiar, e.g. *Æthelwulf*, *Beowulf*, *Cuthwulf*, etc., the transformation was an easy one.

26 This Romano-British place-name is a compound of the British word *gulbio*-, 'beak, headland', with, probably, British *ro*-, 'great'. *Lang. & Hist.*, pp. 559, 661.

27 On the *Notitia Dignitatum* see p. 4, n. 35.

28 'The record of a garrison of *Cohors I Baetasiorum* listed in the *Notitia* has been confirmed by the discovery of four bricks marked by the official stamp of the unit, and this unit may well have built the fort which on good archaeological evidence can now be dated early in the third century.' Jessup, *S.E. England*, pp. 175, 218; and see *Arch. Journ.* CXXVI, 185–6, 223–5 with plan.

29 The fort is of c. A.D. 220, of a new type and almost 8 acres in area (*Brit.*, pp. 184–5). Little is visible now, for much has been eroded by the sea and the ramparts were a ready source of building materials in the Middle Ages.

dug up here. Ethelbert,[30] king of Kent, after he had given Canterbury to Austin the monk,[31] built himself a palace here.[32] Basso a Saxon embellished it with a monastery,[33] from which Brightwald the eighth bishop of Canterbury was called[34] to that see. Hence it was also named *Raculf minster* from the monastery,[35] when Edred, brother to Edmund the elder, gave it to the church of Canterbury.[36] At present it is only a small country village,[37] and owes all its consequence to that monastery, whose church spires are of use to mariners to avoid the shoals and sands in the Thames' mouth.[38] For as the author of the Philippeis[z] sings

z. [*sic*] Hadrian Junius. Holland.[39]

30 On Ethelbert (*Æthelberht*) see p. 48, n. 16.

31 'The story that Ethelbert transferred his capital to Reculver, leaving Canterbury entirely to Augustine (*Anglia Sacra* I, i, ed. H. Wharton, 1691) seems to me an obvious myth...' (Plummer, *H.E.* II, 44).

32 No such remains have been found on the site and Leland mentions none in his day. *Lamb.*, p. 235, says he read of the building of this palace.

33 The *Anglo-Saxon Chronicle* entry for the year 669 records: 'In this year Ecgbryht the king [Egbert I of Kent, 664–73] gave Reculver to the mass-priest Bass to build a church there.'

34 A contemporary charter of A.D. 679 records a grant by Hlothhere, King of Kent (673–c. 685), to Beorhtwald abbot of Reculver of land in Thanet and at Sturry in mainland Kent. See text in *E.H.D.* I, no. 56, 443–4. According to the *Anglo-Saxon Chronicle*, MSS 'A', 'B' and 'C', Beorhtwald succeeded Theodore as archbishop of Canterbury in 690, but in MSS 'E' and 'F' the date is given as 692. (See Plummer, *H.E.* II, 283.) He died in 731. Leland (*L.T.S.* IV, 52) cites Thorne's *Chronicle* for this.

35 On its foundation see n. 33 above. It was built within the walls of *Regulbium*, the Roman fort of the Saxon Shore (see n. 29 above). The original church of C7 was added to in C8 and was further enlarged and modified in C12, C13, and C15. Plan in *Med. Arch.* IX, 25, and see text p. 24. The church was largely demolished in 1805. A plan of the remaining fragments of the ramparts of the Roman fort will be found, with a view of the church shortly before its demolition, in *Roman Forts of the Saxon Shore*, p. 20. *Lamb.*, pp. 235–6, has very little to say of this place. For its state today, see *B. of E., E. Kent*, pp. 414–16. For the most recent excavation of the interior of the church see *Med. Arch.* XIV, 161.

36 This Eadred was son of Edward the Elder and became king of the English (946–55), succeeding his brother Edmund. A forged charter survives in several MSS purporting to be a grant of Reculver Minster by King Eadred to Christchurch, Canterbury. See *A.S. Charters*, no. 546, p. 200 for references. In his will (*E.H.D.* I, no. 107, p. 511) Eadred bequeathed 400 pounds to the archbishop of Canterbury for the relief of the people of Kent, Surrey, Sussex and Berkshire 'to redeem themselves from famine and from a heathen army [of Danes] if they need'. See Leland (*L.T.S.* IV, 52) for similar statements taken from Thorne's *Chronicle*.

37 The marine erosion that has destroyed so much of the Roman fort has also removed most of the village. On the erosion of this coast see *Coastline*, p. 399f. Leland (*L.T.S.* IV, 59–60) noted that

Reculver...stondeth withyn a quarter of a myle or litle more of the se syde. The towne at this tyme is but village lyke.... The old building of the chirch of the abbay remayneth, having ii. goodly spiring steples.

He goes on to describe a great Saxon cross 'yn the enteryng of the quyer' of which fragments are preserved in the crypt of Canterbury Cathedral. For a reassessment of the evidence concerning the minster and the great cross see *Arch. Journ.* CXXV, 291f. Gough (p. 236) records that Reculver church contained an

epitaph to Ralph Brooke, Camden's adversary, under his figure in brass in a tabard;

Here under quit of worldly miseries Ralph Brooke, esq; late York herald lies.
Fifteenth of October he was last alive, One thousande six hundred twenty and five:
Seaventy-three yeares bore he fortune's harmes, And forty-five an officer of armes:
He married Thomsin daughter of Michael Cob of Kent,
Sergiant at armes, by who two daughters God him lent,
Survyvyng Mary, Wylliam Dicken's wife,
Thomasin John Ecton's; happy be their life.

Worse doggerel than this it would be hard to find anywhere.

38 The Corporation of Trinity House objected in 1805 to the demolition of the twin towers of the church, and the lead-covered spires were replaced by skeletal structures of iron to serve as sea-marks. This ironwork has been gone for some years now, but the stone towers remain.

39 Hadrianus Junius (1511–75), the Dutch poet and historian.

40 Thanet is a pre-English place-name. Its earliest recorded forms all have initial 'T' and not 'Th'. See *K.P.N.*, pp. 11–12; *Lang. & Hist.*, p. 331.

41 Thanet remained an island, with a navigable channel, the river Wantsum, between it and the mainland until the Middle Ages. There is evidence already in C11 that it had ceased to be a sea channel (*Arch. Cant.* LIII, 77; LIV, 48), but later, tradition had it that small ships could pass through until the end of C15 (*Coastline*, p. 337, quoting Hasted). In 1485 a bridge was proposed between the mainland and Thanet to replace the ferry ruined by the silting up of the channel (*Oxf. Hist.* VII, 64–5). For a map of the area in Roman times, showing the Wantsum Channel, see *Hist. Geog. Eng.*, p. 39. In Bede's day the name of the whole channel was apparently Wantsum, but today the map shows it to be restricted to the northern arm, from the sea near Reculver to its junction with the Great Stour.

42 Wantsum (like the Norfolk river-name Wensum) is probably from Old English *wændsum*, 'winding'. See *Elements* II, 254 and references there.

43 The Old English word *weald* meant 'woodland'. See p. 52, n. 12, *Sussex*, and *Elements* II, 239–42.

44 Ashford has today a large cattle market and the size of its parish church, rebuilt from mid C14 onwards, suggests that it was a relatively wealthy community during the Middle Ages. *Lamb.*, p. 260f.; *B. of E., W. Kent*, p. 129f. Leland (*L.T.S.* IV, 37):

Assheford is a market towne yn the side or the border of the Weld of Kent. Yt is in quantite as much agayne as Sitingburne, and thereyn is a fayr college of prestes.

45 Wye remains 'a pratie market tounelet' as Leland described it. He

Cernit oleriferum Tamisim sua Doridi amaræ
Flumina miscentem —

It sees the swanny Thames unite its streams
With bitter Doris.

We come now to the isle of *Tanet*[40] separated from the main land by a small channel of the river *Stoure*,[41] called by Bede *Wantsum*,[42] which uniting its two streams in the woody part of the county called the *Weald*,[43] soon after it becomes a large stream passes by *Ashford*[44] and *Wy*,[45] two small but considerable market towns, each having its college of priests; the one[46] founded by John Kemp archbishop of Canterbury,[47] who was born here, the other by Sir Richard *Fogg*,[48] knight.[a] Wie has also a particular well,[50] on which God bestowed some miraculous gift at the prayer of a Norman monk, if we may believe Roger Hoveden,[b] whom the reader that is fond of the

a. This last sentence is omitted by bishop Gibson.[49]
b. P. 457.[51]

adds: 'There is yerely a grete feyre on Seint Grigori's Day at Wye' (*L.T.S.* IV, 37). *Lamb.*, p. 257f.; *B. of E., E. Kent*, p. 485f.

46 Kemp's foundation at Wye largely survives incorporated into the fabric of the Agricultural College. *Lamb.*, p. 259; *B. of E., E. Kent*, p. 486.

47 Kemp became Archbishop of York and Lord Chancellor in 1426, Archbishop of Canterbury and Cardinal-Bishop in 1452. He died two years later. It was in 1447 that he began the rebuilding of Wye church, of which only the nave survives, and he founded a grammar school there as well. Leland (*L.T.S.* IV, 37–8) has much to say of him.

48 'The remarkable Sir *John* Fogge (d. 1490) of Ashford, Kent, who was king's squire and treasurer of the household 1460–69, sat on Kentish commissions from 1450 until his death, and was sheriff of the county …(on three occasions)…' He was one of those who put down Cade's rebellion in 1450. *Oxf. Hist.* VI, 599.

He was also among those against whom an attainder act was passed on the accession of Richard III (ibid., p. 631). He is not mentioned in *D.N.B.* His panelled tomb with a brass, of which only the head remains, is in Ashford parish church. Camden has confused Sir John with the Richard Fogg (d. 1598) to whom there is a brass in Tilmanstone church. Leland (*L.T.S.* IV, 37) tells of 'one Fogge, an gentilman dwelling there about that was controwlar to Edward the Fowrthe etc.'. *Lamb.*, p. 261, speaks of 'Sir Fogge'.

49 On Gibson see Appendix.

50 Called St Eustace's Well after a French monk of C13.

51 Roger of Hoveden or Howden (d. 1201?) wrote a chronicle extending from A.D. 732 (the death of Bede) to 1201. Much of it is drawn from chronicles compiled in the north, but the portion of it extending from 1193 to 1201 is his own work. See *Camb. Hist. Eng. Lit.* I, 174; and *Oxf. Hist.* III, 496.

Chilham Castle in 1773, engraved by Sparrow after Francis Grose

marvellous may consult. Thence we come to *Chilham*,[52] or, as some call it, *Julham*,[53] where are the ruins of an old castle,[54] which one Fulbert de *Dover*[55] is said to have built, whose male line soon ended in a female heir married to Richard[56] natural son of king John, who thus acquired this castle, and had by her two daughters, Lora wife of William *Marmion*,[57] and Isabella[58] wife of David de *Strathbolgy* earl of Athol[59] in Scotland, and mother of that earl of Athol who having been often attainted of high treason was at last, to make his punishment the more exemplary in proportion to his rank, hanged at London on a gallows 50 feet high, beheaded before he was half dead, and his body hrown into the fire;[60] an horrid and among us uncommon kind of punishment. His estate being confiscated, Edward I. generously gave this castle with the *hundred of Felebergh*[61] to Bartholomew de *Badilsmere*, who soon lost both for his treason as before related.[62]

The current tradition among the people here is that Julius Cæsar incamped here in his second expedition against the Britans, and that thence it was called *Julham* or *Julius's Station.* And if I mistake not they have truth on their side. For Cæsar

---

52 Chilham was perhaps 'Ciolla's homestead (*hām*)' in Old English (*P.N. Kent*, pp. 372–3). It is a beautiful place in spite of a touch of self-conscious antiquarianism.

53 One suspects this uncouth form of the name Chilham to be a

B. of E., E. Kent, p. 259f.; *Arch. Journ.* CXXVI, 266.

fictitious 'lead-in' to his fantasies in the next paragraph. See p. 42, nn. 65, 66.

54 The octagonal keep and the fore-building are of C12, though the substructure of the fore-building incorporates the footings of a domestic hall of mid C11. *Ant. Journ.* VIII, 350–53. Plan in *Arch. Journ.* LXXXVI, 303. In Leland's day the castle was 'almost doune' (*L.T.S.* IV, 55).

55 *Lamb.*, p. 255, says merely that the Castle 'fell to the share of Fulbert of Dover' in the reign of John.

56 He 'served as a captain during the baronial revolt'. *King John*, p. 209, n. with references.

57 A member of the family descended from the lords of Fontenayle Marmion in Normandy. Scott's Marmion is a fictitious character.

58 She married, secondly, Alexander de Balliol and continued to hold Chilham in her own right as heir to Richard de Chilham.

59 *Lamb.*, p. 256, says: 'I finde that the Scottish Earle of Ashele [*sic*] enioyed it [the Castle] by marriage with Isabel of Dover.' There is a brass to Philippa de Strabolgi (d. 1395) at West Grinstead. *B. of E. Sussex*, p. 371. Leland (*L.T.S.* IV, 70) says only that 'Cheyney the Lorde Warden [see p. 33, n. 96] hath now Chilham to hym and to his heires males of the Kinges gifte.'

60 This execution followed the revolt of Robert Bruce, the future King Robert II of Scotland, in 1306. See *Oxf. Hist.* IV, 713f.

61 On the hundred as an administrative area see p. 18, n. 59. The Hundred of Felborough includes the parish of Chilham. Its name meant 'Brownish-yellow, or fallow (*fealu*) hill (*beorg*)'.

62 The village of Badlesmere from which the family took its name, is about three miles west of Chilham.

CAN

View of Canterbury, en

BURY

early eighteenth century

41

relates that after marching in the night[c] 12 miles he had his first engagement[d] with the Britans on a river,[e] and having driven them into the woods there, he fortified his camp where by felling a number of trees the Britans had a spot excellently fortified by nature and art.[65] Now this place is exactly 12 miles from the shore,[66] nor is there any other river in the way; so that he must necessarily have made his first encampment here. He staid here 10 days with his army till his fleet which had suffered by a storm was refitted and drawn on shore. Below this town is a tumulus[67] covered with green turf, under which they say was buried many ages since one *Jullaber*, whom some fancy a giant, others a witch. For myself, as I think some antient memorial is concealed under this name, I am almost persuaded that Laberius Durus the military Tribune was buried here, having been slain by the Britans in the march from the fore-mentioned camp, and from him the tumulus was called Jul-laber.[68]

Five miles from hence the Stour parts into two channels, and passes rapidly by DUROVERNUM,[f] the chief city of this county, and gives name to it: *Durwhern* signifying in British a rapid river.[70] Ptolemy[71] instead of *Durovernum* calls it DARVERNUM,[g]

---

63 Gale's correction, which is justified, undermines Camden's identification of the whereabouts of Caesar's first engagement.

64 Of the four Kentish Boughtons, all originally *Bōc-tūn*, 'farm or village among or near beech-trees', or of equal probability 'estate held by written title (book)', (*Elements* I, 39, but cp. *P.N. Kent*, p. 301), only Boughton under Blean is relevant here, as the three others are too far to the west. Of the other places mentioned in Gale's note, only Herhill is identifiable. Herhill is about 2 miles north-east of this Boughton and its meaning is apparently 'gray (*hār*) hill' or possibly 'boundary hill' (*Elements* I, 234). However, Samuel Gale is implying that the first element of Herhill and Herweald was Old English *here*, 'an army', presumably a reference to the events of 54 B.C. The improbability that *here* in these names could refer to an army of six or seven centuries before the formation of these names needs no stressing. In any case, the location of Caesar's first engagement with the Britons is most probably further to the east (n. 66).

65 Probably the pre-Roman fort at Bigbury, four miles north-east of Chilham. *Brit.*, pp. 33–4; a plan in Jessup, *S.E. England*, p. 154.

66 But from what point on the sea-shore? Caesar's landing is believed to have been somewhere between Sandown and Sandwich (*Arch. Kent*, p. 165), or near Walmer Castle (*Oxf. Hist.* I, 43f.; *Brit.*, p. 32f.).

67 This Neolithic long barrow (NG 077533), excavated in 1937, was shown to be of the Wessex type (*Ant. Journ.* XIX, 260f.), unlike Kit's Coty House (p. 26, n. 20) and the other megalithic tombs of the Medway valley. See Jessup, *S.E. England*, pp. 80f., plan 82–3, 95f.; *Arch. Journ.* CXXVI, 239f.; and S. Piggott, *Neolithic Cultures of the British Isles*, 1954, p. 52.

---

c. *about* 12 miles, MS. n. Gale.[63]

d. near *Herhill* and *Herweald down*: so named from the army encamped there before Camden's time, as himself writes. For these are the woods at Bocton and Selrigge and thereabouts. Ib.[64]

e. near Canterbury. Ib. f. Duroaverfus. Peuting. table.[69]

g. Δαρουενον as Ταρουενα. Went. Bede *Wentsum*, i.e. Wentsmuth. MS. n. Gale.[72]

---

68 Caesar, in *The Conquest of Gaul* (v.2), records the death of Quintus Laberius Durus, a military tribune, in a brush with the Britons before the crossing of the Thames. It is very doubtful whether the name of the barrow relates to this man.

69 See p. 18, n. 66.

70 More probably it meant 'town by the alder swamp', *Lang. & Hist.*, pp. 259, 260. This name can hardly refer to the Early Iron Age 'A' fort of c. 250–200 B.C., first discovered during excavations in 1950. (*Arch. News Letter* III, 9, pp. 145–6; IV, 10, p. 157; Jessup, *S.E. England*, pp. 142–3). A Belgic town is, however, known to have existed here about two or three decades before the Roman invasion of A.D. 43 (*Brit.*, p. 47; Jessup, *S.E. England*, pp. 143–4), and this could well account for the British name, *Durovernum Cantiacorum*, of what became a cantonal capital under the Romans. It was surrounded with a wall and inner bank at the end of C3 (*Brit.*, pp. 251–3), enclosing about 130 acres (*Brit.*, p. 257). This made the town a stronghold and the Saxons called it the 'fort or city (*burh*) of the men of Kent (*Cant-ware*)', for the Roman defences were

Bede[73] and others *Dorobernia*,[74] the Saxons 'Cant-wara-byrig', q.d. the *city of the Kentishmen*,[75] Ninnius[76] and the Britans *Caer Kent*, q.d. the *City of Kent*, we *Canterbury*, the Latins *Cantuaria*.[77] It is a very antient city, and was undoubtedly very considerable in the Roman times, "neither very large (as Malmesbury[h] says) nor very small,[79] the situation good, the neighbouring soil exceeding fruitful, the walls entire,[80] well watered with rivers, planted with woods,[81] and by the neighbourhood of the sea well supplied with fish."[82] Under the Saxon heptarchy[83] it

h. De gest. pont. I. prolog.[78]

still effective during the Saxon period and the town began to receive Saxon invaders even in C5 (*Brit.*, p. 377). The 'swamp' of the British name was perhaps a reference to the marshy land beside the river Stour, yet subsidence of the land surface here (*Med. Arch.* II, 7, n. 12) complicates the matter. 'Stour' is a river-name of Old English origin, perhaps meaning 'strong, stiff', i.e. 'rapid'. See *Elements* II, 165; and for the aptness of this meaning, *Eng. River N.*, p. 381. Leland also guessed at this name (*L.T.S.* IV, 69):

Cantorbiry for the most part of the towne stondeth on the farther side of the River of Sture, the which by a probable conjecture I suppose was cawlled in the Britans tyme Avona. For the Romans cawlled Canterbury Duravennum, corruptely, for of Dor and Avona we shuld rather say Doravona, or Doravonum.

71 Claudius Ptolemaeus of C2 was an Egyptian geographer, astronomer and mathematician. His *Geography* takes in the whole of the world then known. See fig. I, 'The British Isles according to Ptolemy', in O.S. *Map of Roman Britain*, text p. 20.

72 What this juggling with names signifies is quite unimportant as a whole, but on Wentsum see p. 38, n. 42. *Darovernon* is the spelling in Ptolemy, on whom see previous note. *Lamb.*, p. 262, is probably the source Camden used.

73 On Bede see Appendix. The earlier MSS of the *Ecclesiastical History*, written within decades of his death, and so more free of scribal errors, have *Doruuern-* consistently as the spelling of the pre-English name for Canterbury. There are about 160 surviving MSS of the *History*, complete or fragmentary, ranging from C8 to C15. The first printed edition came from Strasbourg in about 1475. Camden referred to a late MS or to an edition based on a late MS, which had the form *Dorobern-* (see note following). For these see Plummer's *Bede* I, 426 (p. 45), 428 (p. 113) and cxxix f. On the earlier, more authentic MSS, see ibid., p. lxxxvi f. and B. Colgrave, *The Times* of 7.1.1953.

74 *Dorobernia* is the spelling used by Asser and Geoffrey of Monmouth, among others.

75 See n. 70 opposite.

76 On Nennius see p. 5, n. 53. He uses the form *Cair Ceint*.

77 This is the form used in later Latin MSS. Its abbreviation Cantuar. is still used by the Archbishop, replacing the surname in his signature.

78 See p. 3, n. 33 above.

79 The Roman and superimposed medieval walls enclosed an area of about 130 acres and excluded a large Roman suburb outside the walls on

the western side of the Stour valley. A number of Roman towns were of about 100 acres, but London had 330, Cirencester 240 and Verulamium 200. See *Oxf. Hist.* I, 196–7; *Brit.*, p. 257.

80 Stretches of the city wall, totalling several hundreds of yards, survive on the east and south sides. The whole length of the medieval wall had the remains of the Roman wall of c. A.D. 270-90 beneath it. At points near the Westgate and Riding Gate its base was seven feet thick and like those of a number of other Roman towns, the defences of *Durovernum* were built in late C3. See n. 70 opposite and p. 46, n. 02. The walls were rebuilt in C13 and C14 (*Arch. News Letter* V, 7, p. 134; *Arch. Journ.* CXXVI, 201).

81 There are still extensive tracts of woodland within five miles of the City on all sides except the south-east, but it is doubtful whether they had been artificially planted in or before Malmesbury's day.

82 The nearby Cinque Port of Sandwich, with 'limbs' at Deal, Walmer, Ramsgate, Stonor, Sarre, Fordwich and Reculver and the 'limbs' of Dover at St Peter's (Broadstairs), Margate, Birchington and Kingsdown, were all occupied primarily with fishing and some of them would have provided Canterbury with the large supplies of fish necessitated by fast-days. Demand must have been heavy from seven religious houses and eleven hospitals together with the secular population of the City.

83 'Heptarchy' is a term avoided by most modern historians because it is misleading. It refers to the seven kings and kingdoms of Northumbria, Mercia, East Anglia, Essex, Kent, Sussex and Wessex; but from the time of Edwin of Northumbria, who reigned from 617 to 635, three of them, Northumbria, Mercia and Wessex, overtopped the rest. Even before that time it is difficult to be

43

sure in some periods whether Deira, Lindsey or the Hwicce are to be counted in the seven instead, say, of Essex. But compare *History of the Anglo-Saxons*, p. 274, or *Medieval Foundations of England*, pp. 31–2.

84 Royal manors with their privileges.

85 St Augustine (d. 604) had been prior of the monastery of St Andrew in Rome and was sent by Pope Gregory I as a missionary with 40 monks to evangelize the English. He founded the monastery of Christ Church, later to become the cathedral, in 597 and in the same year St Augustine's Abbey, called the Abbey of St Peter and St Paul until C10. Bede (*H.E.* I, 33) says that Augustine repaired a church said to have been built long before by Roman Christians. It is just possible that a Roman brick pavement seen in C18 beneath the floor of the cathedral nave belonged to this church.

86 On the story of the abandonment of Canterbury by the Kentish kings, see p. 37, n. 31. Leland (*L.T.S.* IV, 52), in Latin, says: 'Augustine had his first dwelling at Canterbury in the place called Stablegate. Ethelbert gave Augustine his palace within the walls and there he built Christ Church.'

87 On this see *Oxf. Hist.* II, 108, 224–5. A letter from Pope Gregory to Augustine in A.D. 601, quoted by Bede, *H.E.* I, 29, instructs him to establish archbishops in London and York, each presiding over twelve bishops. The one archbishop was to take precedence over the other according to priority of consecration. During his lifetime, Augustine was to exercise authority over both provinces.

88 This should read: 'Weever... tells that the fee....' This is presumably John Weever (1576–1632), an antiquary who toured the country as Leland and Camden had

was the head of the kingdom of Kent and residence of the king, till king Ethelbert gave it with the royalty[84] to Austin[85] upon his being consecrated archbishop of the English nation, who fixed here his own and his successors' residence.[86] Though the Pope had fixed at London[87] the metropolitical dignity with the honour of the pall[i] (a part of the pontifical habit falling over the shoulders, and made of sheepskin, in memory of him who sought the lost sheep, and having found it laid it on his shoulders, embroidered with crosses and taken from the body of St. Peter)[89] it was transferred hither in honour of St. Austin. For thus Kenulf king of Mercia[90] writes to pope Leo.[91] "Forasmuch as the body of Augustine of blessed memory who preached the word of God to the people of England, and after having gloriously presided over the churches of Saxony, died in the city of Dorobernia, was deposited in the church of St. Peter the chief of the apostles, which his successor Laurentius[92] had dedicated; it seemed good to all the wise men of our nation that the metropolitan honour should be paid to the first city where his body was laid who planted the true faith in these parts."[93] But whether the archiepiscopal see and metropolitical dignity of our nation was fixed here by the authority of the wise men,[94] or to speak in the modern phrase, of parliament,

i. Weever, p. 198, tells in the fee for a pall from Rome on each election of an archbishop was 5000 florins at 4s. 6d. each, and it was to be buried with the wearer. Gostling p. 179.[88]

done. He is remembered best for his *Ancient Funeral Monuments* of 1631. The antiquary William Gostling (1696–1777) was a minor canon of Canterbury Cathedral and vicar of Littlebourne near by. The reference is to his *Walk in and about the City of Canterbury* of 1774.

89 On the pall and its history, see a long and learned note by Plummer in his *Bede, H.E.* II, 49–52.

90 Cenwulf (796–821), the most powerful English king of his time, was seeking papal sanction for the transfer of the archbishopric from Canterbury to London and to unite with it the archbishopric of Lichfield, established by King Offa of Mercia (757–96) in 788 because of his hatred for Jaenberht, Arch-

bishop of Canterbury and the people of Kent. (*Oxf. Hist.* II, 216 and notes.) London was then part of the Mercian kingdom.

91 Pope Leo III (795–816).

92 The date of Laurentius' succession to St Augustine as archbishop of Canterbury was between 604 and 609 (*Oxf. Hist.* II, 110; Plummer's *Bede* II, 81). He died in 619.

93 For the whole of Cenwulf's letter, which survives only in William of Malmesbury's *De Gestis Regum*, and for Leo's reply, see *E.H.D.* I, 791f.

94 *Witena-gemōt*, 'meeting (council) of wise men', or *witan* simply, was composed of the king, nobles

Canterbury, St Augustine's Monastery, in 1759,
engraved by Godfrey after Francis Grose

or as others think by the authority of Austin himself in his life time,[95] the succeeding popes so confirmed it that they pronounced any attempt to separate it to be a sin deserving excommunication and hell fire. From this time it is incredible how considerable it became, both by the archiepiscopal dignity and the school founded here by Theodore [96] the 7th archbishop, and though it suffered much in the Danish war, and the greatest part of it was burnt by several accidental fires,[97] it always recovered itself with greater splendor.

Since the Norman invasion, when William Rufus, as we find in the registers of St. Austin's monastery, gave the city of Canterbury to the bishops in fee[98] which they held before only by curtesie,[99] by its reputation for sanctity, and the favour

(*ealdormen*), bishops and older retainers. See *Oxf. Hist.* II, 234–5. From being a deliberative assembly (ibid., pp. 347–8) of one of the kingdoms, it developed into a national assembly. One of its main functions was the election of the king (ibid., p. 544 and see pp. 542–6). 'It gave the character of a constitutional monarchy to the Old English state.' Ibid., p. 546.

95 See n. 87 opposite.

96 Theodore (602?–90) of Tarsus had studied in Athens and was a Greek and Latin scholar. He became archbishop in 668 and was the first whom the whole English church recognized as primate. The story of the foundation of a school seems to be merely an implication in Bede's statement (*H.E.* IV, 2) that Theodore and Hadrian attracted to themselves many students to whom they taught scripture, poetry, astronomy and some mathematics. *Lamb.*,

p. 264, has the story but cites no source for it. See *Oxf. Hist.* II, 180–83.

97 *The Anglo-Saxon Chronicle* under the year 754 (which should read 756, see p. 33, n. 03), says that Canterbury was burned down at that time. Leland (*L. T. S.* IV, 52) quotes Marianus Scotus for a similar fire in 776; but Marianus is unreliable for the South. This fire was, presumably, one of Camden's accidental fires. MS 'C' of the *Chronicle*, under 836 (correctly 842) speaks of great slaughter at Canterbury, but the other MSS of the *Chronicle* have *Cwantawic* or *Cantwic*, which was *Quentavic* near Étaples in the Pas de Calais. Continental chronicles confirm that the massacre was at the French place (*Two Saxon Chrons.* II, 76). The Danes stormed Canterbury in 851 (in fact, 850), again according to the *Chronicle*; and a Danish attack was only forestalled in 1009 (MS 'E') by the city suing for peace. In 1011 (MS 'E') they besieged the place and succeeded in taking it by treachery. The martyrdom of Archbishop Ælfheah followed (see p. 9, n. 76). The cathedral was burned down in 1067 (MSS 'D' and 'E') and its choir was destroyed again in 1174. Marianus Scotus, an Irish monk of C11 who lived at Mainz, wrote a chronicle beginning with the Creation and ending in 1082. He drew on Bede, Asser and the *Anglo-Saxon Chronicle*, and his work was a main source for Florence of Worcester (see p. 23, n. 09).

98 To hold by feudal tenure. This story is told by *Lamb.*, p. 263, who cites the *Annals* of St Augustine's Abbey.

99 The archbishops had been acquiring 'lands and haws' in the city, by gift or purchase, from the earliest times. Rufus did not immediately restore the lands of the see of Canterbury on Anselm's

election in 1093. After being held for four years by the king, they were handed back only on the archbishop's firm insistence. *Oxf. Hist.* III, 172–3, and see also *Canterbury under the Angevin Kings*, in which it is apparent that by C12 Christ Church Priory owned half the tenements in the city.

of the prelates (particularly of Simon Sudbury,[01] who repaired the walls)[02] it not only recovered itself, but almost suddenly rose to that splendor as to equal all the cities of Britain for the beauty of private houses,[03] and exceed the most considerable in number and magnificence of sacred structures.[04] Among these the two principal were the monasteries dedicated to Christ and St. Austin, and both filled with Benedictines:

01 Sudbury became archbishop in 1375. He took refuge in the Tower of London during the Peasants' Revolt of 1381, but the mob gained entry and with others he was dragged to Tower Hill and beheaded (*Oxf. Hist.* V, 408f.). He 'initiated the fund for rebuilding the nave [of the cathedral] and himself made generous contributions to it' (ibid., p. 298). He rebuilt the splendid Westgate in about 1380, Henry Yevele being the architect, as he was of the Westgate at Winchester, which is largely of C13, though its western face was remade in C14. The keyhole-shaped gunports are among the earliest extant in England, perhaps of the end of C14 when the south coast was much threatened with French raids. Yevele also built part of the walls of Southampton. Sudbury rebuilt the church of Holy Cross, Canterbury, which had been over the old west gate. In this it was comparable with the surviving church of St Swithun over the Kingsgate at Winchester. Sudbury was buried, headless, in his cathedral. Leland (*L.T.S.* IV, 69): 'Lanfrance, and Sudbury, the wich was hedded [beheaded] by Jakke Strawe, were great repayrers of the cite.' See also the next note.

02 The town wall of Canterbury rests on Roman foundations. In the Domesday Book it is noted that eleven properties were destroyed in making the ramparts, so that the old line of the wall must have been broken and built over in Saxon times. The visible surviving wall is largely of C14, to which were added

semi-circular bastions in C15. See *Med. Arch.* XIV, 182. Leland (*L.T.S.* IV, 59) records in his day:

The town of Cantorbyri ys waulled, and hath v. gates thus named: Westgate, Northgate, Burgate now cawlled Mihelsgate; St George's gate, Rider's gate, the which John Broker, mayr of the town, did so diminisch that now cartes can not for lownes [lowness] pass thorough it; Worthgate, the which leadeth to a streate cawlled Stone streat, and so to Billirica now Curtopstreat [Ibid., p. 69] The river in one place runneth thorowgh the cite walle, the which is made there with ii. or iii. arches for the curse [course] of the stream.... Sudbury builded the west gate, and made new and repaired to gither fro thens to the north gate, and wolde have done lykewise abowt al the town yf he had lyved. The mayr of the town and the aldermen ons a yere cum solemply to his tumbe to pray for his sowle yn memory of his good deade.

He adds that 'long Briton [in fact, Roman] brikes' were to be seen at 'Ryders gate'. These were two Roman arches, or arches built of Roman bricks that had been salvaged from buildings in Durovernum.

03 In spite of German bombs and the even more savage work of the 'developer', this remains a fascinating city. The modern itinerant must spend several days in it before he can enjoy its full savour; and he can return again and again without fear of surfeit. For descriptions of the city's buildings see *Arch. Journ.* CXXVI, 228–38; *B. of E.*, E. Kent, pp. 163–250.

04 Besides the Cathedral and St Augustine's, both Benedictine

houses, there was the Benedictine nunnery of St Sepulchre (destroyed) and Franciscan (Grey) and Dominican (Black) friaries, of which some buildings survive. The Friars Observant, a reformed Franciscan order, took over the house of the Grey Friars here in 1498. The Austin (White) Friars (from 1335) and Austin Canons (from 1084) had houses in the City and the Friars of the Sack, suppressed in 1274, had a brief foothold here.

There were also eight hospitals in medieval Canterbury: St John's, founded by Archbishop Lanfranc in 1084 for poor, sick or aged men and women, the remains of which are well worth seeing; and the hospital of St Thomas, re-established in 1342 for pilgrims, especially those ailing, is equally interesting. The Poor Priests' Hospital, rebuilt in 1373, has surviving remains converted to other uses. Leprous monks were provided for in 1137 in St Laurence's Hospital, of which little survives apart from its name; and in 1317 Maynard's Hospital was established for seven inmates, men and women. Of the other medieval foundations nothing noteworthy survives, but in Camden's day the almshouse called Jesus Hospital was set up by Sir John Boys. Yet another charitable foundation, the King's School of 1541, inhabits buildings of C12 to C14 and later.

There were fifteen parish churches in the medieval City (thirteen in Leland's day) of which twelve survive wholly or in part. On St Martin's see p. 50, n. 29; on Holy Cross see n. 01 above.

Canterbury Cathedral, engraved by Wenceslaus Hollar after Thomas Johnson

but Christ church in the very heart of the city rises with so much magnificence to the clouds, as to inspire even distant beholders with religious awe. Austin beforementioned recovered,[k] according to Bede, this antient building formerly raised by the assistance of the faithful among the Romans,[05] and dedicated it to Christ, and it was the seat of his successors; in which have sat in regular succession 73 archbishops.[06] Of these Lanfranc[07] and William Corboil[08] built the upper part of the church, and their successors, when that more antient part was destroyed by fire, brought the lower part to its present magnificence and size, at a great expence by the contributions of the pious superstition of past ages. Great numbers of all ranks flocked hither with the most costly offerings to visit the tomb of archbishop Thomas Becket, who being slain[09] in

k. *Recuperavit*, repaired. G.

05 See p. 44, n. 85 above. On the evidence for Christianity in Roman Kent see Jessup, *S.E. England*, pp. 196–7.

06 The number is now (1976) a hundred and one.

07 Lanfranc (1005?–89) became the first Norman archbishop of Canterbury, consecrated in the ruins of the Saxon minster in 1070 (n. 67). He had been abbot of the Norman abbey of St Stephen's, Caen, and as archbishop worked in harmony with William the Conqueror. Soon after his appointment to the see, he began rebuilding the cathedral from the foundations.

08 The history of the post-Conquest building of the cathedral may be summarily stated thus: Lanfranc completed a rebuilding in 1077. Between 1096 and 1107 Ernulf the Prior nearly doubled the length of the church and, in the following 19 years, Prior Conrad completed the Choir. This was rebuilt 1175–84. In the following centuries rebuilding and additions took place, with the existing nave reaching completion in 1411. The present central tower, the south-west tower and the Lady Chapel are also of c15. On William de Corbeuil's work at Rochester Castle, see p. 30, n. 61 above. He did little at Canterbury. See *B. of E., E. Kent*, pp. 164–221; *Arch. Journ.* CXXVI, 244–7, with plan.

09 In 1170. On the events leading up to the murder see *Oxf. Hist.* III, 197f.

47

10 *Oxf. Hist.* III, 214:

Four knights of his [Henry II's] household, Reginald Fitz Urse, William de Tracy, Hugh de Morville, and Richard le Breton, without waiting till the king's anger had cooled, hastened to England [from Normandy], and before the messenger sent by the king to prevent any violence could arrive, Thomas Becket was murdered in his cathedral.

Becket was archbishop from 1162.

11 'Religious pilgrimage'. On pilgrimages to Canterbury see *English Wayfaring Life*, p. 198f.

12 Edward, the Black Prince (1330–76), was created Prince of Wales in 1343. He was in command of the van at Crécy in 1346, his father Edward III deliberately holding back so that the Prince should have full credit for the victory. Poitiers, 1356, and Nájera, 1367, were equally decisive victories, but by 1371 his health was failing and his chivalrous reputation was shattered by the wholesale massacre which he ordered after the capture of Limoges in 1370. He died less than a year before his father's death.

13 Henry IV (1367–1413), son of John of Gaunt and grandson of Edward III, was a relatively successful king, but hardly the 'most potent [powerful] monarch of England'. Leland (*L.T.S.* IV, 37f.) gives a long list of those buried in the Cathedral followed by (41f.) notes on the evolution of the fabric.

14 Becket's magnificent shrine was destroyed in 1538 and Prior Goldwell surrendered the monastery in 1540. Although the abbots of other cathedral-monasteries became the first deans of the new secular foundations, Goldwell did not, perhaps because of Archbishop Cranmer's dislike of him. See *English Monks and the Suppression of the Monasteries*, p. 250. Instead, Nicholas Wotton, member of a famous Kentish family (see p. 20, n. 85) became dean.

this church by the courtiers[10] for his obstinate opposition to the king in asserting the liberties of the church, was enrolled among the martyrs by the Pope, and had divine honour paid him, and was so loaded with wealth, that the gold was the least valuable part of the shrine that contained his reliques. "Every thing here (says Erasmus,[1] who saw it) glittered, shone, and sparkled with the choicest and largest jewels, and the whole church was covered with wealth in greater profusion than that of kings;" and the name of Christ was almost sunk in that of St. Thomas. It was distinguished by nothing so much as by his burial and memory, though it has many other monuments to boast of, particularly that of Edward prince of Wales surnamed *the black*, a hero of marvellous military renown,[12] and that of Henry IV.[13] the most potent monarch of England. But Henry VIII. dispersed the accumulated wealth of so many ages, and turned out the monks,[14] in whose stead he placed in this church of Christ a dean, archdeacon, 12 prebendaries, and 6 preachers, to propagate the word of God in the neighbouring places round about. Another church rivalling this stood without the city to the east, known by the name of St. *Austin*, being founded by him[15] and by king Ethelbert[16] by his advice in honour of Peter and Paul for the burying place both of the kings of Kent and of the archbishops;[17] it not being yet

l. Peregrinatio religionis ergo.[11]

15 See p. 44, n. 85.

16 King Æthelberht I of Kent, who ruled from c. 560 to 616, was defeated by the West Saxons in 568 (*Anglo-Saxon Chronicle*), yet became overlord of the southern English kingdoms (Bede, *H.E.* II, 5) a few decades later. He married Bertha, a Frankish princess (*H.E.* I, 25) and the material culture of his kingdom, especially as exhibited by grave-goods, was strongly influenced by Frankish culture. Bertha being a Christian, he gave her St Martin's as a place of worship (*H.E.* I, 26, and p. 50, n. 29) and was himself later converted by St Augustine (*H.E.* I, 26). He made possible the foundation of the churches, later cathedrals, of Canterbury (I, 26), Rochester and

London and endowed them with lands (II, 3). After his death Christianity in Kent nearly came to an end, for his son remained heathen for some time (II, 5). Æthelberht issued a body of laws (II, 5; extracts in *E.H.D.* I, 357–60) which are the earliest surviving in a Germanic language. In his reign 'Kent was the most civilized, and probably the most populous, of all the English kingdoms' (*Oxf. Hist.* II, 109). See also *History* XXVI, 1942, p. 97f., and *Cambridge Hist. Journ.* 7, 1943, p. 101f.

17 King Æthelberht, Queen Bertha and her chaplain were buried in the porticus of St Martin on the south side of the church of St Peter and St Paul. This should not be confused

permitted to bury within the city.[18] The abbot was allowed a mint and right of coining money.[19] Though it is now for the most part buried in its ruins,[20] and the rest turned into a royal mansion it still shews what it once was.[21] Austin himself was buried in the porch with this epitaph according to Thomas Spot,[22]

Inclytus Anglorum præsul pius & decus altum,
Hic Augustinus requiescit corpore sanctus.

Here holy Austin rests so high renown'd.
Whom England for her pious primate own'd.

But, according to Bede,[m] who is more worthy of credit, he had this much older inscription:

HIC REQUIESCIT DOMINUS AUGUSTINVS DOROVERNENSIS ARCHIEPISCOPUS PRIMUS, QUI OLIM HUC A BEATO GREGORIO ROMANÆ URBIS PONTIFICE DIRECTUS, ET A DEO OPERATIONE MIRACULORUM SUFFULTUS, ET ETHELBERTUM REGEM ET GENTEM ILLIUS AB IDOLORUM CULTV AD FIDEM CHRISTI PERDUXIT, ET COMPLETIS IN PACE DIEBUS OFFICII SUI DE-FUNCTUS EST VII KAL. JUNIAS EODEM REGE REGNANTE.[24]

m. Eccl. Hist. II. 3.[23]

with the church of St Martin (on which see p. 50, n. 29). St Augustine and the early bishops Laurentius (604–19), Mellitus (619–24), Justus (624–7), Honorius (627–55) and Deusdedit (d. 663?) were buried in the porticus of St Gregory on the north side of the church. The sites of the tombs of other early Kentish kings, as well as archbishops and abbots, have been located by excavation. See also n. 20 below.

18 This was a Roman law, yet some burials of probably Roman date and a cremation cemetery, certainly of that date, have been found within the line of the Roman walls of Canterbury; but these burials took place before the building of the walls. Outside them at least four Roman cemeteries are known. See *V.C.H.* III, 75f. There were four Romano-British barrows on the southern edge of the city, two within and two outside the walls.

One only remains, incorporated in the Dane John mound. Leland (*L.T.S.* IV, 69) thought that mound to have had a defensive purpose: 'Ther hath bene sum strong fortres by the castel, wher as now the eminent [tall] Dungen [Dane John] Hil risith', though in his previous sentence he noted a sepulchral use for it: 'Many yeres sins [since] men soute [sought] for treasor at a place cauled the Dungen...and ther yn digging thei fownd a Corse [corpse] closed yn leade.'

19 The Laws of Athelstan issued at Grateley (c. A.D. 924–39) state in section 14.2 that 'In Canterbury [there are to be] seven moneyers; four of the king, two of the bishop, one of the abbot; in Rochester, three...' & etc. (*E.H.D.* I, 384, and see *Oxf. Hist.* II, 528).

20 Excavations on the site of St Augustine's Abbey from 1901

onwards have revealed a most interesting complex of buildings. The foundations, and sometimes walls, of four small Saxon apsidal churches (of SS. Peter and Paul, St Mary, St Pancras and another) have been discovered in line running from east to west (plans in *Med. Arch.* IX, 19, 21), comparable with those now known at Glastonbury. St Martin's (p. 50, n. 29) is not far off the alignment. A remarkable discovery not usually mentioned in descriptions of the site, but prominent on it, is of two large stones, one of which is a tall monolith. These may possibly have been pagan Saxon (or Jutish) symbols, for there is a tradition of paganism attached to at least part of the site. Leland (*L.T.S.* IV, 52) records that: 'A temple of idols was converted by [King] Æthelberht into the little church of St Pancras.' He goes on: 'A little later Æthelberht founded the temple [church] of Peter and Paul.' See *Lamb.*, p. 277, and Plummer's *Bede* II, 58–60. The great stones were not known until recent times, for they had been well buried and forgotten.

21 The King's House, begun in 1539, was in part at least a remodelling of the abbot's quarters and adjacent buildings of the monastery. It was one of the three staging posts between Dover and London, the two others being at Rochester and Dartford. To build these royal lodgings (and the contemporary shore-forts) material was taken from the recently dissolved monasteries. On the St Augustine's site as a whole see also *Arch. Journ.* CXXVI, 228–33; *B. of E., E. Kent*, pp. 221–9.

22 On Thomas Sprott (Spott) see p. 7, n. 60.

23 Bede's *Ecclesiastical History*, bk II, ch. 3.

24 For this epitaph see Plummer's *Bede* II, 3, in volume I, p. 86.

25 On these see p. 48, n. 17.

26 Correctly Theodore, on whom see p. 45, n. 96 above.

27 *septem caeloque triones* is literally 'the seven plough oxen in the sky', a reference to the constellation called 'The Wain' or 'The Great and Little Bear'.

28 See previous note.

29 The earliest surviving part of St Martin's church is the western part of the chancel, largely built of Roman bricks. Leland (*L.T.S.*IV, 69) as usual calls them 'Briton brikes'. For a recent study of this church see *Med. Arch.*IX, 11–15 with plans p. 12. See also p. 48, nn. 16, 17; and *Arch. Journ.*CXXVI, 233–5; *B. of E., E. Kent*, pp. 232–4; *Lamb.*, p. 283.

30 The castle was built in the time of Henry II on the site of a Norman castle and for long was used as a county prison. In modern times it was used to store coal, but it has recently been restored. *Arch. Journ.* CXXVI, 238–9, with plan; *B. of E., E. Kent*, pp. 237–8.

31 i.e. before the Reformation.

32 Urban II held the papacy from 1088 until 1099. On his relationship with England see *Oxf. Hist.*III, 173f.

33 Both archbishops, of Canterbury and of York, are Primates, but the former is Primate of all England and the latter is Primate of England. A Metropolitan is a chief bishop.

34 Whitgift (1530?–1604) became Bishop of Worcester in 1577 and archbishop in 1583. At Croydon, Surrey, are a school and almshouse bearing his name and of his foundation. (See p. 19, nn. 30, 31, *Surrey*.) He was buried there in the parish church of St John where an alabaster monument to him still survives. *B. of E. Surrey*, p. 158.

Here rests lord Austin, first archbishop of Canterbury, who formerly directed hither by St. Gregory, Pope of Rome, and supported by God with the gift of miracles converted both king Ethelbert and his people from the worship of idols to the faith of Christ, and ending the days of his ministry in peace, died VII kal. of June* in the same king's reign.

Together with him in the same porch were buried the six succeeding archbishops, and in memory of these seven, viz. Austin, Laurentius, Mellitus, Justus, Honorius, Deus-dedit,[25] and Theodosius,[26] these lines were inscribed in marble:

SEPTEM SUNT ANGLI PRIMATES ET PROTOPATRES,
SEPTEM RECTORES, SEPTEM CÆLOQUE TRIONES,[27]
SEPTEM CISTERNÆ VITÆ, SEPTEMQUE LUCERNÆ,
ET SEPTEM PALMÆ REGNI, SEPTEMQUE CORONÆ:
SEPTEM SUNT STELLÆ, QUAS HÆC TENET ARCA CELLÆ.

Seven patriarch primates were to England given,
Seven rulers, now seven glorious stars[n] of Heaven,
Fountains of life and beaming glories seven,
As many palms, as many crowns of Heaven;
As many stars that once with radiance shin'd
Are here within this vaulted cell inshrin'd.

I need not enlarge on the other church adjoining to this, which, according to Bede,[o] was built by the Romans, and dedicated to St. Martin, in which, before the coming of Austin, Bertha of the royal blood of the Franks wife of Ethelbert used to attend Christian worship.[29] Of the castle on the south side of the city, whose battlements are now decaying apace,[30] nothing memorable occurs, except that it was built by the Normans. Of the dignity of the see of Canterbury, which was antiently by far the largest, I shall only observe, that, as in former ages, during the Roman hierarchy,[31] the archbishops of Canterbury were primates of all Britain, legates of the Pope, and as it were, as Urban II.[32] called them, "patriarchs of another world;" so when the Pope's authority was annulled it was decreed in a council held 1534, that they should lay aside that title, and be called *Primates and Metropolitans of all England*.[33] This dignity was lately enjoyed by the right reverend father in Christ John Whitgift,[34] who, having devoted his

* A.D. 604.
n. *laborers.* G.28
o. Ib. I. 26.

Canterbury Castle in 1761, engraved by Ellis
after Francis Grose

whole life and labours to God and the church, to the great grief of all good men fell asleep in Christ, A.D. 1604. He was succeeded by Richard Bancroft,[35] a prelate of great firmness of mind and extensive experience in all matters relative to discipline and government of the church. The latitude of Canterbury is 51° 16″; its longitude 24° 51″.[36]

The Stour,[37] having now collected its waters into one stream, passes by *Hackington*,[38] where Lora, countess of Leicester, a most respectable lady of her age, renouncing the pleasures of the world, secluded herself from all society to serve God alone.[39] At this time Baldwin, archbishop of Canterbury, began here a church in honour of St. Stephen and Thomas of Canterbury, but, being prevented by the Pope's authority, least it should prejudice the monks of Canterbury, he desisted from his design.[40] The place retained the name of St. Stephen ever since,[41] and sir Roger *Manwood*, knight, chief baron of the exchequer, eminent for his knowledge in our municipal law,[42] to whose bounty the poor inhabitants are

accepted internationally only since 1884. In his Preface Camden defends himself against

> Mathematicians [who] will charge me with egregious mistakes in stating the degrees of longitude and latitude. My answer to these is, I have carefully compared the several astronomical tables, new, old, MSS. Oxford, Cambridge, and those of king Henry V. all which, though they differ greatly in the latitudes from Ptolemy, agree with each other. . . . In the longitude there is no agreement or correspondence. What then could I do? As the modern mathematicians have found that there is no variation of the compass at the Azores, I have followed them in taking the longitude from thence as from the first meridian, though not with a critical exactness.

37 On this river-name see p. 42, n. 70.

38 Hackington is still a pleasant spot on the edge of the City. *B. of E., E. Kent*, p. 236.

39 'Respectable' here means 'worthy of respect'.

40 Baldwin (d. 1190) had been Abbot of Forde in Dorset and Bishop of Worcester before becoming primate in 1180. He came into conflict with the monks of Christ Church, precipitating one of the greatest crises in the history of that house. *Lamb.*, p. 284f. For an account of the matter see *Monastic Order in England*, pp. 317–22. Leland (*L.T.S.* v, 216) quotes the Latin of Gervase of Canterbury to the same effect as the passage in Camden.

41 From the dedication of the Norman church.

42 Sir Roger (1525–92) held legal offices in Kent and represented Hastings and Sandwich successively in Parliament. Queen Elizabeth I granted him the manor of St Stephen's, Hackington, but in the last year of his life he was arraigned before the Privy Council for malpractices. His fine alabaster monument is in the parish church. *B. of E., E. Kent*, p. 236.

35 Bancroft (1544–1610), having been Whitgift's chaplain, was made Bishop of London in 1597 and archbishop in 1604. He was buried in Lambeth parish church where he is commemorated by an inscribed stone let into the chancel floor.

36 Mercator's *Atlas* of 1595 gives a longitude of c. 22° 10′ for Canterbury. On the modern map Canterbury is at Long. c. 1° 5′, Lat. c. 51° 16′ N, which is a reckoning based on a prime meridian through Greenwich,

43 Sir Roger founded the St Stephen's almshouses in 1570 for six poor persons. He was co-founder, with Archbishop Parker, of the grammar school at Sandwich. *B. of E., E. Kent*, pp. 240, 435.

44 Sir Peter (d. 1625) was lawyer, M.P. and antiquary.

45 Fordwich is termed *parvus burgus* in Domesday and is estimated to have had a population of over 400 in 1086. It had 6 burgesses and 80 properties (*masurae*), whereas Canterbury had 438 and 142 respectively. It was the port of Canterbury and a limb of the Cinque Port of Sandwich. The small Moot Hall, a timber-framed building of c. 1544, survives as a token of its former corporate status. In Leland's day it still had 'a poore mayr' (*L.T.S.* IV, 70). See *B. of E., E. Kent*, pp. 315–16.

46 Page, or rather folio, 12 of the Domesday Book. On Domesday for Kent see *History of Kent*, p. 53f.; *Domesday Geog. S.E. Eng.*, p. 483f. For Fordwich see ibid., p. 554.

47 Stourmouth has a church with what are probably Saxon elements in its structure. *Lamb.*, pp. 236–9; *B. of E., E. Kent*, pp. 452–3.

48 On the Wantsum see p. 38, nn. 41, 42 and *Lamb.*, p. 89.

49 C. Julius Solinus (fl. c. A.D. 200) was the author of a short but unreliable geographical treatise, *Collectanea Rerum Memorabilium*, 'Remarks from various sources on noteworthy things'. The passage referred to here is quoted by *Lamb.*, p. 88.

50 The form was probably *Tanatus* in Solinus. See *Dic.*, p. 443, and *P.N. Kent*, p. 593, n. 1.

51 *Ruim*, as in Gough's note *p*, citing Simeon of Durham, is the accepted form. Asser certainly has *Ruim*, which he probably took from Nennius (see p. 5, n. 53). Asser was a Welsh priest from St David's,

greatly indebted,[43] was late its greatest ornament, nor less so, his son sir Peter *Manwood*,[44] knight of the bath, whom, for his proficiency in all virtuous and learned accomplishments, and his regard for men of literature, I cannot but mention with the highest regard. The Stour runs next by *Fordwich*, called the "small *borough of Forewich*"[45] in the Conqueror's survey,° famous for its excellent trout, to *Sturemouth*,[47] where its divided waters taking two courses, lose their first name, and take that of *Wantsume*,[48] making *Thanet* an island on the west and south; the other sides being washed by the ocean. Solinus[49] calls this isle ATHANATOS, and in some copies THANATOS,[50] the Britans *Inis Ruthin*[51] according to Asser,ᵖ perhaps for *Rhutupis*, from the neighbouring city of *Rhutupi*;[56] the Saxons 'Tanet' and 'Tanetland',[57] we *Tenet*. The whole of it consists of white chalk,[58] with fruitful wheat fields, and rich pasture. It is

o. [*sic*] P. 12.[46]

p. *Ruochim.* Nennius; MS. n. G.[52] Insula quæ Saxonum lingua Tened dicitur Britanno sermone *Ruim* appellatur.[53] Sim. Dun. c. 120.[54] Lewis's Hist. of Tenet, p. 2.[55]

Pembrokeshire. He entered King Alfred's service in about 884, wrote a valuable biography of the King and died Bishop of Sherborne in A.D. 910. See *Asser's Life of Alfred*, pp. 84, 186.

52 MS note by Gibson (on whom see Appendix) citing Nennius (p. 5, n. 53).

53 This supplementary MS note, presumably by Gough, gives almost the normally accepted reading of Asser with the form *Ruim* as an alternative British name for Thanet. See nn. 51, 58.

54 Simeon of Durham (*Dunelmensis*), who flourished c. 1130, was precentor of his cathedral. He compiled a Latin *History of the Church of Durham*, which Gough probably cites in this note. The Latin of it may be rendered: 'The island which, in the tongue of the Saxons is called *Tened*, in British speech *Ruim*.' Leland (*L.T.S.* IV, 53): 'The Isle of Thanet [is], be likelihod Toliapis Ptolemaeo.' But Camden,

p. 214 (this edition p. 31), applies this name to Sheppey.

55 John Lewis (1675–1747), vicar of Minster in Thanet, wrote a number of biographies and works on Kentish topography.

56 A worthless suggestion.

57 Old English forms from C7 to C10 are: *Tenid, Tænett, Tenet*. A derivation from a British word is generally suggested. See *Lang. & Hist.*, p. 331. If Ekwall's suggested explanation of its meaning as 'fire island' or 'bright island', from a beacon or lighthouse, is correct, the reference would be to one or more pharos for guiding ships making for the Roman forts at Richborough and Reculver. Two such Roman pharos survive in part at Dover. See p. 69, n. 45.

58 Leland (*L.T.S.* IV, 60) gives the dimensions of Thanet and later (p. 61): 'The shore of the Isle of Thanet, and also the inward part is ful of good quarres [quarries] of chalke.'

eight miles in length, four in breadth, and was formerly supposed to maintain 600[q] families,[r] for which we have in Bede corruptly 600 miles (*miliarum* for *familiarum*). But what Solinus says, that no snakes will breed in this island, and that the earth of it carried elsewhere will kill them, has been found to be false; so that the derivation of it απο του θανατου,[s] from the death of these animals, falls to the ground.[62] The Saxons made their first landing here with leave of Vortigern; here they made their first settlement;[63] here was their retreat; here Vortimer[64] the Britan made a great slaughter of them, driving them in the utmost confusion to their boats[t] at *Lapis Tituli*,[u]

q. Bede, I. c. 25. Now 15 or 1600. G.[59]

r. What was in English called a *Hide* and is thought to have consisted of 100 acres was in Latin formerly *familia*, *mansa*, and *manens*. G. If a *hide* or *family* of land consisted of 64 acres, the lowest computation authors of credit set it at, there will have been in Tenet 38400 acres, which is above double the present number without the marshes. Lewis, p. 3.[60]

s. *Myoparones*.[61]

t. This is *Higden's* derivation. Polichr. I.c. 44. MS. Luv. I.[65]

u. I read Lapis *tumuli*, as Nennius 21. speaks. MS. G. This will relate to the *tomb* rather than the *spot* where it stood.[66]

59 This is Gibson's estimate of the number of families in Thanet in late c17.

60 A hide was a notional area of land adequate to support a free peasant and his household. Leland (*L.T.S.* IV, 61):

Ther hath bene a xi. paroche chyrches in Thanet, of the which iii. be decayed, the residew remayne. In the isle is very litle wodde. Ther cum at certen tymes sum paroches owt of Thanat [the people of some parishes outside Thanet] to Reculver a myle of [off] as to ther mother chyrche. Sum paroches of the isle at certen tymes cummeth to Minstre, being in the isle, as to theyr mother and principal chyrch.

61 This has defeated me as it did Gibson and Gough.

62 Both the adder and the grass snake are recorded from Thanet. See e.g. the distribution map in *Complete Atlas of the British Isles* (*Reader's Digest*), p. 105. Θανατος is

the Greek for '(violent) death, a corpse'. *Lamb.*, p. 88.

63 *The Anglo-Saxon Chronicle*, under the year 449, locates the landing 'on the shore called *Ypwines fleot*' (MS 'A') or '*Heopwines fleot*' (MS 'E'). Ekwall (*Dic.*, p. 152) considers the *Chronicle* forms to be corrupt and suggests an original *Hēopwell*, 'stream where hips grow'; but the collocation of *fleot*, 'sea inlet, stream' with *well(e)*, 'spring, stream' does not make good sense. More probably we are confronted here with a personal name, corrupt in the *Chronicle* forms (*P.N. Kent*, pp. 596–7; *K.P.N.*, pp. 320–22). At some time the name *Ebissa*, of Nennius' *Historia Brittonum*, §38, has probably influenced the development of this place-name. However, as Stenton noted (*Oxf. Hist.* II, 16), 'Ypwines fleot can only mean Ebbsfleet', a minor place in Pegwell Bay. Bede (*H.E.* I, 15) places this landing less precisely. He speaks of

the 'Angles or Saxons' coming to Britain in three long ships and being granted land in the eastern part of the island (of Britain). He is more precise concerning the first landing of St Augustine, which he places (1, 25) in 'Tanatus', a large island to the east of Kent. See also *Lamb.*, pp. 93–4.

64 Vortimer, eldest son of Vortigern, replaced his father as king and won four battles against the Saxons, the last of which was fought in Thanet. He was poisoned by his stepmother Rowena and asked to be buried in a pyramid guarding the port where the Saxons landed (Nennius, *H.B.*, §44). The site of the fourth battle was 'near the stone on the shore of the Gallic sea'. The evidential basis for much of this is quite lacking.

65 Ranulph Higdèn's *Polychronicon*, written at Chester, was a popular work of general history from the Creation down to 1340. It is most unlikely that he drew on early sources, no longer extant, for this incident. He most probably invented it. Higden died in 1364. The MS referred to was apparently in the magnificent university library at Louvain, burnt in 1914. See also p. 20, n. 83.

66 This is another MS note by Gibson with the last sentence added by Gough. The reading *Lapis tumuli* could mean '(grave)-stone of (on) the (burial) mound'; but *lapis* could also mean 'milestone or boundary-stone, marble statue or slab of marble'. It is just possible that *Lapis tituli* ('marble slab with an inscription'?) referred to the great Roman monument of c. A.D. 85, of which the foundation alone survives at Richborough Castle, very near to Stonar. Fragments of marble casing from the monument with a few inscribed letters were found during the excavation of the Roman fort. In c3, the monument was stripped of marble and was perhaps converted to serve as a signalling and look-out

for so Ninnius calls the place which we now call *Stonar* almost in the same sense, and which appears to have been a harbour:[67] in which place, adds he, that hero ordered himself to be buried, to restrain, as he thought, the violences of the Saxons, like Scipio Africanus,[68] who ordered his tomb to be so placed that it might face Africa, thinking this alone would be a terror to the Carthaginians. Here also at *Wippedflete*, so called from *Wipped* a Saxon slain there, Hengist routed the Britans,[69] who had been reduced by many battles.[70] Austin many years after landed here,[71] to whose blessing the credulous priests ascribed the fertility of the island, and Joceline the monk[72] cries out, "Happy Tanet in its own fertility, but most happy by the arrival of so many strangers, who brought God along with them, and by the entertainment of so many citizens of heaven." Egbert, third[x] king of Kent, A.D. 596,[74] to appease Domneva a virgin whom he had before so much injured, granted her an estate here, on which she built a house for 70 nuns,[75] over

x. 8th G.[73]

post. It was certainly not seen by the Saxons of c5 in its original monumental form. See *Richborough, Fourth Report*, p. 38f. and pl. LXXa; also *Archaeology of Roman Britain*, p. 120. The equation of *Lapis tituli* with Stonar occurs in *Lamb.*, p. 94.

67 Stonar, 'stony shore or landing-place', had prospered as a port during the earlier Middle Ages and became a member of the Cinque Port of Sandwich, its near neighbour. In a document of 1359 it was, with Sandwich, Fordwich, Deal and Sarre, under obligation to provide the king with five ships whenever he required the services of the Cinque Ports fleet of 57 ships. In the same year and again in 1365–6 the town was inundated by the sea and in 1385 the French burned it. Recent excavation suggests occupation of the site from 'at least the late 12th until the 14th century'. *Med. Arch.* XIV, 183. In 1693 it was said that the ruins had been lately removed to prepare the land for ploughing. For an account of the site and its excavation see *Arch. Cant.* LIII, 62f., LIV, 41f., LV, 37f.; *Cinque Ports*, p. 242. Leland (*L.T.S.* IV, 48): 'Stonard ys yn Thanet, sumtyme a prety town not far from Sandwich. Now appereth alonly the ruine of the chirch. Sum ignorant people cawle yt Old Sandwiche.'

68 Scipio Africanus Major (234–c. 183 B.C.) was the brilliant Roman general who defeated the Carthaginians.

69 See p. 6, n. 57 above for the text of the *Anglo-Saxon Chronicle* under the year 465. The personal name *Wipped* seems not to occur except in this annal. It is an expanded form of the fairly common name *Wippa*. See *P.N. Herts.*, 1938, p. 46. The place *Wippedesfleot* has not been identified. The killing of the thane *Wipped* was probably invented to explain the place-name. Cp. p. 36, n 25. *Lamb.* pp. 93–4, identifies

Wippedesfleot with Ebbsfleet, for which see p. 53, n. 63.

70 Before the battle at *Wippedesfleot*, only two others against the Britons are recorded in the *Chronicle*, that at *Ǣgæles threp* in 455 (see p. 22, n. 05) and that at *Crecgan ford* in 457 (p. 14, n. 16). For the relevant annals as a whole, see p. 6, n. 57.

71 In 597. Bede, *H.E.* V, 24, 'The Chronological Summary'. Leland (*L.T.S.* IV, 54) cites the Latin chronicle of Joscelin (on whom see next note) to the effect that Augustine came to Richborough; but this is probably a guess. Bede (I, 24) places the first landing merely in Thanet.

72 This is not the famous Jocelin de Brakelond (fl. 1200), monk of Bury St Edmunds, but a contemporary Cistercian monk who wrote a Life of St Patrick and other saints. Leland (*L.T.S.* IV, 58) cites a 'Life of St Sexburga' by *Gotcelinus Monachus*. She founded the monastery at Minster in Sheppey and later became Abbess of Ely.

73 A correction by Gibson, on whom see Appendix.

74 Egbert (664–73) was, as Gibson points out in his footnote, eighth king of Kent. The date 596 is wrong and is taken from *Lamb.*, p. 91.

75 This was the nunnery of Minster in Thanet. Eormenbeorg, a Kentish princess, married Merewalh, ruler of the Magonsæton, whose territory stretched along the Welsh Marches from near Hereford northward to Shropshire. She founded the house at Minster (see n. 80) of which her daughter Mildthryth (Mildreda) was abbess 'before the year 691'. *Oxf. Hist.* II, 46. Thorne, the monk of St Augustine's Abbey, Canterbury (p. 7, n. 61) gives the date of foundation by Domneva, Mildred's mother, as 670. Domneva is probably to be identified with Eormenbeorg. It is noteworthy that Bede makes no mention of these matters, though he had good Kentish informants. Leland (*L.T.S.* IV, 53), quoting Thorne, says:

which presided Mildreda,[76] who was cannonized for her sanctity.[77] The kings of Kent largely endowed it, but chiefly Withred, who (to mention the custom of the age from his original grant)[78] to confirm the gift "laid a turf of the land he had given on the holy altar." This island suffered so much afterwards by the ravages of the Danes,[79] who made this nunnery of Domneva a scene of every species of cruelty,[80] that it did not recover itself till the peaceable times of the Normans.

Nor must I here forget what redounds to the especial praise of the inhabitants, particularly of those who live near the ports of Margate, Ramsgate, and Brodstear.[81] They are excessively industrious getting their living like amphibious animals both by sea and land, making the most of both elements, being both fishermen and ploughmen, farmers and sailors; the same persons that guide the plough in the field, steering the helm at sea. In the different seasons of the year they make nets, catch codd, herrings, mackrel, &c. make trading voyages, manure their land, plough, sow, harrow, reap, and store their corn, expert in both professions, and so carrying on the round of labour. As shipwrecks are very frequent here, those dangerous shoals and shelves called the *Godwyn*[82] (of which by and by among the

In the time of Cuthbert Archbishop of Canterbury (c. 740–60), the Danes laid waste Thanet in certain years and they despoiled the monks of Minster. [Cuthbert is an error for Ceolnoth (833–869 .]

In the year 1011, Sweyn King of the Danes destroyed the Isle of Thanet and the monastery founded by Domneva.

In the year 1027, King Canute gave the estates of St Mary at Minster to the monastery of St Augustine at Canterbury. See *A.S. Charters*, no. 990, p. 296, of doubtful authenticity. During the restoration of the abbey in C19 signs of destruction by fire were found in apparent confirmation of the activities of the Danes in 1011. Furthermore Leland (*L.T.S.* v, 206) records from a *Life of St Eadburg* that in 1085 the tombs of SS Mildred and Eadburg were discovered in Thanet and their remains translated to the church of St Gregory in Canterbury.

76 See previous note.

77 Leland (*L.T.S.* IV, 53), quoting from Thorne, says that King Egbert gave Domneva eighty ploughlands in Thanet as a consolation for the murder of her brothers (at 'Thunnor').

78 There is a surviving charter, probably authentic, which records in 696 a confirmation by Wihtred, who reigned from 690 to 725, to the abbess Mildred, of the privileges previously granted to her nunnery. There survives also a later grant of A.D. 727 by King Eadberht (725–48?) to Mildred and her community, of land *bi Northanuude* (an unidentified Northwood, possibly the one at NG 370670 in Thanet). See *A.S. Charters*, no. 17, p. 75; no. 26, p. 78.

79 According to the *Chronicle* the Danes were in Thanet in 853, 865, 980 and 1011; but see n. 75.

80 Excavations in 1929 revealed some of the foundations of the church of St Peter and St Paul, built by Eadburga, the abbess who succeeded Mildred. It was consecrated in 738. After its destruction by the Danes the monastery was rebuilt as a grange by the monks of St Augustine in early C12. Of this, some of the domestic buildings and part of the conventual church survive, modified in C15 (*B. of E., E. Kent*, pp. 380–81, and see p. 53, n. 28). The place-name Minster is derived from Old English *mynster* (from Latin *monasterium*) which meant 'monastery, mother church'. On the latter see *Oxf. Hist.* II, 148–9, 152–4.

81 Broadstairs. Leland (*L.T.S.* IV, 60):

…at Gore ende is a little staire caullid Broode Staires to go doune the clive: and about this shore is good taking of mullettes. The great raguseis [argosies of Ragusa] ly for defence of wind at Gore ende.

Of Margate he says (IV, 61):

Margate lyith in S. John's paroche yn Thanet a v. myles upward [or more] fro Reculver, and there is a village and a peere for shyppes, but now sore decayed;

and of Ramsgate (ibid.):

Ramsgate a iiii myles upward in Thanet, wher as is a smaul peere for shyppis.

82 The Goodwin Sands lie about six miles off Sandwich, Deal and Walmer, extending from north to south for about twelve miles and are about four miles across. They are partly exposed at low water and have proved treacherous to shipping. There is a traditional association of the sands with Earl Godwine (p. 6, n. 43, *Surrey*; p. 31, n. 25, *Sussex*; *Lamb.*, pp. 94–9), father of King Harold, but Ekwall (*Dic.*, p. 191) suggests that the name may mean 'good friend' used ironically. For legends about them see *Antiquity* v, 1931, pp. 101, 229.

83 The Brake lightship is moored five miles east of Sandwich.

84 The Fourfoote seems to be lost.

85 An inset to Bowen's *Map of Kent* (1746) shows White Dyke at NG 393654 etc., just off Hereson.

86 i.e. the inhabitants of Margate etc.

87 On these topographical changes see *Arch. Cant.* LIII, 62f.; LIV, 41f. Leland was among those who believed in this change of course:

... Richeboro was [existed] or ever the ryver of Sture [the eastern end of the Wantsum, the Stour] dyd turn his botom or old canale [channel] withyn the Isle of Thanet, and by lykelyhod the mayn se [sea] cam to the very foot of the castel. (*L.T.S.* IV, 61.)

88 On Ptolemy, see p. 43, n. 71.

89 On Tacitus, see p. 16, n. 40.

90 Tacitus' *Agricola*.

91 The chapter cited in the *Life of Agricola* relates the Roman victory at *Mons Graupius* against the Caledonians in A.D. 84. The Trutulensian harbour to which the Roman fleet sailed after the victory can hardly be Richborough since the fleet sailed from that harbour on orders to coast round the island. This seems to imply a northward voyage from a point on the east coast of Scotland. See *Brit.*, p. 112; *Oxf. Hist.* I, 115. Recently it has been suggested that the battle was fought a few miles south-east of Perth.

92 Beatus Rhenanus (Rheinauer) was a German humanist and classical scholar (1485–1547) and author of a *History of Germany*.

93 On the Antonine Itinerary see p. 28, n. 46.

94 On Ammianus Marcellinus see p. 4, n. 42.

95 Ammianus Marcellinus' *Historiae*.

islands), the *Brakes*,[83] the *Fourfoote*,[84] the *Whitdick*,[85] &c. lying off this coast, they[86] are very active in recovering lost goods.

At the southern mouth of the Wantsum, which some suppose to have changed its channel,[87] overagainst the island, stood a city called by Ptolomy[88] RHUTUPIÆ,[y] by Tacitus[89] PORTUS TRUTULENSIS[z][91] for RHUTUPENSIS, if B. Rhenanus[92] does not mislead us; by Antoninus[93] RHITUPIS[a] *Portus*, by Ammianus[94] RHUTUPIÆ *statio*,[b] by Orosius[98] the *city and port of* RHUTUBI, by the Saxons, according to Bede,[c] *Reptacester*, by others *Ruptimuth*, by Alfred of Beverley[01] *Richberge*, now *Richborow*: so much has time sported with the change of a single name. Whence this name is derived by no means clear.[02] But as *Sandwich* and *Sandibay* in its neighbourhood

y. Ρουτουπιαι. z. v. Agr. 38.[90] a. *Rhutupæ, Ritupæ.*
b. XX.1.XXVII. 8.[95] *defertur ad* Rutupias, stationem *ex adverso tranquillam.*[96] *Rutupæ* Notit.[97] c. E.H.I. 1.[99]

96 'He [it] was brought to Richborough, outside which is a calm anchorage.'

97 *Notitia Dignitatum*, on which see p. 4, n. 35.

98 Orosius (fl. A.D. 500), historian and theologian, was a disciple of St Augustine of Hippo and wrote a history of the world with the thesis that Christianity was not the cause of the world's woes. It was very freely translated into Old English by King Alfred.

99 The *Ecclesiastical History*, bk I, ch. 1.

01 Alfred of Beverley, who flourished in the first half of C12, compiled a history ending in 1129.

02 Richborough is a name of obscure derivation. See *Lang. & Hist.*, pp. 259, 661–2. The Romano-British name was *Rotupi*, of which the first syllable is the British word *ro*, meaning 'great'. Bede (*H.E.* I, i) in his brief description of Britain, speaks of 'the city which is called *Rutubi portus*, now corruptly called by the English *Reptacæstir*'. By C11 *Repta*- had become *Raette* and in late C12 *Ratteburg*; in C14 it appears as

Retesbrough (*Orig. E.P.N.*, p. 80). With the loss of 'e' between 't' and 's', giving 'ts', the change to the 'ch' of Richborough is easily understood. For these Middle English forms of the place-name see *Dic.*, p. 368. The word *-cæstir* used by Bede is synonymous with *civitas*, 'city', earlier in the same sentence; and it is used also of other Roman forts of the Saxon Shore such as Porchester, *Andredescester* (Pevensey), *Ythencæstir* (at Bradwell, Essex) and Brancaster, Norfolk. From at least C12 the word *burh*, 'fortified place', was applied to the Richborough fort and with equal propriety. See *Elements* I, 59(b), 85–6; *Lamb.*, p. 101f.

Leland (*L.T.S.* IV, 61–2) has this to say of Richborough:

The site of the old town or castel ys wonderful fair apon an hille. The walles wich remayn ther yet be in cumpase almost as much as the Tower of London. They have bene very hye, thykke, stronge and wel embateled. The mater of them is flynt, mervelus and long brykes both white and redde after the Britons fascion. The sement was made of se sand and smaul pible. Ther is a great lykelyhod that the

Richborough Castle, the Castrensian Amphitheatre, engraved by
E. Kirkall after Stukley, published in 1724

have their names from the *sand*,03 and *Rhyd Tufith*04 in
Britan05 signifies the *sandy ford*, I should be for deducing it
from thence if I might. The city stood along the slope of a hill.
The castle on higher ground overhung the sea,06 which is now
so shut out by the sands driven in, that it is near a mile from
it.07 The greatest consequence of this place was in the time of
the Romans.08 From hence was the most usual passage into
Britain,09 and the Roman fleets made10 this port. Lupicinus11
sent by Constantius12 into Britain to check the inroads of the
Scots13 and Picts14 landed here his companies of Heruli, Batavi

goodly hil abowte the castel, and
especially to Sandwich ward hath bene
wel inhabited. Corne groweth on the
hille yn mervelus plenty, and yn going
to plowgh ther hath owte of mynde
bene fownd and now is mo [more]
antiquites of Romayne mony then yn
any place els of England. Surely reason
speaketh that this should be Rutupinum.
... There is, a good flyte shot fro
Ratesburgh toward Sandwich, a great
dike caste yn a rownd cumpas [i.e. an
amphitheatre], as yt had bene for fens
[defence] of menne of warre. The
cumpace of the grownd withyn is not
much above an acre, and it is very holo
by casting up the yerth. They cawle the
place there Lytleborough. Withyn the
castel is a lytle paroche chirch of S.
Augustine, and an heremitage, ... Not
far fro the heremitage is a cave wher

men have sowt [sought] and digged for
treasure. I saw yt by candel withyn, and
there were conys [rabbits]. Yt was so
straite [narrow] that I had no mind to
crepe far yn. In the north side of the
castel ys a hedde yn the walle, now sore
defaced with wether. They cawle yt
Quene Bertha hedde. Nere to that place
hard by the wal was a pot of Romayne
mony fownd.

See *Arch. Journ.* CXXVI, 221f.;
B. of E., E. Kent, p. 416f.; Jessup,
S.E. England, pp. 175–6.

03 Sandwich has indeed 'sand' as its
first element; the second, Old
English *wīc*, probably here meant
'port'. *Names of Towns and Cities*,
p. 205. 'Sandibay' is self-explanatory.

04 *Rhyd* is still the Welsh for 'ford',
but 'sand' is *tywod* or *swnd*.
However, *Tufith* very probably has
no connection with the name
Rhutupiae.

05 'In (Old) British', presumably.
The word 'Britan' could be used
as meaning 'ancient British' in C17.
Cp. 'Britan brikes'.

06 Much of the eastern part of the
site of the Roman fort was long
ago destroyed by erosion, though
the east wall stood until c. 1560.
See *Richborough, Fourth Report*,
p. 81.

07 The sea is now nearly two miles
away.

08 As a military and later as a
naval base with a civil settlement
attached.

09 It was a main supply base for the
armies engaged in the conquest of
Britain and later the main port of
embarkation for the Continent.
Arch. Journ. CXXVI, 185.

10 'made' here is an obsolete usage
meaning to 'reach or arrive at, to
accomplish a distance by travelling'.
S.O.E.D.

11 Lupicinus' expedition was in 360
for the purpose of repelling raids by
Picts and Scots (*Oxf. Hist.* I, 283;
Brit., p. 350).

12 Constantius II was Emperor
from 337 to 361. But it was Julian,
emperor from 360, known as 'The
Apostate', who sent Lupicinus to
Britain.

13 The Scots at this time were a
people of Ireland.

14 The Picts were a people estab-
lished to the north of Hadrian's
Wall in central and northern
Scotland. On their name see *Oxf.
Hist.* I, 282.

15 The Heruli was a tribe settled to the north of the Crimea; the Batavi were in occupation of part of the Low Countries, with the site of Leyden as their capital. The Maesici were presumably Moesians from the lower Danube.

16 Count Theodosius was sent by the Emperor Valentinian in 368 to cope with the inroads of Picts, Scots, Saxons and Franks, who had brought the province of Britain near to disaster. He landed at Richborough with a large force to find the countryside harassed by barbarians and London under siege. With difficulty he restored order and reorganized the government and the defences of the province. *Brit.*, pp. 351f. and fig. 12.

17 Quintus Aurelius Symmachus (c. 345–c. 405) was an orator, writer and administrator, raised to the consulship in 391.

18 Batavi, Heruli (see n. 15), Jovii and Victores. *Brit.*, p. 351.

19 This legion, one of the four engaged in the conquest of Britain from A.D. 43, probably began operations from Richborough. *Isca Silurum* is Caerleon in modern parlance, a name which goes back to a probable Latin origin, *Castra legionis*, 'camp of the (second) legion' (*Dic.*, p. 522). In fact, however, Ptolemy places *Legio II* at *Isca Dumnoniorum*, that is Exeter, where Frere demonstrates that there was probably a small legionary fortress in the sixties of A.D. CI. *Brit.*, p. 75.

20 See *Brit.*, p. 236, and p. 79, n. 48.

21 Magnus Clemens Maximus was Emperor from 383 to 388, but his rule was limited to Gaul, Britain and Spain.

22 Gratian was Emperor of the Western Roman Empire from 367 to 383.

23 Aquileia, to the north-east of Venice, retains fine monuments of

and Mæsici.[15] Theodosius[16] also, father of the Emperor of that name, (to whom, according to Symmachus,[17] the senate voted equestrian statues for restoring tranquillity to Britain), came hither with his Herculian, Jovian, Victorious, and Fidentine cohorts.[18] Afterwards, when the Saxon pirates put a stop to commerce, and made the sea a scene of war, and infested our coasts with their continual ravages, the Legio II. Augusta, which the emperor Claudius had brought out of Germany, and which had been fixed many years at Isca Silurum in Wales, was removed hither,[19] and had its officer here under the Count of the Saxon shore.[20] This command was probably held by that Clemens Maximus,[21] who was chosen emperor by the army in Britan, and put Gratian to death,[22] and was afterwards slain at Aquileia[23] by Theodosius.[24] This man Ausonius[25] in these verses on Aquileia[d] calls the Rhutupine robber:

> *Maximus, armigeri quondam sub nomine lixae.*
> *Fælix, quæ tanti spectatrix læta triumphi*
> *Fudisti Ausonio Rhutupinum Marte latronem.*

> O'er Maximus a common sutler's[27] boy,
> The triumph was to you a source of joy,
> When the Rhutupian robber you beheld
> By Roman valour driven from the field.

The same poet in his *Parentalia*[e] has rescued from oblivion another prefect of *Rhutupiæ*, Fl. Sanctus,[29] of whom he thus sings:

> *Militiam nullo qui turbine sedulus egit;*
> *Præside lætatus quo Rhutupinus ager.**

d. In claris civit.[26] e. 18.[28]

*Some by *Rhutupinus ager* understand Britain in general.

its ancient Roman greatness. Maximus died in 388.

24 Theodosius the Great was Emperor of the Eastern Roman Empire from 378 to 395. He saw military service in Britain under his father. During his reign orthodox Christianity eventually triumphed over other religions in the Empire.

25 Ausonius (d. c. A.D. 395), a poet, had been tutor to Gratian.

26 One might have expected *in clara civitate*, 'in that illustrious city' (of Aquileia).

27 A sutler was an army follower who sold provisions to the soldiers.

28 The *Parentalia* consists of 30 adulatory epigrams on the poet's friends and relatives. Ausonius probably died c. A.D. 395.

29 A governor of Britain in mid C4.

Calm and unwearied in his high command,
A leader he, pride of Rhutupia's land.

His uncle Claudius Contentus, who left at his death an immense fortune at interest in Britain,[30] and involved in foreign mortgages,[f] is thus commemorated by Ausonius in these mournful strains.[g]

> Et patruos elegeia meos reminiscere cantus,
> Contentum tellus quem Rhutupina tegit.

My mournful muse my uncle's praise shall sound,
Contentus buried in Rhutupian ground.

After the coming in of the Saxons Rhutupiæ still continued to be considerable.[32] Historians tell us it was the residence of Ethelbert king of Kent,[33] and Bede honours it with the name of a *city*.[34] It has long since fallen into decay, and its name occurs nowhere but in Alfred of Beverley,[35] who says that Alcher, with the people of Canterbury, fell upon the Danes incumbered with booty, and routed them at this place then called *Richberge*.[36] Time has devoured every trace of it, and to teach us that cities are as perishable as men, it is now a corn field, where, when the corn is grown up, one may see the traces of streets intersecting each other.[37] For wherever the streets have run the corn grows thin, which the common people call *St. Austin's Cross*,[38] and there remain only some half ruined walls

f. *usuris multiplicata extraneis*, and mightily increased the principal by interest. G.[31]   g. Parent. 7.[28]

30 On such investment of money in Britain cp. *Brit.*, p. 291 and n. 1; *Town and Country in Roman Britain*, pp. 68–9.

31 This note is by Gibson, on whom see Appendix.

32 The highly complex history of the Richborough site is set out mainly in *Richborough, Fourth* (1949) and *Fifth* (1968) *Reports*. Summary accounts are obtainable from H.M.S.O. under the title *Richborough Castle, Kent* (1956).
  In the late Roman period the troops in the fort included some of Germanic origin (*Med. Arch.* V, 17,

and see also III, 8), but there are no very early Saxon or Jutish graves yet known from the vicinity of the fort – nothing, that is, before about the second half of c6 (for Saxon finds from the neighbourhood see *Med. Arch.* II, 64–6 and map p. 6). But that the place 'continued to be considerable... after the coming in of the Saxons' might be inferred from the building of a chapel in the north-east corner of the fort. But this in itself does not imply a 'considerable' Saxon settlement near by and there could have been little economic reason for one there as Sandwich had replaced Richborough as a port in Saxon times.

33 'There is no confirmation of this from early records such as the *Chronicle* and Bede, but see p. 37, n. 31.

34 There was probably a Roman civil settlement to the west of the fort and an amphitheatre (Leland, p. 56, n. 02) and two Roman temples are known a short distance to the south-west. *Lamb.*, p. 102; *B. of E., E. Kent*, p. 21.

35 See p. 56, n. 01.

36 The name *Alcher* is presumably Anglo-Saxon *Ealhhere* (also spelt *Ealchere*). A Kentish alderman of that name, with *Æthelstan* sub-king of Kent 'slew the great [Danish] army at Sandwich..., took nine [of their] ships and put the rest to flight' (*Anglo-Saxon Chronicle*, MS 'A', under the year 850). Three years later '*Ealhere* with the men of Kent and *Huda* with the men of Surrey fought in Thanet with the heathen [Danish] army and at first they had the victory and there were many men slain and drowned on both sides' (ibid., 853). Richborough is, of course, close to both Thanet and Sandwich. Leland (*L.T.S.* IV, 54) cites Henry of Huntingdon and Beverley (p. 53) for these events.

37 Camden reports a similar phenomenon at Silchester, Hants. He says that he was told of it by 'the people that live hereabouts', but he had almost certainly read of it in Leland's notes (*L.T.S.* IV, 110). Leland comments also on the fine corn grown at Richborough (p. 56, n. 02).

38 As Gough (p. 242 *Additions*) realized, St Austin's Cross was the name given to the foundation of the great monument of c. A.D. 85 within the fort and close to St Augustine's chapel. Leland (p. 56, n. 02) descended into a gap in the foundation and saw rabbits there. In A.D. C3 the great monument was defaced and was apparently converted into a look-out post

protected by a newly-dug earthwork enclosure. *Archaeology of Roman Britain*, pp. 47, 120; on the chapel see *B. of E., E. Kent*, p. 417.

39 The massive outer walls, with much surviving, are the remains of a fort of the Saxon Shore, one of a chain of Roman forts that extended along the South Coast from the Isle of Wight (Carisbrooke) to the Wash on the East Coast (Brancaster). Garrisoned by mixed bands of troops and seamen, they were bases from which barbarian raiders could be intercepted at sea or attacked if they reached land. This one was probably built in the time of Carausius (287–93), on whom see *Oxf. Hist.* I, 276–7.

40 Leland (see p. 56, n. 02) had also noted this. He added that the place yielded 'mo antiquites of Romayne mony then yn any place els of England'. This was equally true in this century.

41 On the name Sandwich see p. 57, n. 03.

42 Sandwich was one of the original five, a head port with 'limbs' at Deal, Walmer, Ramsgate, Stonar, Sarre, Reculver and Fordwich. Brightlingsea, Essex, became a limb in C15. By mid C14, Sandwich was providing only one ship for the king's service compared with 3 from Hastings, 4 from Romney, 5 each from Hythe and Rye, 10 from Winchelsea and 19 from Dover. See *Cinque Ports*, p. 245 and Appendix II; Leland (*L.T.S.* IV, 49, 56).

43 The medieval defences of this town survive in part. The wall has gone, but two of the gates, The Barbican and Fisher's Gate, remain and the earthen rampart can be followed for much of its original length. See *Arch. Journ.* CXXVI, pp. 220–21, with town plan; *B. of E., E. Kent*, p. 430f.; *Lamb.*, p. 117f. Leland (*L.T.S.* IV, 47) says of its defences that it

of the castle in a square form built with the strongest cement.[39] This may be supposed the citadel, which, from its lofty situation looks down upon the marshy plain in Thanet deserted by the gradual retiring of the sea. The scite of the city now ploughed over discovers Roman gold and silver coins, evidences of its antiquity,[40] and shews a little below its offspring called by the Saxons from the *sand* 'Sondwic', but by us *Sandwich*.[41] This is one of the cinque ports,[42] as they are called, and is defended to the north and west by walls, on the other sides by a rampart, river, and ditch.[43] It formerly felt the ravages of the Danes,[44] and in the last age the fire of the French.[45] It is now sufficiently populous, though the harbour by the sand driven in and a great merchant ship of Pope Paul IV.[46] sunk in the very middle of it, is not capable of admitting large ships.

Below Rhutupia Ptolemy places CANTIUM PROM.[47] as the extreme point of this angle, which some copies give corruptly

is meatly welle walled wher the town stondeth most in jeopardi of ennemies. The residew of the town is dichid and mudde waulled.

He goes on:

Ther be...iiii. principal gates, [and] 3 paroche chyrches [as today] of the which sum suppose that S. Marye's was sumtyme a nunnery. Ther is a place of Whit freres, and an hospital withowt the town fyrst ordened for maryners desesid and hurt. Ther is a place wher the monkes of Christ Chirch did resort when they were lordes of the towne.

44 The *Anglo-Saxon Chronicle* records a defeat of the Danes here in 851 (correctly 850, MS 'A': see p. 59, n. 36); their fleet came here in 993 (MS 'A') and again in 1006, 1009, 1013, 1014, 1015, 1046 (all MS 'E') and in 1048 (MS 'C'). In only the last two of these is there mention of an attack on Sandwich, though it is a fair assumption that it was harried whenever there was booty worth taking from it. On some occasions the Danish fleet was merely using a sheltered anchorage and one convenient for forays along the south and east coasts or up the

Thames. See *Lamb.* p. 120f.; Leland (*L.T.S.* IV, 54).

45 The town was burned in 1216 by the forces of Louis the Dauphin and again in 1456 and 1459 (*Oxf. Hist.* VI, 514, 517; *Lamb.*, p. 118).

46 Paul IV (1555–9). By the later middle ages Sandwich had begun 'to function as an important entrepôt whence Italian produce was re-exported to the Continent'. It was also the port for Canterbury and outport for London. The silting up of harbours was largely a natural process in C15 and C16, but the use of larger ships also contributed to the decline of some small ports. Leland (*L.T.S.* IV, 62) reported that 'Now Sandwich be not celebrated by cawse of Goodwine Sandes [see p. 55, n. 82], and the Decay of the Haven.' He noted also that the 'caryke' of Pope Paul which sank in the haven 'did... gether a great Banke' (ibid., p. 48). Presumably the carrack, a large ship of burden, hastened the natural process of silting. See *Hist. Geog. Eng.*, pp. 303, 311–12, 335–6 and n.

47 *Cantium Promunturium*, the North Foreland (NG 403697).

60

Deal Castle, engraved by Wenceslaus Hollar

Nuncantium[h] and *Acantium*, and Diodorus[49] calls *Carion*, we now the *Foreland*. But all the shore on every side from Rhutupiæ is called by the poets *the Rhutupine shores*. Hence Juvenal[i] lashing Curtius Montanus the epicure about oysters brought from hence to Rome says,

> *nulli major fuit usus edendi*
> *Tempestate mea; Circæis nata forent, an*
> *Lucrinum ad saxum, Rhutupinove edita fundo*
> *Ostrea, callebat primo deprendere morsu.*

> In arts of eating none more early train'd,
> None in my time had equal skill attain'd.
> He whether Circe's rock[51] his oysters bore,
> Or Lucrine lake,[52] or the *Rhutupian shore*,
> Knew at first sight.   Duke.[53]

and Lucan,[k]

> *Aut vaga cum Thetis Rhutupinaque littora fervent*

>   the roar
> Of seas that break on the Rhutupian shore.   Rowe.[55]

From this promontory the shore runs out in a ridge of hills southward for some miles. But when it comes to the neighbouring castles of *Sandon* (q.d. the sand hill) and *Deal*,[l][57] built by Henry VIII. in the last age, it sinks, and presents to the

h. Νεναντων. Marcianus Heracleota.[48] See before, p. 209. [In this edition, pp. 1–2.]
i. IV. 140.[50]
k. VI. 67.[54]
l. Holland adds *Walmar*.[56]

48 This writer is ignored in modern works of reference.

49 Diodorus Siculus, a Sicilian of CI B.C., not a trustworthy authority.

50 Decimus Junius Juvenalis (A.D. ?60–?130+), the greatest Roman satirist. This quotation occurs in Leland (L.T.S. iv, 51).

51 The 'rock' was a legendary island off the Italian coast called *Aeaea*. See *The Odyssey*, Book X.

52 *Lucrinus Lacus* was originally an inner arm of the Gulf of *Baiae*, west of Naples, famous in classical times for the quality of its oysters. In 1538, as a result of volcanic activity, the lake was replaced by a mountain.

53 Richard Duke (1658–1711), clergyman, attempted poetical satire on contemporary topics.

54 Marcus Annaeus Lucanus (A.D. 39–65), a Latin epic poet.

55 Nicholas Rowe (1674–1718), dramatist and Poet Laureate. His translation of Lucan, published in 1718, was, to most readers' taste, superseded by that of A. E. Housman in 1926. This passage is in Leland (L.T.S. IV, 51).

56 On Holland see Appendix. Walmer Castle is the official residence of the Lord Warden of the Cinque Ports. Pitt, Wellington and Churchill are among those who have held this office in recent centuries. Walmer is the best preserved of the three local Henrician castles in spite of the residential additions to it. See *Arch. Journ.* CXXVI, 215, plan p. 216.

57 Sandown Castle, one of those built 1538–40, was largely destroyed in 1864. Deal Castle is largely complete. *Lamb.*, p. 130.

sea an open plain.[58] At *Deal*[59] (which Nennius,[m] and I believe rightly, calls *Dole*, a name still given by our Britans to an open plain on a river or the sea)[64] tradition affirms Cæsar landed,[65] with which agrees Nennius,[66] who, in his barbarous style writes "Cæsar batteled[n] at Dole." A table[68] also hanging in Dover castle proves the same, and Cæsar himself gives it weight when he says he landed on an open plain shore, and was warmly received by the Britans.[69] Hence our countryman Leland in his Cygnea Cantio[70] says,

> *Jactat Dela novas celebris arces,*
> *Notus Cæsareis locus tropheis.*

> Fam'd Deal her new built towers[71] boasts,
> Where Cæsar triumph'd on our coasts.

After that general (to digress a little from the subject) had made himself master of all parts of the world by sea and land, as Pomponius Sabinus[o] observes from Seneca,[72] he turned his views towards the ocean, and as if the Roman world were not sufficient he entertained thoughts of another. In the year before

m. *Tol. Toliapis.* Ptol.[60] Strabo VI. says the Britans paid great tolls for going and coming.[61] There are towns of this name on the opposite coast.[62] MS. n. G.[63]

n. c.14. *bellum pugnavit.* Gale's printed copy read "pugnavit contra *Dolobellum* qui erat proconsul regi Britannico:" he corrects it "pugnabat apud *Dole* contra *Bellinum.*"[67]

o. A commentator on Virgil.

58 Called Lydden Valley. It is to be distinguished from Lydden in Thanet and from the village near Dover. All three are derived by Ekwall (*Dic.*, p. 293) from *hlēo-denn*, 'pasture with a shelter'; alternatively 'sheltered valley' (*P.N. Kent*, p. 452).

59 Deal may well be derived from Old English (Kentish dialect) *dēl*, 'a share of land, a district', cognate with 'dole', although a derivation from OE(Kt) *del*, 'a valley', is not impossible. See *Elements* I, 126. The town of 'Deal is a post-medieval plantation' (*New Towns*, p. 457). Leland (*L.T.S.* IV, 42), in an aside, observes on this place-name: 'The chirch of Dale, corruptely caullid Dele, was a prebende longging of auncient tyme to St. Martines College in Dovor.'

60 This must be a reference to *Toliatis Ins.*, an island which Ptolemy places north-east of the North Foreland in the southern Northern Sea. See 'The British Isles according to Ptolemy', p. 20 of the O.S. *Map of Roman Britain*. On Ptolemy see p. 43, n. 71. It is very doubtful indeed whether the place-name *Toliatis* has any connection with the place-name Deal.

61 See *Oxf. Hist.* I, 70–71.

62 Only Dol in eastern Brittany comes to mind, but it is hardly likely to be related to the name Deal.

63 Manuscript note by Bishop Gibson, on whom see Appendix.

64 Modern Welsh *dol* means 'meadow'.

65 Caesar landed 'in the neighbourhood of Walmer and Deal'. *Brit.*, p. 31.

66 On Nennius, see p. 5, n. 53.

67 This name may well be derived from Nennius. Geoffrey of Monmouth has a city called Dorobellum, presumably in Kent, where Cassivellaunus was said to have held a council at the time of

Caesar's first invasion. See *History of the Kings of Britain*, p. 319. Aaron Thompson's translation of the *History* of 1718 identifies Dorobellum as probably Deal, perhaps influenced by this passage of Camden.

68 'Table' is here used in the sense 'picture' (cp. French *tableau*). *S.O.E.D.* I, d,3, p. 2117.

69 After proceeding for about seven miles from the cliffs (presumably near Dover), where a landing would have been dangerous, he 'ran his ships aground on an evenly sloping beach, free from obstacles'. The Britons vigorously opposed the Roman landing (*Conquest of Gaul*). Camden's 'warmly received' is ambiguous in translation.

70 The *Cygnea Cantio*, printed in 1545, consists of a description of the Thames from Oxford to Greenwich as seen by a swan. It concludes with a history of the palace of Greenwich and the virtues of Henry VIII.

71 Deal Castle (*Arch. Journ.* CXXVI, 217–19 with plans, and see p. 201f. for the coastal defences of the South-East as a whole) was finished only five years before the publication of the *Cygnea* in 1545. *Lamb.*, p. 131, quotes these same lines of Leland.

72 Whether this refers to the elder Seneca (55 B.C.–A.D. 40?), the 'Orator', or to his son, Seneca the Younger (4 B.C.–A.D. 65) matters little in British topography.

Christ 54,[73] and the following, with a fleet of 2000 sail,[74] as Athenæus[p] says from Cotta,[76] invaded Britain either to be revenged on its inhabitants who had assisted the Gauls,[77] as Strabo[q] relates, or to get some of the British pearls,[79] as Suetonius[r] says, or, as others, fired with the love of glory. He had before informed himself of the harbours and passage, not as Roger Bacon fables,[*] by glasses disposed along the coast of Gaul and by the catoptric art[82] which multiplies obscure images, but by scouts, as himself[83] and Suetonius[84] testify. His proceedings here are related at large by his own pen, and by me already in brief from his account,[85] and Suetonius' memoirs of Scæva now[86] lost, whose valour displayed itself in the civil war at Dyrrhachium, and whom our poet Joseph[87] in his Antiocheis in these lines about Britain mistakenly makes a Britan:

> Hinc & Scæva satus, pars non obscura tumultus
> Civilis, Magnum solus qui mole soluta
> Obsedit, meliorque stetit pro Cæsare murus.
>
> Hence Scæva sprang; no common part he bore
> In civil discords, tottering from the shore
> The solid mole by Pompey's force he view'd
> Himself instead a wall for Cæsar stood.

p. VI. 273.b.[75]

q. IV. 200. Mr. Camden mistakes Strabo's words, which say that Cæsar landed twice in Britain without doing mischief or advancing far, δια τας εν τοις Κελταις στασεις, on account of disturbances in Gaul; which refers to his *success* and *progress*, not to his *motive*.[78]

r. J. Cæs. c. 47. of which was made a breastplate which he dedicated in the temple of Venus Genetrix, Plin. IX. 35.[80]

*De arte & natura.[81]

73 In fact, 55 and 54 B.C., not 54 and 53.

74 In 55 B.C. the expedition used over 800 ships according to an original addition to the text of the *Gallic War*. In 54 B.C. Caesar had 600 vessels built to a new design and 28 warships in support. See *The Gallic War*, V, 1 and 2. Camden's 2000 is very wide of the mark for either year.

75 Athenaeus was a Greek grammarian and author who flourished c. A.D. 230. The chief interest of his work consists in the preservation of excerpts from classical authors whose writings are otherwise lost.

76 Presumably Lucius Aurunculeius Cotta, one of Caesar's generals. He did not take part in either expedition to Britain, but was in Gaul and should have been well acquainted with the facts.

77 Caesar himself (V, 1) explicitly says that 'he made active preparations for an expedition because he knew that in almost all the Gallic campaigns the Gauls had received reinforce- ments from the Britons'. Economic gain for Rome and personal prestige were other, unavowed motives. See *Brit.*, p. 28.

78 Strabo (c. 64 B.C.–c. A.D. 24), of Pontus in Asia Minor, was a historical geographer and traveller.

79 Tacitus, *Agricola* 12, reported that British pearls were of poor quality. See *Brit.*, p. 294.

80 The first part of this note perhaps means: 'Julius Caesar, in about the year 47 B.C....' The final reference is to Pliny's *Natural History* (on which see p. 12, n. 98), of which books VIII–XI deal with fishes, birds, insects and animals.

81 Roger Bacon (1214?–94) was described by Diderot as 'one of the most surprising geniuses that nature had ever produced, and one of the most unfortunate of men'. For what little is known of his life and writings see e.g. *Camb. Hist. Eng. Lit.* I, 205f. The work cited by Camden, *On Art and Nature*, was published in the original Latin at Paris in 1542 under the title *De Mirabili potestate artis et naturae*; and in translation at London in 1593.

82 Catoptrics is that part of the study of optics which relates to the reflection of light, especially by mirrors.

83 Caesar (V, 1), having failed to get the desired information from traders, sent a warship under Volusenus to make a general reconnaissance.

84 Suetonius was born in c. A.D. 69. His book *The Twelve Caesars*, who include Claudius and Vespasian, is available as a Penguin Classic in a translation by Robert Graves.

85 In one of his introductory chapters, 'The Romans in Britain', in the Gough ed., pp. xxvi–lxiv.

86 On Suetonius see n. 84 above. Scaeva was a centurion in Caesar's army. The battle of Dyrrachium occured in 48 B.C. when Caesar was defeated.

87 Joseph of Exeter, who wrote Latin poetry in late C12.

88 Marcus Fabius Quintilianus (A.D. c. 35–c. 100) was a Roman educationist and rhetorician. Only his *Institutio Oratoria* (Training of an Orator) has survived.

89 For an account of this coast see *Arch. Cant.* LIII, 62f., especially p. 74. Leland (*L.T.S.* IV, 48):

Deale, half a myle fro the shore of the se, a fisscher village iii. myles or more above Sandwice, is apon a flat shore and very open to the se, wher is a fosse or a great bank artificial betwixt the towne and the se, and beginneth aboute Deale, and rennith a great way up toward S. Margaret's Clyfe, yn so much that sum suppose that this is the place where Caesar landed *in aperto litore* [on the open shore]. Surely the fosse was made to kepe owte ennemyes there, or to defend the rage of the se; or I think rather the castinge up beche or pible.

A natural pebble ridge thrown up by the sea was until lately the accepted explanation for this phenomenon. However, a different explanation of these earthworks is that they linked Deal Castle with both Sandown and Walmer Castles and were part of Henry VIII's defensive system here. *Arch. Journ.* CXXVI, 218–19. *Lamb.*, p. 130, attributes the earthworks to Caesar.

90 Caesar's *Gallic War*, V, 21.

91 See p. 62, n. 65.

92 John Horsley (1685–1732) in his *Britannia Romana* (1732). 'It may be regarded as the first and in many ways the best book on Roman Britain as a whole.' So Collingwood in *Oxf. Hist.* I, 466.

93 Julius Celsus Constantinus. See *Scribes and Scholars*, pp. 33–5, for a discussion of 'subscriptions' such as these.

94 This is an echo of Caesar, V, I:

The lie of the land at this point was such that javelins could be hurled from the cliffs right on to the narrow beach enclosed between them and the sea. Caesar thought this a quite unsuitable place for landing...

But I must refer the reader for the account of Cæsar's proceedings here to his own and the other relations before-mentioned; not having met with that long-lived Britan whom M. Aper, according to Quintilian[88] found in this island, who acknowledged he had been in that battle when his countrymen endeavoured to repulse Cæsar in his first descent; nor intending now to write history.

For a considerable length under this shore are a number of heaps like banks which some suppose to have been blown up by the wind;[89] but I rather take them for the fortifications or defences for ships which Cæsar was ten days and nights throwing up to draw his shattered ships into, and secure them from storms and the Britans who attacked them in vain.[s] I understand that the inhabitants call these banks *Romesworke*, q.d. *the work of the Romans*. And I the rather think Cæsar landed here,[91] because he says seven miles[t] from hence (as it stands in an antient MS. corrected by Fl. Constantine a person of consular rank),[93] the sea is so confined by narrow mountains that a spear may be thrown from the high grounds upon the coast.[94] Certain it is, that soon after you leave Deal, a ridge of cliffs (those *moles magnificæ*,[95] as Cicero[u] calls them), covered with *Crythmus*, or Samphire,[97] runs on for about seven miles to Dover, where it divides and opens a passage, and the place exactly answers to Cæsar's description of it as admitting and confining the sea between two hills. In this opening of the cliffs lies DUBRIS[98] mentioned by Antoninus,[99] called by the Saxons 'Dofra',[01] by us *Dover*. Darell[02] from Eadmer[03] says it

s. Cæs. B.G. V. 21.[90] t. 8. the common Editions & Horsley. p. 13.[92]

u. Ep. ad Att. IV. 16.[96]

95 'Splendid sea cliffs'. Much of this is an echo of Leland (*L.T.S.* IV, 49).

96 *Epistolae ad Atticum* (Letters to Atticus).

97 *Crithmum maritimum*, common on limestone cliffs by the sea. William Turner (d. 1568), Dean of Wells, whose *Names of Herbs* (1548) is the first work of scientific botany in England, remarks on the growth of samphire on the cliffs at Dover. See J. E. Lousley, *Wild Flowers of the Chalk and Limestone*, 1950, p. 50, and Shakespeare's *King Lear*, IV, vi, 15.

98 *Dubris* is a Romano-British locative plural meaning 'at the waters'. See *Lang. & Hist.*, pp. 259, 577, 629. The river Dour, at the mouth of which Dover stands, is from the same Celtic word-root as 'Dover'.

99 On the *Antonine Itinerary* see p. 28, n. 46.

01 In fact Old English *Dofras*, on which see *Dic.*, pp. 142–3. Camden probably took the form *Dofra* from *Lamb.*, p. 131.

02 This is William Darrel (d. 1580) who wrote a book in Latin on the castles of Kent.

had its name from its being close and difficult of access.[04] For as antiently the sea thereabouts spreading itself very wide forms a large bay,[05] it was obliged to be confined within straiter bounds. William Lambarde,[06] however, derives it more probably from *Dufyrrha*,[w] which in British signifies *a steep place*.[08] The town lying among the cliffs where the harbour antiently was (when the sea came up thither, as may be inferred from the anchors and planks dug up there),[09] is more famous for the convenience of its harbour and the passage from it to France, than for its beauty or populousness.[10] This is the most noted passage, and it was antiently by law provided[x] that no person going abroad on pilgrimage should take shipping from any other place.[12] It is one of the cinque ports, and was obliged antiently to furnish twenty-one[13] ships for war fitted out in the same manner as Hastings already mentioned.[14] On the side next the sea now shut out by a gravelly beach, it was surrounded by walls, of which some part still remains.[15] It had

w. *Dwy bryn*, two rocks. MS. n. G.[07]
x. 4 E.III. c. 8. 9 E.III. c. 8. 4 E.IV. c. 10.[11]

03 Eadmer (d. 1124?) was a Canterbury monk who wrote a biography of St Anselm, whose chaplain he was, and a chronicle of contemporary events entitled *Historia Novorum*. 'Eadmer is almost modern in his deliberate limitation of himself to a period and special subject upon which he could speak as a first-hand authority'. *Camb. Hist. Eng. Lit.* I, 162–3.

04 On the meaning of 'Dover' see n. 98 opposite.

05 There is no large bay here though there was earlier an inlet between two chalk headlands. In later paragraphs (p. 70) Camden debates the former existence of a land-link with the Continent where the Strait of Dover is now; and he may have been thinking of the bay existing before the sea broke through this land-link.

06 See p. 1, n. 01. *Lamb.*, p. 131, gives also the correct derivation.

07 This is a MS note by Gibson, on whom see Appendix.

08 This, too, is from *Lamb.*, p. 131.

09 Leland (*L. T. S.* IV, 49):

There hath bene a haven yn tyme past, and yn token therof the ground that lyith up betwyxt the hilles is yet in digging fownd wosye [muddy]. Ther hath be fownd also peces of cabelles and anchores, and *Itinerarium Antonini* cawleth hyt by the name of a havon.

10 Much of this is still true of Dover. See *B. of E., E. Kent*, p. 288f. Leland (*L. T. S.* IV, 50):

The towne is devided in to vi. paroches, whereof iii. be under one rofe at S. Martines yn the hart of the town. The other iii. stand abrode [further afield], of the which one is cawled S. James of Rudby, or more likely Rodeby, *à statione navium* [roadstead for ships].

He goes on to assert that Dover cannot be the Roman port of

Rutupiae, which must have been at Richborough.

11 Statutes enacted in the fourth year of the reign of Edward III (1330); in his ninth year (1335); and in the fourth year of Edward IV's reign (1464/5).

12 Jusserand, in his *English Wayfaring Life*, p. 213 and n., refers to an enactment of 1389 which allowed Plymouth as an alternative to Dover for departure on pilgrimage. It would certainly have been more convenient for those going to St James of Compostella in Spain.

13 Letters Patent of 1359, confirming a record of 1303, give the Dover contribution as 19 ships, but together with its corporate members, Folkestone and Faversham, it had the obligation of providing 21 ships. See *Cinque Ports*, pp. 143, 242. Dover was the chief of the Cinque Ports and today is the only one of them that survives, in any real sense, as a port.

14 The fleet required from all of the Cinque Ports was of 57 ships, as for example in 1294 (*Oxf. Hist.* IV, 655). See *E.H.D.* II, 968 for a charter of Henry II to Hastings.

15 One section of them is no doubt commemorated in the name Townwall Street, but I could find no remains of them in 1969. Leland (*L. T. S.* IV, 49–50):

The towne on the front toward the se hath bene right strongly walled and embateled, and almost al the residew [i.e. the sections not facing the sea]; but now that is partly fawlen downe, and broken downe. Cou [Cow] gate, Crosse gate, Bochery gate, stoode with toures toward the se. There is beside Betingate and Westegate. The residew of the town, as far as I can perceyve, was never waulled. (Howbeyt M. Tuine [on whom see p. 69, n. 44] tol me a late that yt hath be walled abowt, but not dyked) [i.e. there was no ditch outside the wall].

Elsewhere (*L.T.S.*IV, 63), Leland includes other gates:

Gates in Dovar sumtime to the se side: Cumming first from the Castel Crossegate, Segate, Tinkeresgate, Bocherygate, Snoregate, Boldersgate to the Wikeward [i.e. towards Wick]. On the other side of the toun: Cougate, Waullegate, to entre into Dovar cumming from London.

16 Some time before 640 a house of secular canons was instituted perhaps within the walls of a fort of the Saxon Shore at Dover, but in 696 it was moved to the site where Dover College now stands. The church was rebuilt after the Norman Conquest and replaced again from 1135 by Archbishop Corbeuil (on whom see p. 30, n. 61 above) as a Benedictine priory. Leland (*L.T.S.*IV, 55) transcribed some of the Latin chronicle of this monastery, including a paragraph relating how King Eadbald of Kent (616–40) established a house of canons in the *castrum* of Dover through the initiative of Laurentius, Archbishop of Canterbury (604–19). The canons were transferred by King Wihtred (690–725), who built for them St Martin's in the town of Dover and there they remained for more than 400 years. Henry I (1100–1135) converted it from a house of canons to a house of Benedictine monks. Of the medieval buildings a gatehouse, refectory and part of the dormitory remain. See *B. of E., E. Kent*, pp. 287–8 and pl. 18a; *Lamb.*, pp. 143–4.

17 See previous note.

18 Not completely. The lower parts of the walls of the circular nave and rectangular chancel survive (NG 315412). Leland (*L.T.S.*IV, 50) merely says that near the western pharos 'was a place of Templarys'; and see *B. of E., E. Kent*, p. 530.

19 Assistant. There is still a Bishop Suffragan whose cure is at St Martin's, Dover.

Dover castle in 1762, engraved by Godfrey after Francis Grose

a church dedicated to St. Martin[16] built by Whitred king of Kent,[17] also an house of knights templars now gone;[18] and it furnished a see for a suffragan[19] to the archbishop of Canterbury, who, when the archbishop had more important affairs on his hands, acted for him in the article of orders without interfering with episcopal jurisdiction. On the hill, or rather rock, which rises to the right, inaccessible on almost every side, to an amazing height overhanging the sea, stands a large castle like a little city, strongly fortified by art, and thick set with towers threatening the chanel below.[20] Mathew Paris[21] calls it the key and bar of England.[y] The common people fancy it

y. [Left blank by Gough.][22]

20 Dover Castle is a highly complex group of structures ranging in date from the second half of C12 down to the Tudor period and later. The most authoritative recent description of it is in the Official Guide-Book, *Dover Castle*, with a useful short bibliography. See also *Arch Journ.* CXXVI, 262–3.

21 Matthew Paris (d. 1259), a chronicler at the monastery of St Alban's, revised and continued the *Chronica Majora* of his predecessor there, Roger of Wendover. Matthew is considered to have surpassed 'all the chroniclers of the twelfth century'. The position of St Alban's on a medieval main route, the Watling Street, kept him in touch with the court of Henry III and with the trends of political affairs including those of Europe. See *Camb. Hist. Eng. Lit.*I, 178–80. The *Chronica Majora* was readily available to Camden in the edition produced by Archbishop Parker in 1571.

22 Leland (*L.T.S.*IV, 57): 'Kent is the key of al Englande.' His editor equates 'key' with 'quay'; and certainly 'key' is a possible spelling for modern 'quay' down to C18

was built by Julius Cæsar.[23] I believe it was first built by the Romans, from the British bricks[24] in the chapel[25] such as they used in their foundations.[z] Upon the decline of the Roman empire in Britain, a party of Tungricani,[27] who are reckoned among the Palatine auxiliaries,[28] was stationed here, part of whose armoury those great arrows may have been which the people of the castle shew with wonder, and which used to be shot out of basiliscæ.[29] From the coming in of the Saxons to the end of their government, I do not find the least mention of this castle[30] or town, except in certain loose papers copied from a table hung up here, which say that Cæsar, after he landed at Deal, and had routed the Britans at *Baramdown*,[31] a neighbouring plain fit for horse, and therefore for drawing up an army,

z. *Substructionibus*, larger buildings. G.[26]

(*S.O.E.D.*, s. n. key, sb²). The sense of modern 'key' is necessary in the Leland because of its being associated with 'bar' (of a gateway or door). A number of writers from William of Malmesbury onwards use this phrase of Dover. *Lamb.*, p. 135, actually quotes Malmesbury.

23 The *castrum* (n. 16 above) mentioned in pre-Norman documents is a late Roman Fort of the Saxon Shore now overlaid by the modern town. The history of Dover Castle may, however, extend back to the late Saxon period if three of the Norman chroniclers are to be relied upon. Then the Early Iron Age earthworks on the site were adapted for purposes of defence by King Harold. See *Dover Castle*, p. 4. There is a further possibility, that the prehistoric earthwork had been refashioned as a Saxon *burh* and that William I put his castle within it as he did at Pevensey and Porchester. See *Arch. Journ.* CXXVI, 265; *The Normans*, p. 119, n. 48, and p. 237; *Med. Arch.* VI–VII, 322; VIII, 254–5; IX, 190; X, 190–91.

24 As before noted, these are Roman

bricks, probably prised from ruined buildings in the Roman town.

25 This is the late C10 or early C11 church of St Mary-in-Castro, one of the most complete of Saxon churches, though badly mauled in C19 after use as a coal-store. Its structure contains much Roman brick and at its west end stands a much-altered Roman pharos, probably of A.D. C1. It served as a bell-tower to the church until C18. Leland (*L.T.S.* IV, 55) notes a passage from the Latin Chronicle of the Monastery of Dover to the effect that Lucius the [British] King built the church in Dover Castle. *Arch. Journ.* CXXVI, 265; *B. of E., E. Kent*, pp. 278–9.

26 The classical meaning of *substructio* was 'foundations'. Gibson ('G') was perhaps thinking that brick substructures were normally provided only for 'larger buildings'.

27 Camden had this from the *Notitia Dignitatum*, on which see p. 4, n. 35; and *Arch. Journ.* XCVII, 140. The *milites Tungrecani* were recruited into the Roman army from what is now part of Belgium.

28 Originally 'palace troops'; later, troops serving under immediate imperial control as opposed to those serving under a general to whom the emperor had delegated control.

29 In the England of C16, a basilisk was a cannon that discharged shot of about 200 lbs. Probably Camden had in mind a *ballista*, a large catapult for hurling iron bolts or stones. The sockets for such, or similar engines, are still visible in the tops of the bastions of some Roman forts, e.g., Burgh, Suffolk. For the missiles cast by these engines see R. E. M. Wheeler, *Maiden Castle*, 1943, pp. 281–2 and figs. 93, 1–13; for the engines themselves *Archaeology of Roman Britain*, pp. 306–7.

30 *The Anglo-Saxon Chronicle*, MSS 'E' and 'F', refer to incidents at Dover in 1051 (misdated 1048) and 1052 (correctly dated).

31 Barham Downs is traversed by the main Roman road from Dover to Canterbury, built about a century after Caesar's expeditions to Britain. The Latin *Chronicle of Dover Priory*, quoted by Leland (*L.T.S.* IV, 55) says:

Julius Caesar fought with the Britons and Cassivellaunus on Barham Down, as is evident from the barrows (*acervos*) heaped up over the bodies of the slain not far from the village of Bridge.

There are still barrows in this area, some possibly of the Bronze Age, some Romano-British and some Saxon. Leland (*L.T.S.* IV, 41) also notes:

In the paroche of Barehamdoune a litle from the wood side, and about a 6. (myles) from Dovar, apperith a dikid campe [NG 206517?] of men of warre. Sum say that it was Caesar's cam[p]: sum thinke that it was a campe of the Danes. It hath 3. diches.

Lamb., p. 245, brings Caesar from Deal to 'Baramdowne'.

32 'The Britans' of the Early Iron Age had certainly constructed a hill-fort there (see p. 67, n. 23), but not a castle. Leland (*L.T.S.* IV, 55), again quoting from the Latin *Chronicle of Dover Priory*, records:

Arviragus strengthened (or established, *firmavit*) the castle (*castrum*) of Dover against the Romans, and (similarly) that of Richborough.

33 Arviragus, second son of Cymbeline, figures in Geoffrey of Monmouth's *History of the Kings of Britain*, but this incident at Dover is not mentioned there. *Lamb.*, p. 135, cites Juvenal for Arviragus and makes him founder of Dover castle.

34 This is not, as one would expect, from Geoffrey of Monmouth. However, Leland (*L.T.S.* IV, 55) notes that Guinevere's bower (*camera*), Arthur's Hall and the bones of Gawain (*Walwanus*) are to be found in Dover Castle (*castrum*).

35 Both Eadmer, the Canterbury chronicler, and the Norman chronicler William of Poitiers, assert this. See *The Normans*, pp. 128–32.

36 The order of events as stated here is wrong. William proceeded from Hastings via Romney to Dover, where he built fortifications, perhaps the still visible motte and bailey castle, then on to Canterbury and Southwark. From there he made a wide circuit through Surrey and Hampshire to Wallingford in Berkshire and thence to Berkhamsted in Hertfordshire, before he made straight for London. See *Oxf. Hist.* II, 588–90.

37 The Conqueror's half-brother Odo, Bishop of Bayeux (see p. 30, n. 62) was made Earl of Kent and established in Dover Castle where he could control the Channel crossing. Haimo the royal seneschal and later dapifer, Richard de Clare (p. 68, n. 60, *Sussex*) and Hugh de Montfort were important tenants-in-chief who held lands in Kent. The

Roman warfare: the assault troops make a *testudo* by coming to close order and locking their shields together over their heads: from a seventeenth-century engraving

began to build Dover castle,[32] which was afterwards fortified against the Romans, and the harbour shut up by Arviragus.[33] Afterwards Arthur and his soldiers overcame certain unknown rebels here.[34] However a little before the coming of the Normans this was accounted the chief fortress of England, and on that account William the Norman obliged Harold to swear that he would surrender to him this castle with its wall when he aspired to the crown;[35] and as soon as he had settled matters in London, his first thought was to fortify this place,[36] and to assign to his nobles lands in Kent[37] upon condition they were ready for its defence with a certain number of soldiers, instead of which a sum of money is now paid yearly.[38] "For

Archbishop and Christ Church, Canterbury, were the principal ecclesiastical holders of land. Nevertheless, the King retained for himself the largest share, including the enormous manor of Milton Regis, as well as Faversham, Aylesford and Dartford, with the boroughs of Dover, Canterbury and Rochester, thus keeping in his own hands the main lines of communication between London and Normandy.

38 On feudal tenure see *Oxf. Hist.* II, 626, and on the commutation of military service for money payment see *Oxf. Hist.* III, 16: 'There is abundant evidence of it in [i.e. as early as] the reign of Henry I.'

68

when Hubert de Burg[39] was appointed constable of this castle," to borrow the words of an antient writer, "he, considering it was not safe for the castle to have a new set of guards on duty every month, procured by the consent of the king and all the knights, that every knight should send for one month's duty ten shillings, and that therewith should be paid certain men chosen and sworn, both horse and foot,[a] to guard the castle."[41] Philip Augustus king of France[42] is reported to have said when his son Louis was raising disturbances in England, and had made himself master of some cities,[43] that his son would not have any footing in England if he did not possess himself of Dover castle, as being the strongest fortification in the whole kingdom, and most conveniently situated with respect to France. On the other opposite rock which is almost level on the top are remains of a very antient building. Somebody, on what authority I know not, has called it *Cæsar's Altar*: but John Twine of Canterbury,[44] a learned old man, who, in his youth had seen it almost intire, assured me it was a Pharos to direct ships by fire in the night.[45] Such another was on the opposite coast of France at Bologne, built by the Romans, and repaired long after by Charlemagne,[46] (according to Regino,[47] who corruptly wrote it *Phanos* for *Pharos*), now called by the French *Tour d'Ordre*,[48] and by the English *the Old man of Bullen*.[49] At the foot of this rock, in the last age that potent prince Henry VIII. at great pains and infinite expence by driving down piles in the sea, banding boards and timbers together, and covering them with huge stones, made the mole, which we call the *Peere*, for the security of ships.[50] But this design of that excellent prince was soon broken down by the fury of the raging ocean, which, by the violence of its waves loosened the joints of the work. Queen Elizabeth

a. *Tam milites quam pedites.*[40]

1203–6 and put an end to English suzerainty over them. *Lamb.*, p. 140.

43 For the French invasion of England led by the Dauphin Louis in 1216, see *Oxf. Hist.* III, 483f. and n. 39. Leland (*L.T.S.* IV, 54) cites briefly two medieval chroniclers for these events.

44 John Twine (1501?–81) was a Canterbury schoolmaster, M.P. and antiquary. He was one of the few who perceived the falsity of much of Geoffrey of Monmouth. See *British Antiquity*, p. 105.

45 On the western heights only a few scraps of masonry survive from this second pharos at Dover. See p. 67, n. 25 above.
Leland (*L.T.S.* IV, 50):

On the toppe of the hye clive betwene the towne and the peere remayneth yet, abowt a flyte shot up into the land fro the very brymme of the se clyffe, a ruine of a towr, the which hath bene as a pharos or a mark to shyppes on the se.

The much better preserved Roman lighthouse in the precincts of the Castle was not recognized for what it had been presumably because its adaptation as a belfry obscured its original function. See *Archaeology of Roman Britain*, p. 66.

46 Charles the Great (742–815), king of France and Holy Roman Emperor.

47 Presumably the chronicler Reginon, abbot of Prum in the Eifel, who died in 915.

48 The name survives in Boulogne in the 'Rue de la Tour d'Ordre'. This pharos was 200 feet high. *Archaeology of Roman Britain*, p. 66.

49 The former English name for Boulogne. Leland (*L.T.S.* IV, 64, 65) calls it Boleyn. The surnames Bullen and Boleyn originally meant 'man of Boulogne'.

50 For a view of Dover harbour in the time of Henry VIII see G. M. Trevelyan, *Illustrated Social History* I, 1949, pl. 157.

39 Hubert de Burgh (d. 1243) was chief justiciar of England from 1215. As custodian (Constable, according to Leland, *L.T.S.* IV, 54) of the Castle he defended it against Louis the Dauphin in 1216 and was created Earl of Kent in 1227. *Lamb.*, pp. 140–41.

40 Literally, 'as many knights as foot-soldiers'.

41 On castle-guard and its commutation for money payment see *Oxf. Hist.* III, 18. Leland (*L.T.S.* IV, 64): 'The knight service of castellegarde in Dover Castle was institutid about King John's tyme.' But this is too late.

42 Philip II Augustus (1180–1223) conquered Normandy, Anjou and Poitou in campaigns waged during

51 See *The England of Elizabeth*, p. 207 and reference there.

52 The immediate cause of the severing of the land-bridge was a change in the relative levels of land and sea. See p. 65 where Camden mentions that 'as antiently the sea thereabouts spreading itself very wide forms a large bay, it was obliged to be confined within straiter bounds': he may have been thinking of the bay existing before the sea broke through the land-link.

53 C. Julius Solinus (fl. c. A.D. 200) was the author of a short but unreliable geographical treatise, *Collectanea Rerum Memorabilium*, 'Remarks from various sources on noteworthy things'.

54 Cornelius Tacitus (b. circa A.D. 55) held high office in Rome and the provinces. In 77 he married the daughter of Agricola whose biography he wrote in 98. This work is significant in the history of Britain in that Agricola had been its governor. The *Germania*, also of A.D. 98, is a study of the German tribes, including those which were ancestral to the Angles, Saxons and Jutes. The *Agricola* and *Germania* have appeared as a Penguin Classic (*On Britain and Germany*).

55 Ammianus Marcellinus wrote a history of the Roman Empire covering the period from A.D. 96 to 378. Only the sections from the year 353 survive. The second reference is to Robert Ainsworth (1660–1743), antiquarian and lexicographer who compiled a Latin–English dictionary published in 1736.

56 Grattius Faliscus, a contemporary of Ovid (n. 63 opposite), is known only for a poem on hunting.

57 Now in English 'The Strait of Dover'.

The Old Church in Dover Castle, with the pharos at the West end, in 1758, engraved by Godfrey after Francis Grose

expended a great sum of money for its repair,[51] and the parliament laid a tax for seven years on every English ship that imported and exported goods.

This coast is separated from the continent of Europe by a strait where some suppose the sea forced its way through the land.[52] Solinus[b] calls it *Fretum Gallicum*, Tacitus[c] and Ammianus[d] *Fretum Oceani* and *Oceanum fretalem*; the poet Gratius,[e]

> *Freta Morinum dubio refluentia ponto;*
>
> The Morine strait, uncertain in its tide;

the Dutch *Dehofden*, from the two points, we the *Strait of Calleis*,[57] the French *Pas de Callais*. This is the place of which a poet of the present age says,

> *gemini qua janua ponti*
> *Faucibus angustis, lateque frementibus undis,*
> *Gallorum Anglorumque vetat concurrere terras.*
>
> Of either sea the gate,
> Where the waves echo in the narrow strait,
> And France and England's shoars eternal distance keep.

b. [Left blank by Gough.][53]   c. [Left blank by Gough.][54]
d. I do not find this in Ammianus; Ainsworth quotes him for *fretalis* without pointing out the place.[55]   e. I. 174.[56]

Marcellinus truly says, "this strait is subject to dreadful storms, and presently resumes the smoothest and most level surface, like a plain field having two tides both of ebb and flood between two risings of the moon."[f] For when the moon is in the meridian, and then again below the opposite horizon, the ocean is here uncommonly turbulent, and so great a body of water breaks with such noise on the shore, that the poet Lucan,[g] not without reason, said,

> *Rhutupinaque littora fervent.*
>
> And shores Rhutupian boil.

and S. Paulinus,* speaking of the country of the Morini,[61] which he calls "the extremity of the world," says "the ocean rages with barbarous waves."

Here arises a question worthy the consideration of any learned and ingenious man who has leisure, whether in place of this strait which now parts France from Britain was once an isthmus uniting the two kingdoms, and afterwards being torn asunder by the general deluge, or the violence of the waves, or an earthquake, gave passage to the water.[62] That the face of the globe has been greatly altered by the flood, by length of time, and other causes, and that islands by earthquakes or by the retreat of the waters have been united to the continent, is disputed by none: and on the other hand nothing is more certain, from the most credible authors than that by earthquakes and the inroads of the sea islands have been torn from the continent. Whence Pythagoras in Ovid[h]:

> *Vidi ego quod quondam fuerat solidissima tellus*
> *Esse fretum; vidi factas ex æquore terras.*
>
> The face of places and their forms decay,
> And that is solid earth that once was sea;
> Seas in their turn retreating from the shore,
> Make solid land what ocean was before.   Dryden.

Strabo,[i] inferring what may happen from what has happened, concludes that isthmus's have been and may be cut through. "You see, says Seneca,[k] whole countries torn from their foundations and places that stood on the edge of the sea, removed across it: you see the separation of cities and nations, when part of Nature rises of itself, or a great storm drives in

f. XXVII. 8.[58]   g. VI. 67.[59]   *Epist. 2 ad Victricium.[60]
h. Met. XV. 262.[63]   i. I. 59.[64]   k. Nat. Quæst. VI. c. 29.[65]

58 On Ammianus Marcellinus see n. 55.

59 Marcus Annaeus Lucanus (A.D. 39–65) was author of the heroic poem in 10 books entitled *Pharsalia*, whose subject is the rivalry between Julius Caesar and Pompey. There is a translation by Robert Graves in the Penguin Classics.

60 The second letter to Victricius, written by Paulinus of Nola (A.D. 353–431). His surviving works include 51 letters.

61 In Julius Caesar's time this tribe was in occupation of much of the territory now called the Pas de Calais.

62 Britain has been separated from the Continent more than once, but the final breaking through of the sea to form the Strait of Dover occurred perhaps between 7000 and 6000 B.C. or even later. See F. E. Zeuner, *Dating the Past*, 3rd ed., 1952, pp. 100–101. *Lamb.*, p. 11, cites Twine (p. 69, n. 44) on the subject of the former existence of a land bridge.

63 Publius Ovidius Naso (43 B.C.–A.D. 18), one of the greatest of Roman poets, is perhaps remembered best for the *Metamorphoses*, which is a re-telling in verse of tales from ancient mythology. See the translation by Mary Innes in the Penguin Classics.

64 Strabo (c. 64 B.C.–c. A.D. 24), of Pontus in Asia Minor, was a historical geographer and also a traveller.

65 *Natural Questions* by Seneca (c. 4 B.C.–A.D. 65) concerns natural phenomena and was used in the Middle Ages as a text-book of natural science.

71

66 *resecta*, 'cut off'; *rejecta*, 'cast off'.

67 The *Aeneid*, bk III, l. 415f.

68 Christopher Pitt's translation of the *Aeneid* was published in 1740.

69 Pliny's *Natural History*, bk 1, §88. On Pliny see p. 12, n. 98.

70 Eubœa or Negroponte is the largest of the Aegean islands and is situated off the south-eastern coast of Greece opposite Boeotia on the mainland. The two are separated by a narrow channel.

71 The small island of Besbicos is in the Sea of Marmora about 12 miles off the nearest point of the coast of Bithynia in Asia Minor.

72 Claudius Claudianus (d. c. A.D. 408), the last of the Roman classical poets, enjoyed the patronage of Stilıcho (d. A.D. 408), a Vandal, who became an outstanding general and statesman.

73 Servius was a Latin grammarian and commentator on Virgil of c. A.D. 400. Camden's statement in his introduction (Gough edn, p. 1) states: 'Servius says, "Britain was antiently joined to the Continent." '

74 He is not mentioned in the usual books of reference, but his opinions are unimportant in this context.

75 On John Twine see p. 69, n. 44.

76 On W. Somner see p. 7, n. 65. Richard Verstegan or Rowlands (c. 1550–c. 1640) in his *Restitution of Decayed Intelligence: In antiquities. Concerning the most notable and renowned English nation* of 1605 also speaks of this land bridge and may have been another of Camden's sources for this theory. See *Late Tudor and Early Stuart Geography*, pp. 91–2.

77 John Wallis (1616–1703), Fellow of the Royal Society and polymath.

the sea, whose force, as derived from the whole body, is wonderful. For though it rages only in part it is with the violence of the whole world. Thus the sea has torn Spain from Africa: and thus by an inundation recorded by the greatest poets Sicily has been cut off[1] from Italy. Whence Virgil[m]

Hæc loca vi quondam & vasta convulsa ruina
(Tantum ævi longinqua valet mutare vetustas)
Dissiluisse ferunt, cum protinus utraque tellus
Una foret, venit medio vi pontus, & undis
Hesperium Siculo latus abscidit, arvaque & urbes
Littore diductas angusto interluit astu.

That realm of old a ruin huge was rent
In length of ages from the continent;
With force convulsive burst the isle away;
Through the dread opening broke the thundering sea:
At once the thundering sea Sicilia tore,
And sunder'd from the fair Hesperian shore;
And still the neighbouring coasts the town divides,
With scanty channels and contracted tides.   Pitt.[68]

Pliny[n] also informs us that Cyprus was torn from Syria, Eubæa from Bæotia,[70] Besbicus from Bithynia,[71] having all been part of the respective continents. But none of the antients mention such a separation of Britain from the continent. Those lines indeed of Virgil and others of Claudian,[72] with the conjecture of Servius mentioned in the introduction to this work,[73] insinuate as much. But Dominicus Marius Niger,[74] the learned John Twine,[75] and the author, whoever he was, that applied these lines about Sicily to Britain, are of this opinion.[o]

Britannia quondam
Gallorum pars una fuit, sed pontus & æstus
Mutavere situm; rupit confinia Nereus
Victor, & abscissos interluit æquore montes.

l. *resecta*. Some copies read *rejecta*.[66]   m. En. III. 415.[67]   n. I. 88.[69]
o. Of the same opinion are Mr Somner[76] and Dr Wallis.[77] Phil. Trans. 275. 275. 376. See Chartham. G.[78]

This is a reference to contributions he made to the Philosophical Transactions of the Royal Society which began to be published in 1665. On Wallis see *English Literature in the Earlier Seventeenth Century*, pp. 269f., 603.

78 This note of Gibson's refers to Chartham, Kent. In his additions to Camden, retained by Gough, is a reference to discoveries at the place indicating, as it was then thought, that the Stour valley was once an arm of the sea.

Britain was once to antient Gallia join'd,
But sever'd since by rage of sea and wind:
Victorious Nereus[79] by his furious shocks
Has burst the bound, and laves the sever'd rocks.

Since therefore we have here no historical authority to proceed upon, the learned by comparing the similar appearances in such kind of straits, in order to trace out the truth have proposed these and the like particulars to be more maturely considered.

Whether the soil is the same on both coasts? This is the case here, both coasts rising with bold cliffs of the same materials and colour in the narrowest part as if they had been forced asunder.[80]

What is the breadth of the strait? It is certain these straits are not much wider than that at Gibraltar or Sicily, about twenty-four miles; so that at first sight one would suspect the land was parted by the furious tides of the ocean that now beat on both sides. For I dare not suppose it subsided by an earthquake, such shocks being very uncommon in our northern latitudes, and never very violent.[81]

What is the depth? As that of the Sicilian strait is 80 paces, ours is scarce 25 fathom, though the sea on both sides is much deeper.[82]

What is the bottom, sandy, gravelly, or clayey, and are there many shoals in the strait? Sailors know of but one,[p] and that always the same in the middle of the channel which at low water is scarce three fathom deep.[83]

Lastly; has any place on either shore its name in the antient language from *tearing asunder*, *division*, *separation*, or the like, as *Rhegium*,[84] in the Sicilian strait from the Greek *Ρηγνυμι*, *to break*, because there by the violence of the waves Sicily was broken off from Italy? I can think of none unless we suppose *Witsan*[85] on the French coast has its name from *Gwith*, a British word for separation.[q]

Those who suppose Britain joined to Gaul after the general deluge argue from the circumstance of wolves being formerly

p. Frowen shoal. Not in any modern chart. G.

q. Against this it may be urged, that the Saxons called this place 'Whitsand' from its *White sand*, discerned as we may suppose from the coast of Kent, and that the meaning of the name should rather be sought for in the lesser division than the greater, as the name of Sicily was given to Trinacria and not to Italy. G.   How then came *Rhegium*?[84]

79 *Nereus* was the old man of the sea and father of the fifty *Nereides*, the sea-nymphs.

80 See *The Weald*, p. 22, fig. 5, for a sketch-map of the extent of the Wealden formation. It stretches south-eastwards from the Pas de Calais to far beyond Paris.

81 The immediate cause of the severing of the land-bridge was a change in the relative levels of land and sea.

82 The greatest depth in the Strait of Dover is between 20 and 30 fathoms. The phrase 'on both sides' must mean to the north-east and south-west.

83 On a line almost due south from Dover to Le Tréport there are now six shoals at 5 fathoms or less deep. There are three smaller ones immediately west of this line.

84 Rhegium is modern Reggio. Camden's argument assumes that the language in use at the time of the separation is still in use or still recognizable. This is not true for England.

85 Wissant, Pas de Calais, is in a region settled by Saxons during the migration period. The name was given by people on the Gaulish side of the Strait and is paralleled by other local place-names of Germanic origin, such as Hardinghem and Maninghem, comparable with our place-names in -ingham; Bonningues (-ingas); Landrethun and Baincthun (-ton); Clenleu (-ley) and others, Saxon or Frankish. The form *Gwith* or *Guith* is cited by Camden (Gough edn, p. 123) as one used 'by the Britans' for the (Isle of) Wight and he gives the meaning as 'separation'. The form comes from Nennius (p. 5, n. 53) and the meaning is not accepted by modern scholars. See e.g. *Orig. E.P.N.*, p. 71, or *Lang. & Hist.*, p. 409.

86 It is said that the last wolf was killed in England in C15.

87 Augustine of Hippo (345–430), *The City of God*, which provided the doctrinal basis for the teaching of Luther and Calvin.

88 'Repair' here means 'to maintain and increase'.

89 The sense here seems to be that the various kinds of animals in the ark symbolized the various nations in the Church.

90 This may well be so. *Moridunum* (Carmarthen) meant 'sea fort' (*Lang. & Hist.*, p. 225), though it must be said that it was situated some twelve miles from the open sea.

91 *Portus Itius*, later known as *Gesoriacum*, was the harbour of Boulogne (*Brit.*, p. 31). It was formerly believed that *Portus Itius* was on the site of later Wissant. *Bononia* was an alternative name for *Gesoriacum*, it seems; and it was the Latin name for Bologna in Italy.

92 *The Gallic War*, v, 2: '[he] ordered all the ships to be assembled at Portus Itius, the starting-point for the crossing to Britain, a run of about 30 miles'.

93 Michel de l'Hospital (1507–73) became Chancellor of France in 1560.

94 'Small market town'.

95 In 1347. Calais, 'Though a small town...had strong natural defences...; its ramparts were solid.' *Oxf. Hist.* v, 136.

96 See n. 85 on previous page.

97 Cap Gris-Nez, literally 'Cape Grey-Nose'. The 'ness' of Blackness is a word related to 'nose'. See *Elements* II, 49.

74

as common among us[86] as now in Scotland and Ireland. How, say they, could they come into islands when all animals, except those in the ark, perished, unless the land had been contiguous long after, and there had been no islands. This difficulty perplexed St. Austin,[r] who observes upon it: "It may be supposed wolves and other animals swam over to the islands that were nearest as deer do every year from Italy to Sicily to feed. But some are so far from land that it seems impossible for any beast to reach them by swimming. If men caught them alive, and brought them over, this seems very consistent with a fondness for the chace: though it cannot be denied but they might be conveyed over by angels by the divine command or permission. If they sprung from the earth as at first when God said, Let the earth bring forth living creatures, it will more clearly appear that there were in the ark all kinds of animals, not only to repair[88] the several species, but to figure out the various nations as an emblem of the church,[s] if the earth has produced many animals in islands to which they could not get." Thus he. Nor could any person have expressed himself more clearly or elegantly on the subject. It is enough for me to have proposed it: let the reader consider it at his leisure: and he that comes nearest the truth in this question will seem to me the most enlightened and sagacious.

On the opposite continent were the MORINI, so called in the antient Celtic language from their maritime situation,[90] q.d. *dwellers on the sea*. Their country is now called *Contè de Guisnes* and *Contè de Bolonois*, and had antiently two places of considerable note, GESSORIACUM and ITIUM,[91] from which last Cæsar says is the best passage from Gaul to Britain,[92] and many suppose it to have been where now is *Calais*; but the great and learned chancellor of France, L'Hospital,[93] well versed in matters of antiquity, asserts that Calais is a place of no great antiquity, and was only a small village such as the French call *Bourgade*,[94] till Philip earl of Bologne enclosed it with walls not many years before the English took it.[95] Nor will you any where find that any persons crossed from thence into Britain before that time.[t] We must, therefore, I think, look for *Itius* elsewhere, namely at *Witsan*, which we called *Whitsan*,[96] a name not very remote from *Itium*, lower down near Blackness.[97] At this place it appears by our historians all who went

r. De Civit. Dei xvi. 7.[87]   s. Propter sacramentum ecclesiæ.[89]

t. See also Le Febure; Hist. de Calais I. 105–107 & 646.

from Britain landed, insomuch that Louis le Jeune king of France[98] when he went on pilgrimage to Thomas of Canterbury humbly besought that saint that no person might be shipwrecked between Dover and Witsan, as if this was the best passage at the time; nor is the strait so narrow any where else: though it is to be presumed the persons who crossed did not regard the shortness of the passage,[99] but the convenience of the harbours on each coast. Thus though the strait is narrowest between *Blackness* in France and the *Nesse*[01] in England, they now cross between Dover and Calais, and in former ages before Vitsan harbor was blocked up, between it and Dover; and before that between *Rhutupiæ* and *Gessoriacum*,[02] whence the emperor Claudius, and the other generals already mentioned, crossed over into Britan. Pliny[u] seems to call this Gessoriacum *"the British port of the Morini,"*[04] perhaps from the passage from it to Britain. Ptolemy,[05] in whom it has crept in instead of Itium, *Gessoriacum navale*, in which sense the Britans call it *Bowling Long*.[06] For I will maintain against Boethius the Scot[07] and Turnebus[08] that *Gessoriacum* was the maritime town which Ammianus[09] calls *Bononia*, the French *Bolongue*, the Dutch *Beunen*, and we *Bolen*; on the authority of Rhenanus,[10] who had seen the antient Peutinger table[11] since published by Velser, in which stands *Gessoriacum, quod nunc Bononia*,[12] as well as from the distance in the Itinerary which exactly answers to that in Antoninus[13] between the *Ambiani*[14] and *Gessoriacum*. But what is of greatest weight, the Panegyric[15] addressed to Constantius Augustus[16] says that the army of pirates under Carausius were besieged and reduced in *Gessoriacum*,[17] and the other addressed to Constantine the

u. N.H. IV. ad fin. Cellar. Γεσσοριακον επινειον. – Γησοριακ, Terræ fines. See Chiflet de portu Iccio, p. 13. MS. n. G. Hence Somner pronounces *Gessoriacum* or Bologne the place whence Cæsar sailed. G.[03]

98 Louis VII (1137–80). He made the pilgrimage to Canterbury in 1179.

99 About 21 miles direct.

01 Presumably the slight headland, less eroded in Camden's day, now called Shakespeare's Cliff. It is the only local promontory that could properly be termed a 'ness'.

02 Richborough and Boulogne.

03 N.H. refers to Pliny's *Natural History*. The rest of Gibson's note has no relevance to English topography.

04 A tribe in occupation of the coast round Boulogne in Caesar's day. See n. 90 opposite.

05 On Ptolemy see p. 43, n. 71.

06 This sounds like the anglicization of a foreign name in Tudor times comparable with Wipers (Ypres), Eatapples (Étaples) and Hellfire (Halfaya) in C20.

07 Hector Boece (1465?–1536). His Latin *History of Scotland* was translated into English by William Harrison for inclusion in Holinshed's *Chronicles*, published in 1578.

08 Adrien Tournebu (1512–65), a French philologist.

09 On Ammianus Marcellinus see p. 4, n. 42, and n. 12 below.

10 Beatus Rhenanus on whom see p. 56, n. 92.

11 For the Peutinger Table see p. 18, n. 66.

12 In fact, the Peutinger scribe (probably of C13, but copying an original MS of C4) erred and wrote *Gesogiaco quod nunc Bononia xviiii*, as is clearly apparent in the photograph of the relevant part of the Table in *Antiquity* I, facing p. 189.

13 There is confusion here, for the *Itinerary* and *Antoninus* are the same work. See p. 28, n. 46.

14 The *Ambiani* was one of the Belgic tribes settled near the mouth of the river Somme. Amiens takes its name from them.

15 Twelve of these Latin Panegyrics survive, four of them from the time of Constantine. See *XII Panegyrici Latini*, ed. R. A. B. Mynors, 1964.

16 Constantius I Chlorus, Emperor (A.D. 305–6). At the very end of C3 A.D. he restored Britain to the Empire by defeating rebels who had seized control in Britain. A commemorative medal was struck in his honour as *Redditor Lucis Aeternae*, 'restorer of the eternal light' (of Roman civilization). See *Brit.*, p. 339f.

17 See *Oxf. Hist.* I, 276–7 for the background to these events.

18 Presumably an edition of the *Panegyrici* published at Basel, the classical *Basilia*.

19 *Sic.*

20 See p. 74, n. 95.

21 Calais fell to the French in 1557. See *Oxf. Hist.* VII, 558, for details. This should mean that it was in English possession for 210 years.

22 On Gibson and Holland see Appendix.

23 Folkestone. Two Roman buildings were excavated on the Warren in 1924, the coins recovered extending to A.D. 353. Besides these, separate groups of cremation and inhumation burials are known and another possible Roman building. See *Roman Folkestone*, and pl. VIII of *Arch. Kent.*

24 Gildas was probably referring to the Forts of the Saxon Shore (see p. 60, n. 39), the nearest of which were at Dover to the east and Lympne to the west; but there is no evidence for one at Folkestone. Theodosius the younger, Emperor of the East from A.D. 378 to 395, was not the builder of these forts, but most probably Carausius (287–93). See *Brit.*, p. 189. Some of these forts were built earlier in C3. Ibid., p. 184–5. On modern Folkestone, see *B. of E., E. Kent*, p. 309f.

25 Eadbald's accession in 616 imperilled the conversion of Kent to Christianity (Bede, *H.E.* II, 5) by his persisting in heathen practices. He was later converted by a miracle (II, 6). Eanswith died in 640. Her relics, discovered in the parish church in C19, are still preserved there. Leland has several references to this nunnery. He cites (*L.T.S.* V, 205), from the Latin of Gervase of Canterbury, a passage describing Eanswith's choice of a remote spot by the sea where she built a church and domestic offices for the nunnery. By his own day all had disappeared through marine erosion. Elsewhere (ibid., IV, 64) he says:

Great his son says they were routed at *Bononia*,* so that *Bononia* and *Gessoriacum* must be one and the same town, and the older name seems to have been grown into disuse about that time. For we can hardly suppose such authors addressing themselves to such princes, could have mistaken this place so lately make [19] remarkable. But what have I to do with France? I was induced to mention these places as the valor of our ancestors so often distinguished itself on this coast, when they took Calais and Bologne from the French,[20] restoring the latter on their earnest solicitation eight years after for a sum of money, and having held the former 212 years [21] in spite of all the efforts of France. I return now with the tide[x] to Britain.

From Dover the chalk cliffs run on in one continued ridge for five miles to *Folkstone*, a place of consequence antiently, as appears by the Roman coins daily found there, but under what name is uncertain.[23] It was probably one of those towers which the Romans "erected at intervals" according to Gildas "on the south coast of Britain along the shore to guard the coast" against the Saxons under Theodosius the younger.[24] It was eminent among the Saxons on a religious account, for the nunnery founded by Eanswida, daughter of Eadbald king of Kent.[25] At present it is a small village, the greatest part being carried off by the sea. It was however the barony[y] of the family of *Abrincis*,[27] from whom it came to Hamo de *Crevequer*,[28]

*Edit. Basil, p. 272. & 251.[18]

x. *secundo æstu*, omitted by Gibson. with full sails and a favourable tide. Holland.[22]

y. Dugd. I. 467.[26]

The towne shore be al lykelihod is mervelusly sore wasted with the violens of the se; yn so much that there they say that one paroche chyrch of Our Lady, and a nother of S. Paule ys clene destroyed and etin by the se. Hard upon the shore ys a place cawled the Castel Yarde, the which on the one side is dyked, and ther yn be great ruines of a solenne old nunnery, yn the walles wherof yn divers places apere gret and long Briton [Roman] brikes; and on the right hond of the quier a grave trunce [*trusse*, 'formed of'?] squared stone. The castel yard hath bene a place of great burial; yn so much as wher the se hath woren on the banke bones apere half stykyng owt. The paroch chyrch is therby, made also of sum newer worke of an abbay. Ther is

S. Eanswide buried, and a late therby was a visage [semblance] of a priory. He notes (IV, 55), also from Gervase, that Canute gave back the vill of Folkestone, with its appurtenances, to the church of Canterbury. See also *Lamb.*, p. 151f.

26 William Dugdale, *Baronage of England*, vol. I, p. 467.

27 The best-known member of this family was Hugh of Avranches, Earl of Chester, who died in 1101. He contributed 60 ships to the invasion of 1066 and was rewarded with lands in 20 shires. He endowed the monastery of St Werburgh at Chester and was the conqueror of

Saltwood Castle, engraved by D. Lerpiniere after Francis Grose

and by his daughter to John de *Sandwich*,[29] whose son John's daughter Juliana brought it in dower to John de *Segrave*.[30]

The shore turns to the west near *Saltwood*, a castle of the archbishops of Canterbury, which archbishop William Courtenay enlarged;[31] and *Ostenhanger*,[32] where Edward baron *Poinings*,[33] father of a numerous illegitimate race,[34] began a noble house.[35] Four miles off is *Hith*,[36] one of the

north Wales and Anglesey. *Lamb.*, p.154. Gough in his *Additions* (p.246) speaks of a castle 'rebuilt by William de Abrincis about 1068'. The place close to the church called 'The Bail' (Leland's 'Castel Yarde etc.', n.25 opposite) is no doubt its site. To the north of the town (at NG 213380) is Castle Hill with an excavated Norman castle earthwork, possibly somewhat later in the period. Gough, however, presumably meant Hugh d'Avranches, for William d'Avranches was the founder of the present parish church in 1138.

28 The Crèvecoeurs were also at Leeds, Kent. See p.20 n.90. Hugh de Crèvecoeur was appointed in 1235 as one of the two *Custodes* ('wardens', but not quite in the

later sense) of the Cinque Ports. *Cinque Ports*, p.79.

29 Perhaps a member of the family which included Thomas, seneschal of Ponthieu, and the brothers Henry (d.1273) and Ralph (d.1308?). Henry was Bishop of London; Ralph held several important offices, including that of Constable of the Tower and Warden of London.

30 John de Segrave came of a distinguished family most active in C13 and early C14. See *Oxf. Hist.* IV, 332, 707–11. The unnamed tomb with a recumbent effigy of a knight placed against the north wall of the chancel of the parish church almost certainly commemorates the Sir John de Segrave who died in 1343. For a description of the tomb see *B. of E., E. Kent*, p.310.

31 Saltwood Castle was granted to the Archbishop in John's reign. Archbishop Courtenay (1381–96), to whom the indent of a brass survives in Maidstone parish church, made it his chief residence; the gatehouse is his main surviving work. An earthquake in 1580 severely damaged much of the fabric, which was well restored in late C19. Leland (*L.T.S.* IV, 65) adds: '. . . at this day Hithe is but a chapel perteining to Saltwood parish'; and (ibid., p.55) he quotes the *Chronicle of Christ Church Canterbury* to the effect that Halfden, one of Canute's nobles, gave Saltwood to Christ Church. See *Lamb.*, p.162f., and *B. of E., E. Kent*, p.425f.

32 Westenhanger in its modern spelling represents an irregular development from either Old English *ōster*, 'hillock' or possibly from *eowestre*, 'sheepfold'. The word '-hanger' means 'wood on a steep hillside'. Leland (*L.T.S.* IV, 44) speaks of 'Ostinghaungre . . . now corruptely caullid Westenanger'. Camden's spelling is therefore nearer to the original than the modern form. See *Elements* II, 56; I, 233; and *P.N. Kent*, pp.428–9.

33 Sir Edward Poynings (1459–1521), Lord Deputy of Ireland, Comptroller of the Royal Household and Warden of the Cinque Ports. Leland (*L.T.S.* IV, 44) says: 'Ostinghaungre was Creals lordship. Poynings a late hald it. The King hath it now.' The castle, begun in 1343, had four towers on its curtain wall and a gatehouse. What remains of it is a splendid ruin. *B. of E., E. Kent*, pp.473–4.

34 Of them, Thomas alone achieved distinction, especially in the military expedition to France in 1544. He was made a baron in 1545, the year of his death.

35 This early C16 house was much damaged in 1701. *B. of E., E. Kent*, p.473.

36 Hythe retains some scraps of its former individuality, especially in its old nucleus near the fine parish church. The town had been founded by 1086. If Camden's view be accepted, that Hythe throve on the decline of West Hythe, the process is paralleled by the emergence of New Romney as Old Romney declined. See *New Towns*, p. 457. Leland (*L.T.S.* IV, 64–5):

Hithe hath bene a very great towne yn lenght, and conteyned iiii. paroches that now be clene destroied, that is to say S. Nicolas paroche, our Lady paroch, S. Michael's paroche, and our Lady of Westhithe.... And yt may be well supposed that after the haven of Lymme, and the great old town ther fayled, that Hithe strayte therby encresed and was yn price [enhanced in prosperity]. Finally to cownt for Westhyve to the place wher the substans of the towne ys now ys ii. good myles yn lenght, al along on the shore to the which the se cam ful sumtyme, but now by bankinge of woose [silt, mud] and great casting up of shyngel the se ys sumtyme a quarter, sumtyme *dim.* [half] a myle fro the old shore. In the tyme of King Edward the 2. there were burned by casuelte [accident] xviii. score howses and mo [more], and strayt folowed great pestilens, and thes ii. thinges minished the towne. Ther remayne yet the ruines of the chyrches and chyrch yardes. It evidently apereth that wher the paroch chirch is now was sumtyme a fayr abbay. Yn the quire be fayre and many pylers of marble, and under the quier a very fair vaute, also a faire old dore of stone, by the which religius folkes cam yn [to the church] at mydnight. In the top of the chirch yard is a fayr spring, and therby ruines of howses of office of the abbey; and not far of was an hospital of a gentilman infected with lepre.

See also *Lamb.*, p. 159f.; *B. of E., E. Kent*, p. 344f.

37 In the time of Edward I it was required to contribute five ships towards the 57 from all the Cinque Ports. A charter of Henry II to Hythe, dated January 1155–6, survives. See *Cinque Ports*, pp. 242, 233.

Ostenhanger House, engraved by Godfrey after Francis Grose

cinque ports,[37] whence its name, which signifies a port or station:[38] though at present it can hardly maintain that name against the heaps of sand which shut out the sea for a great way.[39] Nor is it long since it was very considerable by the decline of *West Hythe*, a little neighbouring town to the west,[40] which was a harbour till the sea withdrew itself two centuries ago.[z] It owes its origin, as well as West Hythe, to the adjoining

z. *proavorum memoria.*[41]

38 The Old English word *hȳth* meant 'port, haven, landing-place'. Leland (*L.T.S.* IV, 65):

The havyn is a prety rode [anchorage], and liith [lies] meatly strayt [conveniently opposite] for passage owt of Boleyn [Boulogne]. Yt croketh yn [curves inland] so by the shore a long, and is so bakked fro the mayn [open] se with casting of shinggil, that smaul shippes may cum up a larg myle toward Folkestan as yn a sure gut [safe narrow channel].

39 On marine deposition at Hythe see *Coastline*, p. 318f. The site of its harbour is now about a third of a mile from the sea.

40 The second 'it' refers to Hythe and the meaning seems to be that

Hythe became 'very considerable' as a port because of the decline of West Hythe. The idea comes from Leland (n. 36 above). The word 'town' is not here used in its modern sense, but means roughly 'a community'. West Hythe was a limb of the Cinque Port of Hythe. See *Cinque Ports*, pp. 242, 233. Leland (*L.T.S.* IV, 46) says:

Mastar Twyne [p.69, n.44] saythe that this ('Holde Hithe alias West Hithe') was the towne that was burnid alonge on the shore, where the ruines of the churche yet remayne.

It remains a ruin to this day. *B. of E., W. Kent*, p. 574.

41 Within the recollection of our great-grandfathers (or ancestors).

78

Lyme Castle, with the ruins of Stutfall Castle, below,
engraved by T. Morris after Francis Grose

little village of *Lime*,[42] formerly a very famous harbour, till the
sands thrown up by the sea choked it up.[43] Antoninus[44] and
the Notitia[45] call it PORTUS LEMANIS, Ptolemy[46] *ΛΙΜΗΝ*,
which being a significative word in Greek the copyists to supply
a supposed omission wrote *Καινος λιμην*,[47] and the Latin translators rendered *Novus portus*: whereas the name of the place
was *Limen* or *Leman*, as now *Lime*. The commander of a company of Turnacenses was stationed here under the count of the
Saxon shore.[48] A military road paved with stones runs hence
to Canterbury, easily known to be a Roman work,[49] as also the
neighbouring castle called *Stutfall*[50] inclosing about ten acres
on the slope of a hill, and fragments of the walls remain built
of British bricks, flints, and chalk, with sand and pebbles inter-
mixt, so strong as to have still resisted time.[51] At present

44 The *Antonine Itinerary*, on which
see p. 28, n. 46.

45 The *Notitia Dignitatum*, on which
see p. 4, n. 35.

46 On Ptolemy see p. 43, n. 71.

47 'New port'. The frequent
English place-name Newport meant
either 'new (market) town' or 'new
harbour'. *Elements* II, 70–71, *port*[1]
and *port*[2]. Some towns of this name,
e.g. in Bucks., Essex and Salop, are
far inland and could not have had
harbours.

48 The *Turnacences* were originally
recruited as auxiliary troops for the
Roman army from the district round
Tournai (*Turnacum*). The office of
the Count of the Saxon Shore was
not established before early C4 and
was reorganized at the end of that
century. The Count had command
of a mixed force of troops and
sailors based on the Forts of the
Saxon Shore. See p. 60, n. 39.
 It was their function to intercept
raiders at sea or, if they eluded the
naval patrols, to engage them on
land. See *Roman Britain*, pp. 61–3.

49 Although this Roman road,
later known as the Stone Street, is
overlaid by modern metalling for
most of its length, its characteristics
are unmistakably Roman. See
Roman Roads in Britain I, 35–6; *Lamb.*,
pp. 166–7. Leland (*L.T.S.* IV, 66):

Ther went fro Lymme to Cantorbury a
streate fayr paved, wherof at this day yt
is cawled Stony Streat. Yt is the
straytest that ever I sawe, and toward
Cantorbury ward the pavement
continually appereth a iiii. or v. myles.

50 From Old English *stōdfald*,
'horse enclosure'. *P.N. Kent*, p. 467.

51 The walls and bastions are very
fragmentary, long since tumbled by
landslips. Much material, flints,
stone and Roman bricks, was no
doubt taken from the ruins to build
the Norman church and fortified
house at the top of the steep slope.

42 Lympne is in origin a British
river-name applied to a locality
with the meaning 'place of elms'
(*Lemanis*). *English Place-Names*, p. 35.

43 That it was a naval harbour in
Roman times is certain, for tiles
stamped CL. BR. (*Classis Britannica*,
'British fleet') were found there in
C19, together with an altar dedicated
by a naval commander. *Arch. Kent*,
pp. 190–94, plan p. 188. There may

well have been a civil settlement and
a port before the Roman fort was
built and continuing alongside it.
Leland (*L.T.S.* IV, 65):

Lymme Hill or Lyme was sumtyme a
famose haven, and good for shyppes
that myght [were able to] cum to the
foote of the hille.... The place ys yet
cawled Shypwey and Old Haven.
 Of sum yt is cawlled the old rode
[anchorage]. Ibid., p. 49.

though it is not a harbour it retains no small shadow of its former dignity; for here at *Shipway* the warden of the ports takes a solemn oath when he enters on his office, and here courts are held on certain days to determine controversies among the inhabitants of the ports.[52]

Some have supposed that a great river here emptied itself into the sea, because some writers have mentioned the river *Leman*[53] and the mouth of the *Leman*, where the Danish fleet anchored A.D. 892.[54] But I suspect they are mistaken in the description of the place, both because here is no river except a very small one, which dwindles away as soon as it makes its appearance, and because the archdeacon of Huntingdon, a writer of strict veracity, says[a] this fleet came to the *Portus Lemanis*,[56] and has not a word of the *River*. Unless we should suppose, which is more than I take upon me to do, that the river *Rother*, which falls into the sea below Rhie,[57] ran down hither, and has gradually changed its course[58] as that marshy plain *Rumney marsh* landed up.[59] This level tract reaching

a. Henry of Hunt. V. p. 201.[55]

For a reference see p. 79 n. 43 and see *B. of E., W. Kent*, p. 379. Leland (*L.T.S.* IV, 65–6):

Ther remayneth at this day the ruines of a stronge fortresse of the Britons hangging on the hil, and cummyng down to the very fote. The cumpase of the forteresse semeth to be x. acres, and be lykelyhod yt had sum walle beside [in addition] that strecchid up to the very top of the hille, wher now ys the paroch chirche and the archidiacon's howse of Cantorbury. The old walles of the [blank] made of Britons brikes, very large and great flynt set togyther almost indissolubely with morters made of smaule pybble. The walles be very thikke, and yn the west end of the castel appereth the base of an old towre. Abowt this castel yn tyme of mind were fownd antiquites of mony [money] of the Romaynes.

See also *Lamb.*, p. 166. For a plan of the fort see *Archaeology of Roman Britain*, p. 50.

52 On the growth and functions of the Shipway Court see *Cinque Ports*, chap. V, p. 60f. This place-name meant 'sheep-way', that is, a drove-way for sheep brought up from Romney Marsh. For the etymology see *Elements* II, 101, 249. *Lamb.*, p. 165f. Leland (*L.T.S.* IV, 65):

Lymme Hille or Lyme was sumtyme a famose haven, and good for shyppes that myght cum to the foote of the hille. The old castel of Lyme longed to Richard Knight of Hyve [Hythe] late decesid. The place ys yet cawled Shypwey and Old Haven. Farther at this day the Lord of the v. Portes [Cinque Ports] kepeth his principal cowrt a lytle by est fro Lymmehil.

53 See p. 79, n. 42.

54 The *Anglo-Saxon Chronicle*, MS 'A', under the year 893 reads:

In this year [correctly 892] the great army [of Danes] went... westward to Boulogne and there were [so well] provided with ships that they crossed over in one voyage with their horses and all and then came up into the mouth of the Limen with 250 ships. This estuary is in east Kent... [and] the river of

which we spoke before flows out from the forest [the Weald]. They dragged their ships up the river as far as the forest, four miles up from the river mouth and there destroyed a fortress within the fen.

Recent investigations make it probable that this fortress, hitherto unidentified, is represented by the earthwork now called Castle Toll at Newenden (NG 853284) (see *Med. Arch.* XIII, 84, n. 3; VIII, 74f.). It appears to be a Norman motte-and-bailey castle superimposed on a Saxon defensive work. It might well be the lost Saxon *burh* of *Eorpeburnan* listed in the Burghal Hidage. See a sketch-plan of the site in *Earthwork of England*, p. 419.

55 Henry of Huntingdon (1084?–1155) wrote a *History of the English* in Latin carrying the narrative down to the year of his death. His work is perfunctory and much inferior to that of William of Malmesbury (p. 3, n. 33).

56 This port was on the river. In any case, Henry of Huntingdon is so much later (he died in 1155) as an authority that he cannot be preferred to a contemporary chronicler.

57 Rye, in east Sussex.

58 This is no doubt the true explanation. The Royal Military Canal of early C19 follows the old course of the river, at least for much of the way.

59 That is, 'became land'. The process was a combination of silting by the river and marine deposition, forming Romney Marsh. See *Coastline*, p. 318f.; Jessup, *S.E. England*, p. 22; *Lamb.*, p. 180. Leland (*L.T.S.* IV, 67) gives the dimensions of the Marsh as about ten miles by five and goes on:

The marsch of Rumney encresith dayly in breede [breadth] . . . It is mervelus rank [rich] grownd for fedyng of catel, by the reason that the gresse groweth so plentefully upon the wose [mud, silt] sumtyme cast up ther by the se.

from Lime[60] 14 miles long by eight broad, having two towns,[61] 19 parishes, and about 44200 acres,[62] whose luxurious verdure is excellently adapted for fattening cattle,[63] has by the bounty of the sea been by degrees added to the land. So that I may not without reason call it the Gift of the Sea, as Herodotus[b] calls Egypt the Gift of the Nile, and a very learned man[c] the pastures of Holland the Gifts of Boreas[66] and the Rhine. For the sea to make amends for what is has swallowed up in other places of this coast, has restored it here by retreating, or by bringing up mud from time to time, so that several places which two centuries[d] ago stood on the sea are now a mile or two from it. None but those who have seen it can believe how rich the soil is, what great herds of cattle it feeds, which are driven here to fatten from the furthest part of England, or with what art it is embanked against the sea.[68] For the better government of it Edward IV. made it a corporation consisting of a bailiff, jurors, and commoners.[69] In the Saxon times the inhabitants of this tract were called 'Merscware',[70] *Marshmen*, a name perfectly suiting the place. I do not understand that antient writer Ethelwald,[e] when he says that "Cinulph king of Mercia[72] ravaged Kent, and the country called *Mersc warum*," and elsewhere[f] "that an officer named Herbyth was beheaded by the Danes in the placed called *Merscwarum*;"[74] if he does not mean this marshy little tract. *Rumney* or *Romeney*, antiently *Romenal*,[75] which some, from its name, think a work of the

b. II. 5.[64]

c. Peter Nannius of Alcmar, a learned painter, schoolmaster, and canon of Arras. His writings are Dialogues between illustrious women, and translations of various authors. Hoffm. Lex.[65]

d. *avorum memoria*.[67] e. III. 478.a.[71] f. III. 478.b. A.D. 839.[73]

60 Lympne. See p. 79, n. 42.

61 New Romney and Lydd.

62 43,821 acres according to Bartholomew's *Gazetteer of the British Isles. Lamb.*, p. 180, says 24,000 acres.

63 This is equally true today. 'The Romney Marsh pastures, perhaps the most intensively stocked in the world....' *The Weald*, p. 240. The Marsh feeds sheep mainly.

64 Herodotus (c. 484–c. 420 B.C.) was a Greek historian and a great traveller. His *History*, in nine books, was intended to give a full account of the struggle between Asia and Europe ending with the invasion of Greece by Xerxes.

65 The reference here is to Hoffman's *Lexicon*.

66 The north wind.

67 Within the memory of our grandfathers (or forefathers).

68 The Rhee and Dymchurch Walls are ancient and a Roman origin has been suggested for them. Traces of Roman occupation have been found at Lydd and Dymchurch. For the Roman coastline in this region see *Hist. Geog. Eng.*, fig. 9, p. 39.

69 There is an extant charter of the corporation of 1253 which indicates that it had a still earlier history. It was largely concerned with land drainage, but the corporation of c. 1462 mentioned by Camden had judicial functions also. *Lamb.*, pp. 181–2.

70 The *Merscware* are known from two references in the *Anglo-Saxon Chronicle*: MS 'E' 796 (correctly 798) when *Ceolwulf* (correctly *Cænwulf*) King of the Mercians, harried the men of Kent as far as (or including) the Marshdwellers; and in 838 (correctly 841) when *Herebryht*, alderman (of Mercia) was slain by the heathen men (the Danish army) in the territory of the Marshdwellers. The latter reference may, however, be to the men of the Lincolnshire marshes. See *Parker Chronicle*, p. 19. For a charter reference to them see *K.P.N.*, pp. 55–6.

71 Æthelweard (d. 998), alderman of Wessex beyond Selwood, translated the *Chronicle* into execrable Latin. It was edited by Savile in 1596 and was probably well known to Camden, though not perhaps in time for his earlier editions of the *Britannia* unless he saw Savile's work in MS or the MS of Æthelweard's Chronicle. See *Oxf. Hist.* II, 455.

72 See n. 70 above.

73 See n. 70 above.

74 See n. 70 above.

75 New Romney takes its name from Old Romney. The final syllable -ey is from Old English *ēa*, 'a river'; the first element is doubtful. See *Dic.*, p. 373; *P.N. Kent*, pp. 485–6. The 'curious fact that a priest named Romanus... was once

Romans, is the principal town of this tract, and one of the cinque ports, of which *Old Romney*[76] and *Lid*[77] are accounted members, which were bound jointly to furnish five[78] ships of war in the manner afore cited. It stands on a high hill[79] of sand and gravel, and had before the sea withdrew itself a very spacious harbour to the west defended from most winds. The inhabitants, as appears in the Conqueror's survey,[g] "were, on account of their serving at sea, exempt from all custom but robbery, breach of peace and forstel."[h] At that time it was very considerable, being divided into twelve wards, and having five parish churches, a priory and an hospital.[82] In the time of Edward I. the sea driven by violent winds overwhelmed this tract and made great havock of men, cattle, and buildings,[83] and having destroyed the little populous village of *Promhill*,[84] changed the channel of the Rother,[85] which here emptied itself into the sea and filled up its mouth, making it a new and shorter course by *Rhie*:[86] so that it gradually deserted this town, which

g. P. 11.b.[80]   h. *forestalling*. Spelman.[81]

owner of land in Lydd', need be no more than a curious coincidence. The forms *Romenal* (1247) or *Romenel* (1086, 1130) have an unetymological 'l' as a result of Anglo-Norman linguistic influence. See Zachrisson in *E.P.N.S.*, *Introduction to the Survey*..., pt I, p. 113, §6. OE *Rumenea* would normally have become *Romene(e)* or -*ei* or -*ey* in C13 and C14. Winchelsea was written *Winchensel* in a number of documents of C12 and early C13. *P.N. Sussex* II, 537–8, and p. 52, n. 12, *Sussex*.

76 Old Romney is little more than a church and a few scattered cottages in a quiet pastoral setting. *B. of E., W. Kent*, pp. 423–4. 'The port of Old Romney was silted up even before the Norman Conquest', *New Towns*, p. 459.

77 Besides Old Romney and Lydd, Romney had as its members Denge Marsh (south-east of Lydd), Orlestone and Broomhill (see n. 84 below and *Cinque Ports*, p. 245). Of these only New Romney and Lydd survive with more than a handful of population.

78 A document of 1359, confirming one of late C13, states that four ships were due from Romney and Old Romney and one from Lydd. *Cinque Ports*, pp. 242, 725. Leland (*L.T.S.* IV, 67) says:
Rumeney is one of the v. portes, and hath bene a metely good haven, yn so much that withyn remembrance of men shyppes have cum hard up to the towne, and cast ancres yn one of the chyrch yardes. The se is now a ii. myles fro the towne, so sore therby now decayed that where ther wher iii. great paroches and chirches sumtyme, is now scant one wel may(n)teined.... The very towne of Rumeney, and a ii. myles abowt yt, was always by lykelyhod dry land, and ons [once], as yt is supposed, the se cam abowte hyt, or at the lest abowt the greatest part of yt.

The town of New Romney had been established by 960. On its history and topography see *New Towns*,

p. 459; *Med. Eng.*, pp. 188–90 and figs. 77A, 77B.

79 It is very doubtful whether Camden saw the place for himself. There is no 'high hill' here.

80 The Domesday Book, folio 11b.

81 There may be some confusion here between OE *for(e)steall*, 'an interception, waylaying or ambush', which is the sense required in Domesday Book, and *forstelan*, 'to steal'. Spelman is thinking of a later meaning of *forsteall*, that of 'buying up goods in order to corner the market and secure a higher price' or 'pre-emption'. Sir Henry Spelman (1564?–1641) published a Glossary of obsolete Latin and Old English terms in 2 volumes (1626, 1664) as well as *Councils of the Church* and *Tenures of Knight Service*. Camden knew him as a fellow-member of the Society of Antiquaries.

82 There were two parish churches, St Martin and St Laurence, besides the surviving fine church of St

Nicholas, which is mainly Norman and 'Decorated' of later C14. It must have been in this churchyard that ships cast anchor, as it is beside the former quay. Before the Dissolution, there were two small religious houses and a hospital for lepers. *B. of E., W. Kent*, p. 415f.

83 See Winchelsea, *Sussex*, p. 61, n. 95. The storms of 1287 seem to have been the most destructive. On the changes in coastline see *Coastline*, p. 318f.

84 The name Promhill perhaps goes back to Old English *prūme*, 'a plum' (*Elements* II, 73), with the addition of 'hill'. Already in C13 it was being called *Bromehell*, -*hill*, but *Promehill al Bromehill* occurs as late as mid C17 (*P.N. Sussex*, p. 529). There is no village remaining, but the parish name survives on the map as Broomhill (NG 980190).

85 On the river Rother see *Sussex*, p. 65, n. 18.

86 On Rye see *Sussex*, p. 64, n. 13.

from that time declined, and lost much of its antient populousness and dignity.

Below this the land runs out a great way east, which we call *Ness*,[87] q.d. *Nose*,[88] on which stands *Lid*,[89] a pretty populous place since the inhabitants of Promhill removed to it after that inundation. On the extremity of the point which we call *Dengenesse*, where is nothing but gravel and pebbles, grows plentifully Holm oak[90] with its evergreen prickly leaves like a low forest for above a mile. Among the pebbles near *Stonend*[91] is an heap of larger stones, which the neighbours call the tomb of the saints Crispin and Crispinian, who they pretend were shipwreckt here, and called to heaven.[92] The shore retiring from hence runs strait west, producing pease[93] among the pebbles which spring up spontaneously in large clusters,[h] and differ little in taste from field pease, to the mouth of the Rother which divides Kent and Sussex.

Its course from this last county we have briefly followed above. In its Kentish course it has *Newenden*, which I am almost apt to believe is the long sought-for harbour which the Notitia calls ANDERIDA, the Britans *Caer Andred*, the Saxons 'Andredsceaster':[94] first, because the inhabitants affirm it to have been a very antient town and harbour:[95] next, because of its

h. [*sic*] See in Sussex.

87 Dungeness. On its geological history see *The Weald*, pp. 103–5 and diagram p. 104. *Lamb.*, p. 183.

88 The Kentish and Mercian dialects of Old English had *ness* as against *næss* in West Saxon and some Anglian dialects. The OE word for 'nose' was *nesu*, *nasu*, or *nosu*, all closely related to *næss*. Leland (*L.T.S.* IV, 67) says:

In the mydde way (or ther abowt) betwixt Rumney town and Lyd the marsh land beginneth to nesse and arme [to project like a crooked arm] yn to the se, and contynueth a pretty way beyond Lydd, and runnyng ynto a poynt yt standeth as an arme, a foreland, or a nesse.

Denge remains the name of the Marsh.

89 Lydd, which

is countid as a parte of Rumeney, is a 2. myles beyond Rumeney town, and is a market. The town is of a prety quantite, and the townesch men use botes to the se, the which at this tyme is a myle of. The hole town is conteyned yn one paroche, but that is very large. (*L.T.S.* IV, 67.)

The Saxon church of Lydd had more in common with the Romano-British church at Silchester than with the Saxon churches of Kent. See *Journ. British Archaeological Association*, XXII, 1959; and *B. of E., W. Kent*, p. 374f., for church and town.

90 This is almost certainly an error. The Holm Oak (*Quercus ilex*) is said to have been introduced from the Mediterranean region only in 1580 (*Royal Horticultural Society Dictionary of Gardening*, IV, 2nd edn, 1956, p. 1728), but 'holm-oak', as a word, is recorded from 1552 (*S.O.E.D.*). Leland (*L.T.S.* IV, 67) observes that

Ther is a place beyond Lydde, wher as a great number of holme trees groueth apon a bank of baches [pebbles] throwen up by the se, and there they bat [beat for] fowle and kil many birdes.

The word 'holm' could be used of holm-oak or of holly in C16 (*Etym. Dic.*, p. 445), but Leland, followed incorrectly by Camden, is surely referring to stunted holly, for holm-oak could hardly survive in the poor soil and gale-swept conditions of Dungeness. However, Tansley in his *British Islands and their Vegetation* II, 891, does not include holly among the scrub growing there, yet the place-name Holmstone, shown on Speed's map of 1612, on a tract of shingle, may suggest that Leland's observation was not at fault. Artillery ranges now make the area inaccessible. The sea holly (*Eryngium maritimum*), up to 2 feet high, cannot be meant.

91 Speed's *Map of Kent* of 1612 shows this place to have been at about NG 080230, somewhere near the modern Greatstone.

92 Traditionally these were Roman brothers who migrated to Soissons to preach Christianity and lived there as shoemakers. They were put to death by the Emperor Maximian (286–305) and became the patron saints of shoemakers. Cp. Shakespeare's *Henry V*, IV, iii, 40f.

93 Probably *Lathyrus japonicus* (syn. *L. maritimus*), the Sea Pea, now found in Britain only on south-eastern shingle beaches. It is said to have saved Suffolk people in mid-C16 from starvation in time of famine. J. Hutchinson, *More Common Wild Flowers*, 1948, pp. 54–5.

94 Newenden was not *Anderitum*. See p. 52, n. 12, *Sussex*.

95 *Lamb.*, pp. 189, 190, says much the same: '…at, or neare Newendene, as it is thought, there stood sometime a Citie, called… Andredes Chester…'

96 The Weald (which name itself means 'forest'). *Lamb.*, p. 189f.

97 A most unlikely etymology in this region.

98 A Roman fort near Caernarvon.

99 This may possibly mean 'Selebeorht's swine-pasture (*denn*)' (*P.N. Kent*, p. 346), though the personal name seems to be otherwise unrecorded. This place-name will not bear Camden's implication. *Lamb.*, p. 37, has Selbritendene.

01 On the *Notitia Dignitatum* see p. 4, n. 35.

02 The forms with 't' are correct: the letters 'c' and 't' were easily confused by scribes. On this name and the Albuci see *Arch. Journ.* XCVII, 136–7.

03 On Gale see p. 28, n. 39.

04 The *Anglo-Saxon Chronicle* under the year 491 records that 'Ælle and Cissa besieged Andredesceaster and slew all the Britons occupying it'. Far from their utterly destroying the Roman fort, much survives even today. See p. 53, n. 17, *Sussex*.

05 Much of this is mere embroidery on the plain fabric of the traditions recorded in the earliest source, the *Chronicle*.

06 This friary was founded at Lossenham in 1241 in the reign of Henry III. No buildings remain. *B. of E., W. Kent*, p. 414. See *Lamb.*, p. 188.

07 He is not apparently otherwise noteworthy. The family name became Aucher. There are brasses of early C16 at Rainham and Otterden, Kent. Otterden Place was their main residence in mid C16. *B. of E., W. Kent*, pp. 448, 397–8. Sir Anthony Aucher was 'one of the principal recipients in Kent of Henry VIII's largesse after the dissolution of the monasteries' (ibid., p. 398).

08 Early forms of this place-name show that it could not have meant

situation on the forest of *Andredswald*[96] to which it gives name: lastly, because the Saxons seem to have called it *Brittenden* or the *Britons valley*[97] (as they did also *Segontium*[98] before described) whence the whole adjoining hundred has the name of *Selbrittenden*.[99] The Romans to defend this coast against the Saxon pirates, placed here a company of the *Abulci* with their officer.[i] Afterwards the Saxons utterly destroyed it:[04] for Hengist when he determined to drive the Britans entirely out of Kent, and thought it necessary for this purpose to increase his forces, sent for Ella out of Germany with a large body of Saxons who violently assaulting this Anderida, the Britans who lay in ambush in the neighbouring wood so harrast them, that when at last after great loss on both sides, they divided their forces and routed the Britans in the woods, and at the same time assailed the town, the barbarians breathed such a spirit of vengeance that they put all the inhabitants to the sword and razed the place.[05] "It was shewn in this desolate state for many ages" says Henry of Huntingdon,[k] till under Edward I. certain Carmelite friars lately come from Carmel in Palestine, and seeking solitary places erected a monastery here[06] at the expence of Sir Thomas Albuger,[07] and a town presently sprung up, which with respect to the antient ruined one was called *Newenden*, q.d. *New town in the valley*.[08] The river Rother dividing its streams lower down surrounds the grassey isle of *Oxney*,[09] and near its mouth stands *Apuldore*,[10] where a swarm of Danish and Norman pirates, which

i. The Notitia[01] mentions *Andereciani milites. Anderetiani & Andereniciani*,[02] sect. 40, 64, 65. ed. Labbe. Gale MS. n.[03]

k. [Left blank by Gough.]

'new town...', but most probably 'new swine-pasture (*denn*)'. Camden has confused *denn* with *denu*, 'a valley'. See *Dic.*, p. 324. On the place see *B. of E., W. Kent*, p. 414.

09 Leland (*L.T.S.* IV, 63):

To Oxney feri over from Kent to it, and on the farther ripe [bank] in Oxeney is a village. Yet parte of Oxeney in Kent, and part in Southsax. Sum say that it is or hath bene al in Southsax. Sum caulle it Forsworen Kent, by cause that were [*sic*] the inhabitantes of it were of Southsax they revoltid to have the privileges of Kent.

The Isle of Oxney is now entirely in Kent. Leland (IV, 68) adds:

Oxoney Isle is toward [nearly] a x. myles yn cumpace [circumference], and ys cumpassed abowt with salt water excepte where yt is devided by the fresch water fro the Continent.

10 Appledore is now nearly seven miles from the mouth of the Rother. On the village see *B. of E., W. Kent*, pp. 126–7. Leland (*L.T.S.* IV, 68) records that

Appledor (of sum is contid as a membre of Rumeney) ys yn Kent a market

under Hastings had infested the French coast, landed laden with booty, and built a castle; but by the valor of king Alfred were compelled to sue for peace.[11]

Near it in the woodland are *Cranbrook, Tenterden, Benenden,*[12] and other neighbouring towns, in which the woollen manufacture first flourished from the time of Edward III. who by premiums and many privileges invited the Flemings into England in his 10th year to teach our people that manufacture, which now is deservedly accounted one of the pillars of the state.[13]

To recite now the earls of Kent in their order, omitting the Saxon ones, *Godwin,*[14] and others who were not earls by inheritance but by office: *Odo*[15] own[l] brother to William I. is reckoned the first earl of Kent of Norman descent. He was also bishop of Bayeux, a man of a bad and restless disposition, always busy in raising disturbances, whence after that violent rebellion of his stirring up he was stript of his estates and property in England[17] by his nephew Rufus.[m] Afterwards when the usurper Stephen endeavoured to attach the soldiery to his interest by favours, he bestowed that honour on *William of Ipres*[19] a Fleming,[n] that insupportable burthen[o] on Kent, as Fitz-Stephens[22] calls him, who was by Henry II. forced to leave it with tears.[p] The son of Henry II. whom his father had crowned king,[24] for the same reason when he was forming

l. *uterinus frater*; brother by the mother's side. G.[16]

m. He died in Normandy A.D. 1096.[18]   n. A.D. 1141.[20]

o. *violentus Cantii incubator,* Fitz Steph. p. 13, ed. Sparke. *over-pressor.* Holland.[21]

p. He died a monk at Laon in Flanders 1162. Meyer ap. Dugd. I. 612.[23]

worthy of attention than the better-known 'sights' of Kent. See *B. of E., W. Kent,* pp. 234–7, 540–44, 146–8. *Lamb.* ignores these places; Leland (*L.T.S.* IV, 62) mentions Cranbrook and Tenterden, but adds nothing significant.

13 See *Oxf. Hist.* V, 366–8. By Gibson's time the industry was already 'much decayed'.

14 Godwine (d. 1053,) earl of the West Saxons and father of King Harold. See p. 31, n. 25, *Sussex.*

15 Odo (d. 1097) on whom see p. 30, n. 62.

16 Gibson, on whom see Appendix.

17 In 1082. See *Oxf. Hist.* II, 608 and notes.

18 See n. 15 above and the reference there.

19 William of Ypres (d. 1165?) was not Earl of Kent though he held much land there. See p. 64, n. 10, *Sussex.* Henry II, for reasons of policy, was rather more lenient than Camden suggests, for he allowed William to retain his Kentish estates until 1157. *Oxf. Hist.* III, 321.

20 See n. 22 below.

21 'The violent oppressor of Kent'. On FitzStephen see next note. Joseph Sparke(s) edited FitzStephen's *Life of Becket* in 1723 with other sources of medieval history. On Holland see Appendix.

22 William FitzStephen (d. 1190?) was an early biographer of Becket, having been present at his murder. See pp. 47–8, nn. 09, 10.

23 On Dugdale see p. 17, n. 50.

24 Henry 'the young king' (1155–83) was the second son of Henry II. Refused a grant of lands, he turned traitor and betook himself to the court of France in 1172 after his second coronation at Winchester. He was not reconciled with his father until 1174. *Oxf. Hist.* III, 332f.

town, and hath a goodly church riding [?] yn Kent, and our Lady of Ebny yn Oxeneye. ... Fro Appledor to the mayne se or pudle [*sic*] vi. myle.

11 This is from the *Anglo-Saxon Chronicle* under the year 893 (correctly 892). The earthwork ('castle') has not been identified unless it be that at Kenardington two miles away. But it is now so slight a work that a search for it in pouring rain gave no sight of it, although it is marked on the O.S. One-Inch Map. Leland (*L.T.S.* IV, 56) cites Asser, but see p. 80, n. 54;

Lamb., pp. 184–5 who relies on the *Chronicle*; and *Med. Arch.* XVI, 123f, where it is suggested that the site is at Castle Toll (NG 853284).

12 Cranbrook, Tenterden and Benenden, with other small towns and villages in this part of the Weald of Kent, are all worthy of a visit by the modern antiquary. If he will follow the by-ways and the back streets, as well as savouring the main streets, he will be well rewarded with much architecture of a simple unaffected kind and no less

25 William de Ypres was a grandson of Robert I, Count of Flanders and son of Philip Count of Ypres. On Dugdale see p. 17, n. 50.

26 Gervase of Canterbury (fl. 1188), a monk of Christ Church, whose works (ed. W. Stubbs, 2 vols., 1879, 1880) include a chronicle of the reigns of Stephen, Henry II and Richard I, a history of the arch-bishops of Canterbury and a Canterbury chronicle (1100–99). *Inter X Script.* is a reference to Sir Henry Savile's *Rerum Anglicarum Scriptores post Bedam* of 1596. It is not to be confused with Roger Twysden's *Historiae Anglicanae Scriptores Decem* of 1652. Camden himself, in 1603, published a collection of chronicles including those of Asser, Thomas Walsingham, Giraldus Cambrensis and William of Jumièges. This collection was entitled *Anglica, Hibernica, Normannica, Cambrica a veteribus scripta*.

27 Leland (*L.T.S.* IV, 55) quotes from chronicles of the library of St Peter's in Cornhill, London, to the effect that 'Henry the king, son of Henry II, gave the whole of Kent with the castles of Dover and Rochester to Philip, Count of Flanders.' Leland himself adds: 'but Philip never had possession of them'.

28 Hubert de Burgh (d. 1243) successfully defended Dover Castle against the French in 1216 and was created Earl of Kent in 1227. On his character and administration as justiciar see *Oxf. Hist.* IV, 23f., 39f. On his fall from the king's favour see ibid., p. 45f. See also p. 69, n. 39.

29 In 1226/7. See previous note.

30 Stow, in his *Survey of London*, p. 391, suggests that Hubert died either at Banstead or Berkhamsted, Herts.

31 According to Stow (ibid., p. 303) the Black Friars had their house in Holborn from 1221 to 1276. On Dugdale see p. 17, n. 50.

designs against his father, bestowed this additional title on *Philip earl of Flanders*;[q] but this man was earl of Kent only by title and promise. For as Gervase Dorobornensis[r] expresses it, "Philip earl of Flanders promised all the assistance in his power to the young king, doing homage to him with oath: to whom for his service the king promised with all Kent a revenue of £.1000. and Rochester and Dover castles."[27] Not long after, *Hubert de Berg*[28] for his eminent services to the state received as the reward of his own desert the same honour from Henry III.[s] He was a true lover of his country, and in all the storms of his adverse fortune discharged fully all the duties that the state can require from the best of subjects. He died[t] divested of his honour,[u] which remained dormant till the reign of Edward II. That king in his 15th year[32] conferred it on his younger brother *Edmund of Wodstock*,[33] who having the care of his nephew Edward III. fell under the storm of false and unjust envy, and was beheaded[x] for expressing an unreserved brotherly affection to his deposed brother, and attempting to rescue him from his confinement, not knowing he was made away.[35] His two sons *Edmund*[y] and *John*[z] succeeded however in their turn, and dying without issue,[37] their sister who survived them, and was called for her beauty *the fair maid of Kent*,[38] conveyed it to the knightly family of *Holand*; for Thomas Holand her husband[39] was called earl of Kent,[a]

q. Query, if the father of William de Ipre. Dugd. I. 611.[25]

r. Inter X Script. 1424.[26]   s. 11 Henry III.[29]

t. At Bansted, Surrey,[30] 1243, and was buried in the Black friars church, Holborn. Dugd. I. 699.[31]

u. Dugdale says only of his high posts, (I. 696,) but his son John did not succeed to the title. Ib. 700.   x. 4 Edward III.[34]

y. He was restored 4 Edward III. and died in his minority soon after. Dugd. II. 94.   z. He died 26 Edw. III. Ib.[36]

a. in her right 34 Edw. III.[40] and died the same year. Ib. 73.

32 In 1321/2.

33 Edmund (1301–30) was the youngest of Edward I's sons. He held the Wardenship of the Cinque Ports.

34 In 1330.

35 On this plot by Edward II's widow and Roger de Mortimer in 1330 see *Oxf. Hist.* V, 100.

36 In 1352.

37 In 1352.

38 Joan (1328–85) married as her second husband the Black Prince in 1361.

39 Sir Thomas Holland (d. 1360) was an eminent soldier and one of the original Knights of the Garter.

40 In 1360.

and was succeeded in that honour by his son *Thomas*,[41] who died 20 Richard II.[42] and was succeeded by his two sons, *Thomas*, created duke of Surrey,[b] and soon after beheaded[c] for plotting against king Henry IV. and after him *Edmund* High admiral of England, who died of a wound received 1408 at the siege of St. Brien in Bretagne.[d] With these the title becoming extinct for a time, and the estate being divided between their sisters, Edward IV. conferred it first on *William Nevill* lord *Fauconberg*,[e] and after his death upon *Edmund Grey*[f] lord *Hastings, Weisford* and *Ruthyn*, who was succeeded by his son *George*.[g] He had by his first wife Anne *Widevile, Richard* earl of Kent, who died[h] without issue, having spent his estate. By his second wife Catharine, daughter of William Herbert earl of Pembroke,[51] he had sir Henry *Grey*, knight,[i] whose son Henry's son Reginald was advanced[k] to the earldom of Kent by queen Elizabeth A.D. 1572, and dying without issue was succeeded by his brother Henry, a most accomplished nobleman.

This county has 398 parishes.

b. 21 Rich. II.[43] which honour he was deprived of 1 Hen. IV.[44]
c. At Cirencester 1 Hen. IV.[45]
d. Thomas Walsingham, Ypod. Neust. p. 179. Dugd. II. 77.[46]
e. 1 Edw. IV. He died the same year. Ib. I. 308.[47]
f. 5 Edw. IV. He died 4 Hen. VII. Ib. I. 718.[48]
g. He died 20 Hen. VII. Ib.[49]
h. 15 Hen. VIII. Ib.[50]
i. of Wrest c. Bedford, who by reason of his slender estate declined taking the title, and died 1562. Ib. His son Henry died in his life time. MS. n. of Le Neve. Ib.[52]
k. He reassumed the title and died the same year. Ib.

41 The second Thomas was Richard II's half-brother. He became Earl of Kent in 1381 and was Earl Marshal 1350–55.

42 In 1396/7.

43 In 1397/8.

44 In 1400.

45 See *Oxf. Hist.* VI, 24–5.

46 Edmund Holland, fourth Earl, second son of Sir Thomas (d. 1400). Edmund died at Briant. On Walsingham see p. 63, n. 07, *Sussex*.

47 He was son of the first Earl of Westmoreland and became Earl of Kent in 1460 and died in 1463. The first year of Edward IV's reign lies between March 1461 and March 1462.

48 Created Earl 1465, died 1489.

49 In 1504/5.

50 In 1523/4.

51 The first Earl of the second creation (1501?–70).

52 There were three antiquaries with the name Le Neve, but only Peter (1661–1729) and John (1679–1741) could have added a note to Dugdale's *Baronage*, which was published 1675–6. See p. 24, n. 76, *Surrey*.

APPENDIX

THE ANGLO-SAXON CHRONICLE 'is the most fruitful source for the history of England between Bede and the Norman Conquest'. Seven manuscripts survive, but after the annal for 915 they show much independence of each other. The earlier annals are derived from Bede, from oral traditions, some of which had been preserved in verse, and from brief notices of events in Latin. The assembly of the material began in the late ninth century and the chronicles were continued year by year with the addition of the main events in national or regional history inscribed soon after they had occurred.

MS 'A' The Parker Chronicle, was kept at Winchester in C10 and was transferred to Canterbury in C11. It ends in 1070. It is now Corpus Christi College, Cambridge, MS 173, folios 1–32.

MS 'B' A copy of a lost MS which may have been at Abingdon. The copy was made c. A.D. 1000 and kept at Canterbury, but it was not continued after 977. It is now British Museum, Cotton MS Tiberius A vi, folios 1–34.

MS 'C' Another copy of the lost Abingdon Chronicle, made in mid C11 and continued to 1066. It is now British Museum, Cotton MS Tiberius B i, folios 115–64.

MS 'D' A copy made in mid C11 of a lost chronicle kept in northern England, which had been expanded by matter taken from Bede and other northern sources. The copy was sent to the diocese of Worcester and there continued to 1079. It is now British Museum, Cotton MS Tiberius B iv.

MS 'E' The Laud or Peterborough Chronicle has affinities with 'D'. It was sent to Canterbury and remained there until after 1066. A copy of it was made at Peterborough in about 1122. It was continued until 1154. It is now Bodleian MS Laud 636.

MS 'F' A twelfth-century epitome of 'E', in English and Latin, made at Canterbury after the Conquest. It ends in the middle of the annal for 1058; how much is lost is unknown. It is now British Museum, Cotton MS Domitian A viii.

See *Oxf. Hist.* II, 679–84; G. N. Garmonsway (trans.), *The Anglo-Saxon Chronicle*, 1953; *E.H.D.* I, 109f.; *E.H.D.* II, 107f.; and C. Plummer, *Two of the Saxon Chronicles Parallel*, 2 vols., 1892 and 1899.

THE VENERABLE BEDE (673–735) lived most of his life in the Northumbrian monastery of Jarrow. Among his numerous works, all in Latin, the *Historia Ecclesiastica Gentis Anglorum* (Ecclesiastical History of the English People), finished in 731, stands out as the work of a great scholar. Stenton has said that 'in regard to all the normal substance of history his work can be judged as strictly as any historical writing of any time'. His collection of evidence and critical use of it is essentially modern. See e.g. *Oxf. Hist.* II, 185f.; the translation of 1955 by L. Sherley-Price; and the standard edition of all Bede's historical works: *Venerabilis Baedae Opera Historica*, ed. C. Plummer, 2 vols., 1896.

DOMESDAY BOOK is the record of an agrarian survey made in 1086, 'deliberately planned so as to reveal the territorial basis on which English feudalism rested'. 'As an ordered description of a national economy it is unique among the records of the medieval world.' See *Oxf. Hist.* II, 644f. and references there; and *E.H.D.* II, 198f.

EDMUND GIBSON (1669–1748) was librarian at Lambeth Palace, archdeacon of Surrey, bishop of Lincoln and then of London (1723–48). He declined the archbishopric of Canterbury a year before his death. Among his published works were editions of the *Saxon Chronicle* (1692), of Camden's *Britannia* (1695) and some of Spelman's writings. His *Britannia* appeared when he was only twenty-six years of age, the translation being undertaken by a team of scholars each of whom had local knowledge of the shire allotted to him. As editor he revised and collated their contributions. Their work has a directness and strength of idiom characteristic of the English language of the time, but, as Gough was to find, they were not always accurate in their renderings of Camden's Latin. The work has been republished in facsimile in 1971.

RICHARD GOUGH (1735–1809) made antiquarian excursions through the English shires over a period of twenty years. Most noteworthy among his publications is the translation of Camden's *Britannia* (1789) incorporating most of what was worthy of preservation from the editions of Holland and Gibson, and with lengthy additions of his own. It has been considered the best of the translations and, as a whole, is the truest rendering of Camden's original Latin text.

PHILEMON HOLLAND (1552–1637) qualified in medicine, but is remembered for his translations of Livy (1600), Pliny's *Natural History* (1601), Plutarch, Suetonius, Ammianus Marcellinus and other authors, as well as for his somewhat free rendering of Camden's *Britannia* of 1610. See D. Bush, *English Literature in the Earlier Seventeenth Century*, 1945, pp. 57 and 553.

JOHN LELAND (1506?–52) was the first of the modern English antiquaries. He journeyed round England from about 1535 to 1543, noting antiquities of all kinds with the intention of writing a great work on ancient Britain (*De Antiquitate Britannica*). He was fanatical in his patriotism and in his belief in the truth of Geoffrey of Monmouth's *History of the Kings of Britain*. In 1544 he made a savage attack in print on Polydore Vergil's *Anglica Historica* (1534), which had cast doubt on Geoffrey's accuracy. One of Camden's few acknowledgements to Leland cites the Latin poem *Cygnea Cantio* (1545), which opens with a description of the Thames between Oxford and Greenwich as seen from the river. The *Itinerary*, a record of his travels, survives in a fragmentary state, much of it consisting of hasty jottings in need of revision and some of them repetitive of earlier notes. Intermixed with them are extracts from medieval chronicles that would have provided sources for his history, as the topographical notes would have been the basis of his observations on antiquities. He became insane in 1550 before he could organize his vast mass of materials and write them up. Although he lacked aesthetic sense, he was well endowed with sharp powers of visual awareness and a directness of expression that make his *Itinerary* fascinating to read. Camden used this work very considerably in the *Britannia*, but without acknowledgement. The *Itinerary* was first published in 1710 and again in 1906–7 by L. Toulmin Smith. This edition was reproduced in 1964 and in cheaper format in 1971. For Leland's life and a discussion of his work see the foreword by T. D. Kendrick. His *Collec-*

tanea, which consists of extracts from histories, annals, chronicles, and of genealogical notes and catalogues of manuscripts, was published in 1715. The MS had been available to Camden.

JOHN STOW (1525–1605), a London tailor, was the acquaintance or friend of most of his contemporary antiquaries and his valuable library, like Sir Robert Cotton's, was open to them. Unworldly and industrious in his researches, he experienced great poverty late in life, yet persevered in his main task, *The Survey of London*, published first in 1598 and enlarged in 1603. His earlier publications were of medieval chronicles, including that of the so-called Matthew of Westminster in 1567; the *Chronica Majora* of Matthew Paris in 1571; and the *Historia Anglicana* of Thomas of Walsingham in 1574. The *Survey* was edited in 1908 by C. L. Kingsford with full critical apparatus, and in 1912 by H. B. Wheatley in a cheap edition.

GENERAL BIBLIOGRAPHY

JOURNALS

Antiquity
  I, 1927, 'Ancient Writers on Britain', C.E.Stevens,
    189f.
  XII, 1938, 'Nennius and the Twenty-Eight Cities of
    Britain', K.Jackson, 44f.
  XXXII, 1959
Archaeologia
  XCIII, 1949, 'The British Section of the Ravenna Cos-
    mography', I. A. Richmond and O. G. S. Craw-
    ford
Archaeological Journal
  XCII, 1935, 'Norman Domestic Architecture', M.
    Wood, 167f.
  XCVII, 1940, 'The British Sections of the Notitia Dig-
    nitatum', C.E.Stevens, 125f.
  CV, 1950, Supplement, 'Thirteenth Century Domes-
    tic Architecture in England', M.Wood
  CXII, 1955, 'The Reorganisation of the Defences of
    Romano-British Towns in the Fourth Century',
    P. Corder, 20f.
  CXIX, 1962, 'A Survey of Romano-British Town
    Defences of the Early and Middle Second Cen-
    tury', J. Wacher, 103f.
  CXXIII, 1966, 'Medieval Undercrofts and Town
    Houses', P. A. Faulkner, 120f.
  CXXIV, 1967, 'The Origins of the Castle in England',
    B. K. Davison, 202f.
  CXXVI, 1969, 'The Coastal Defences of the South-
    East', A. D. Saunders, 201f.
  CXXVI, 1969, 'An Historian's Approach to the
    Origins of the Castle in England', R. A. Brown,
    131f.
Archaeological News Letter, 1948–65
Essays and Studies of the English Association
  XIX, 1934, 'English Names and Old English Heathen-
    ism', B.Dickins, 148f.
Journal of Roman Studies
  XXXVIII, 1948, 'On some Romano-British Place-
    Names', K.Jackson, 54f.

Medieval Archaeology
  II, 1958, 'Medieval Inquisitions and the Archaeolo-
    gist', M. Beresford, 171f.
  V, 1961, 'Soldiers and Settlers in Britain, fourth to
    fifth century . . .', S. C. Hawkes and G. C. Dunn-
    ing, 1f.
  VI–VII, 1962–3, 'Medieval English town-house plans',
    W. Pantin, 202f.
  VIII, 1964, 'The Unidentified Forts of the Burghal
    Hidage', N. Brooks, 74f.
  XIII, 1969, 'The Burghal Hidage: The Establishment
    of a Text', D. Hill, 84f.
  XIV, 1970, 'The Later Pre-Conquest Boroughs and
    their Defences', G. A. Ralegh Radford, 83f.
Proceedings of the British Academy
  1935, 'Laurence Nowell and the Discovery of Eng-
    land in Tudor Times', R. Flower, 47f.
  1951, 'William Camden and the Britannia', S.
    Piggott, 199f.

BOOKS AND MAPS

*Abbeys: An Introduction to the Religious Houses of England
  and Wales*, R. Gilyard-Beer, 1959
Ancient Burial-Mounds of England, The, L. V. Grinsell,
  2nd edn, 1953
Anglo-Saxon Charters, P. H. Sawyer, 1968
Anglo-Saxon Chronicle, The, G. N. Garmonsway (trans.),
  1953
Archaeology and Place-Names and History, F. T. Wain-
  wright, 1962
Archaeology in the Field, O. G. S. Crawford, 1952
Archaeology of Roman Britain, The, R. G. Collingwood
  and I. A. Richmond, 2nd edn, 1969
Archaeology of South-East England, An, G. J. Copley,
  1958
Archaeology of Wessex, The, L. V. Grinsell, 1958
Architecture in Britain, 1530–1830, J. Summerson, re-
  vised edn, 1955
Asser's Life of King Alfred, W. H. Stevenson (ed.), 1904

Atlas of Tudor England and Wales, An (from John Speed's Pocket Atlas of 1627), E. G. R. Taylor, 1951

Bayeux Tapestry, The, E. Maclagan, 1943

Bede, His Life and Writings, A. Hamilton Thompson (ed.), 1935: 'Bede as Historian', W. Levison

Beginnings of English Society, The, D. Whitelock, 1952

Black Death, The, P. Ziegler, 1969

Brass Rubbings (Victoria and Albert Museum), M. Clayton, 1968

Britannia, a History of Roman Britain, S. Frere, 1967

British Antiquity, T. D. Kendrick, 1950

British Islands and their Vegetation, The, A. G. Tansley, 2 vols., revised edn, 1949

British Plants and their Uses, H. L. Edlin, 1951

Buildings of England, The, N. Pevsner (ed.), 1951–74. Complete in forty-six volumes. Page references are to first editions.

Cambridge History of English Literature, Vol. I: 'From the Beginnings to the Cycles of Romance', A. W. Ward and A. R. Waller (eds.), 1949

Castles: An Introduction to the Castles of England and Wales, B. H. St J. O'Neil, 1953

Catalogue of Manuscripts containing Anglo-Saxon, N. R. Ker, 1957

Chronica Majora, Matthew Paris (H. R. Luard ed.), 7 vols., 1872–84

Chronicles, J. Froissart (G. Brereton sel., ed., trans.), 1968

Chronicles and Annals, R. L. Poole, 1926

Chronicon ex Chronicis, Florence of Worcester (B. Thorpe ed.), 2 vols., 1848–9

Chronicon Monasterii de Abingdon, J. Stevenson (ed.), 2 vols., 1858

Coastline of England and Wales, The, J. A. Steers, 1946

Complete Atlas of the British Isles (Reader's Digest), n.d.

Concise Oxford Dictionary of English Place-Names, The, E. Ekwall, 2nd edn, 1940

Conquest of Gaul, The, Caesar (S. A. Handford trans.), 1951

Conquest of Wessex in the Sixth Century, The, G. J. Copley, 1954

Crawford Collection of Early Charters and Documents, W. H. Stevenson and A. S. Napier (eds.), 1895

Dark Age Britain, D. B. Harden (ed.), 1956: 'The Jutes of Kent', C. F. C. Hawkes; 'Romano-Saxon Pottery', J. N. L. Myres; 'Coinage in Britain in the Fifth and Sixth Centuries', C. H. V. Sutherland

Description of England, The, W. Harrison (G. Edelen ed.), 1969

Development of the Castle in England and Wales, The, F. M. Stenton, 1933

Dictionary of National Biography: The Beginnings to 1900, 22 vols., 1885–1900

Domesday Book and Beyond, F. Maitland, 1897

Domesday Geography of South-East England, The, H. C. Darby and E. M. J. Campbell (eds.), 1962

Earthwork of England, A. H. Allcroft, 1908

Ecclesiastical History of the English People, The, Bede (C. Plummer ed.), 2 vols., 1896

England in the Late Middle Ages, A. R. Myers, 1952

England of Elizabeth, The, A. L. Rowse, 1950

English Abbey, The, H. Crossley, 2nd edn, 1939

English Church Monuments (1510–1840), K. A. Esdaile, 1946

English Coins, G. C. Brooke, 3rd edn, 1950

English Field Systems, H. L. Gray, 1915

English Historical Documents, Vol. I: c. A.D. 500–1042, D. Whitelock (ed.), 1955: 'The Anglo-Saxon Laws', 327f.; 'Charters', 337f. – Vol. II: 1042–1189, D. C. Douglas and G. W. Greenaway (eds.), 1953 – Vol. III: 1189–1327, H. Rothwell (ed.), 1975

English Hundred-Names, The, O. S. Anderson, 1934

English Hundred-Names, The: The South-Eastern Counties, O. S. Anderson, 1939

English Literature in the Earlier Seventeenth Century, D. Bush, 1945

English Monks and the Suppression of the Monasteries, G. Baskerville, 1937

English Place-Name Elements, A. H. Smith, 2 vols., 1956

English Place-Name Society

Vol. I, pt I: *Introduction to the Survey of English Place-Names*, A. Mawer and F. M. Stenton (eds.), 1933: 'The Celtic Element', E. Ekwall, 15f.; 'The English Element', F. M. Stenton, 36f.; 'The Feudal Element', J. Tait, 115f.; 'The French Element', R. E. Zachrisson, 93f.; 'Personal Names in Place-Names', F. M. Stenton, 165f.; 'Place-Names and Archaeology', O. G. S. Crawford, 143f.

Vol. I, pt II: *The Chief Elements in English Place-Names* superseded by *English Place-Name Elements*, q.v.

Journal 1, 1968–9, to V, 1973.

English Place-Names, K. Cameron, 1961

English Place-Names and Their Origins, G. J. Copley, revised edn, 1971

English Pronouncing Dictionary, D. Jones, 11th ed., 1958

English River-Names, E. Ekwall, 1928

English Scholars, D. C. Douglas, 2nd edn, 1951

English Society in the Early Middle Ages, D. Stenton, 1951

English Wayfaring Life in the Middle Ages, J. J. Jusserand, 4th edn, 1950

Flores Historiarum, Roger of Wendover (H. O. Coxe ed.), 5 vols., 1841–4

Gesta Guillelmi ducis Normannorum et regis Anglorum, William of Poitiers (R. Foreville ed.), 1952

Gesta Normannorum Ducum, William of Jumièges (J. Marx ed.), 1914

Gesta Pontificum Anglorum, William of Malmesbury (N. Hamilton ed.), 1870

Gesta Regum Anglorum and *Historia Novella*, William of Malmesbury (W. Stubbs ed.), 1887–9

Handbook of British Chronology, M. Powicke and E. B. Fryde, 2nd edn, 1961

Handbook of Greek and Latin Palaeography, E. M. Thompson, 1906

Heraldry in England, A. Wagner, 1946

Historia Anglicana, Thomas of Walsingham (H. T. Riley ed.), 2 vols., 1863

Historia Anglorum, Henry of Huntingdon (T. Arnold ed.), 1879

Historia Ecclesiastica, Ordericus Vitalis (A. le Prevost ed.), 1838–55

Historia Minor (Historia Anglorum), Matthew Paris (F. H. Madden ed.), 3 vols., 1866–9

Historia Novorum in Anglia, Eadmer (M. Rule ed.), 1884

Historic Towns and Cities in the British Isles . . . from earliest times to 1800, Vol. I, M. D. Lobel (ed.), 1969

Historical Geography of England before A.D. 1800, An, H. C. Darby (ed.), 1951: 'Camden's England', E. G. R. Taylor; 'Leland's England', E. G. R. Taylor; 'Medieval Trade: Eastern Ports', R. A. Pelham

History of the Anglo-Saxons, A, R. H. Hodgkin, 2 vols., 2nd edn, 1939

History of the English Church and People, Bede (L. Sherley-Price trans.), 1955

History of the Kings of Britain, The, Geoffrey of Monmouth (L. Thorpe trans.), 1966

Introduction to the Use of the Public Records, An, V. H. Galbraith, 1934

Itinerary in England and Wales in or about the Years 1535–1543, John Leland (L. T. Smith ed.), 5 vols., 1964

King John, W. L. Warren, 1961

Language and History in Early Britain, K. Jackson, 1953

Late Tudor and Early Stuart Geography, E. G. R. Taylor, 1934, Appendix of MSS and Printed Books

Laws of the Earliest English Kings, The, F. L. Attenborough (ed.), 1922

Lost Villages of England, The, M. Beresford, 1954

Making of Domesday Book, The, V. H. Galbraith, 1961

Medieval England: an aerial survey, M. Beresford and J. K. S. St Joseph, 1958

Medieval Foundations of England, The, G. O. Sayles, 1964

Methods of Chronology, A. E. Stamp, 1933

Monastic Order in England, The, D. Knowles, 2nd edn, 1966

Monasticon Anglicanum, William Dugdale (J. Caley, H. Ellis, B. Bandinel eds.), 1817–30

Monumental Brasses, J. Mann, 1957

Names of Towns and Cities in Britain, The, W. F. H. Nicolaisen, Margaret Gelling and Melville Richards, 1970

New Towns of the Middle Ages: Town Plantations in England, Wales and Gascony, M. Beresford, 1967

Norman Conquest, The, E. A. Freeman, 6 vols., 1867–79

Norman Conquest, The: Its Setting and Impact, D. Whitelock et al., 1966: 'The Anglo-Saxon Achievement', D. Whitelock; 'The Campaign of 1066', C. H. Lemmon; 'The Effects of the Norman Conquest', F. Barlow; 'William the Conqueror: Duke and King', D. C. Douglas

Normans and the Norman Conquest, The, R. A. Brown, 1969

Old Towns of England, The, C. Rouse, 2nd edn, 1943–4

On Britain and Germany (The Agricola and the Germania), Tacitus (H. Mattingly trans.), 1948

Opera, Simeon of Durham (T. Arnold ed.), 2 vols., 1882, 1885

Ordnance Survey
 Map of Britain in the Dark Ages, 2nd edn, 1954
 Map of Monastic Britain, South Sheet, 2nd edn, 1954
 Map of Roman Britain, 3rd edn, 1956
 Map of Southern Britain in the Iron Age, 1967

Origin of English Place-Names, The, P. H. Reaney, 1960

Origin of the English Nation, The, H. M. Chadwick, 1924

Oxford Companion to English Literature (especially the 'Perpetual Calendar' with English Regnal Years), P. Harvey, 3rd edn, 1936, p. 909f.

Oxford Dictionary of English Etymology, The, C. T. Onions (ed.), 1966

Oxford History of England, G. Clark (ed.), Vol. I: *Roman Britain and the English Settlements*, R. G. Collingwood and J. N. L. Myres, 2nd edn, 1937 – Vol. II: *Anglo-Saxon England*, F. M. Stenton, 1943 – Vol. III: *From Domesday Book to Magna Carta, 1087–1216*, A. L. Poole, 2nd edn, 1955 – Vol. IV: *The Thirteenth Century, 1216–1307*, M. Powicke, 2nd edn, 1962 – Vol.

v: *The Fourteenth Century, 1307–99*, M. McKisack, 1959 – Vol. VI: *The Fifteenth Century, 1399–1485*, E. F. Jacob, 1961 – Vol. VII: *The Earlier Tudors, 1485–1558*, J. D. Mackie, 1952

Parker Chronicle (832–900), The, A. H. Smith, 2nd edn, 1939

Parker Chronicle and Laws, The, R. Flower and A. H. Smith, 1941

Penguin Dictionary of Surnames, The, B. Cottle, 1967

Perambulation of Kent, A, W. Lambarde, 1570, edn of 1826, rep. 1970

Personality of Britain, The, C. Fox, 4th edn, 1943

Polychronicon, Ranulf Higden (C. Babington and J. R. Lumbry eds.), 9 vols., 1865f.

Pre-Feudal England: The Jutes, J. E. A. Jolliffe, 1933

Prehistoric Communities of the British Isles, V. G. Childe, 3rd edn, 1949

Printed Book, The, H. G. Aldis, 2nd edn, 1947

Roman Britain (Britain in Pictures), I. A. Richmond, 1947

Roman Britain, I. A. Richmond, 1955

Roman Forts of the Saxon Shore, The (H.M.S.O.), L. Cottrell, 1954

Roman Roads in Britain, Vol. I, I. D. Margary, 1955

Roman Silchester, G. C. Boon, 1958

Roman Ways in the Weald, I. D. Margary, 1948

Romans, Kelts and Saxons in Ancient Britain, R. E. Zachrisson, 1927

Scribes and Scholars, L. D. Reynolds and N. G. Wilson, 1968

Select Charters . . ., W. Stubbs (ed.), 8th edn, 1905

South-East England: Ancient Peoples and Places, R. F. Jessup, 1970

Studies in Chronology and History, R. L. Poole, 1934

Survey Gazetteer of the British Isles, The, J. Bartholomew (ed.), 9th edn, 1943

Survey of London, 1598, John Stow (H. B. Wheatley ed.), 1912

Tour through the Whole Island of Great Britain, A, D. Defoe, 2 vols., revised edn, 1962

Town and Country in Roman Britain, A. L. F. Rivet, 2nd edn, 1964

Tudor Geography, E. G. R. Taylor, 1930, Appendix I

Twelve Caesars, The, Suetonius (R. Graves trans.), 1957

Two of the Saxon Chronicles Parallel, C. Plummer (ed.), 2 vols., 1892, 1899

Venerabilis Baedae Opera Historica, C. Plummer (ed.), 2 vols., 1896

Wandering Scholars, The, H. Waddell, 6th edn, 1932

Weald, The, S. W. Wooldridge and F. Golding, 1953

Woodlands and Marshlands of England, The, H. A. Wilcox, 1933

INDEX OF PLACES

National Grid numbers in Italic